Praise for
Superminds

"*Superminds* is the first book I have seen that deeply explores the power of information technology to enable truly new forms of human organization. I really love the premise and thoughtfulness of the book, and I highly recommend it if you want to understand and make sense of what we are likely to see in the next few years!"

—Jimmy Wales, Wikipedia founder

"From the father of collective intelligence, a refreshingly realistic view of how computers will supercharge collective intelligence and how these superminds can help us tackle the most complex problems that face the world today."   —Joi Ito, director of the MIT Media Lab

"Thomas Malone was a decade ahead of most of the rest of us in thinking about the future of work. Now—in this fascinating book—he has done it again, looking ahead to a hyperconnected world and introducing us to new vistas of human capability and creativity achievable through collective intelligence. By thinking imaginatively about our future, Malone helps us think differently about the present."

—Anne-Marie Slaughter, CEO of New America and
author of *Unfinished Business*

"Tom Malone puts worries about artificial intelligence in perspective, explaining why AI works best when combined with humans in superminds. What makes a supermind more or less intelligent is just one of many surprises in this fascinating book."

—Patrick Winston, former director of the
MIT Artificial Intelligence Laboratory and
author of *Artificial Intelligence*

"As Tom Malone observes, it's usually harder to create the future than to imagine it, but in the case of interacting, networked people (as with Facebook), sometimes it's the other way around. The wonderful essence of Tom's book is to imagine how people and computers will interact on a massive scale to create intelligent systems. And by imagining them in advance, we have some hope of nudging them in a positive direction."

—Esther Dyson, executive founder of
Way to Wellville and author of *Release 2.1*

"After helping introduce the phrase 'future of work' in his 2004 book with that name, Tom Malone is back to remind us that the real impact of technology will come not only from AI but also from harnessing human minds at hyperscale. In this terrific, well-researched, and highly readable book, he explores provocatively and practically the opportunities and challenges that superminds will help us address in businesses and society. Leaders who care about harnessing the power of human minds in a world enabled by digital technologies must read this book."

—James Manyika, chairman of the
McKinsey Global Institute

"Humans plus computers and networks have enormous potential. How can such wee creatures as ourselves take advantage of this potential? In his new book, Malone addresses this question in a concrete way, laying the foundation for a new discipline: the systems engineering of superminds."

—Vernor Vinge, Hugo Award–winning
science fiction author and originator of the
"technological singularity" concept

"Malone takes us on an intentional journey into thinking about thought, intelligence, reasoning, and consciousness. He sees these notions in extremely broad terms that have changed my views of what it means to 'think'—a property that emerges from aggregations and organized structures. I may never see a four-legged table the same way again!"

—Vint Cerf, vice president at Google and one of the "fathers of the Internet"

"A remarkable journey into the basic structures—markets, hierarchies, democracies, and more—that have advanced civilization throughout history and now bring us to a turning point where the complex problems facing humanity can be addressed by people and computers working together in totally new ways. A must-read for anyone interested in a fresh look at artificial intelligence."

—Amy Edmondson, professor at Harvard Business School and author of *Building the Future*

Superminds

THE SURPRISING POWER OF PEOPLE AND COMPUTERS THINKING TOGETHER

Thomas W. Malone

LITTLE, BROWN AND COMPANY

New York Boston London

To my parents, Ernest and Virginia Malone

Little, Brown and Company
Hachette Book Group
1290 Avenue of the Americas, New York, NY 10104
littlebrown.com

First Edition: May 2018

Little, Brown and Company is a division of Hachette Book Group, Inc. The Little, Brown name and logo are trademarks of Hachette Book Group, Inc.

The Hachette Speakers Bureau provides a wide range of authors for speaking events. To find out more, go to hachettespeakersbureau.com or call (866) 376-6591.

All image credits appear in the endnotes.

ISBN 978-0-316-34913-0
LCCN 2017964059

10 9 8 7 6 5 4 3 2 1

LSC-C

Printed in the United States of America

Contents

CONTENTS

Superminds

Preface

Supermind is an English word that means "a powerful combination of many individual minds."[1] This book is the story of superminds on our planet. We'll see that the history of humanity is largely the history of human superminds, of how humans in groups—like hierarchies, communities, markets, and democracies—accomplished things that individual humans could never have done alone.

More important, we'll see how crucial computers will be for the superminds in our future. For a long time, the most important contribution of computers won't be artificial intelligence; it will be *hyperconnectivity*—connecting human minds to each other in new ways and at unprecedented scales. But over time, computers will also do more and more of the complex kinds of thinking that only humans do today.

This book is not primarily about how computers will do things people used to do. It's about how people and computers together will do things that were never possible before. It's about how human-computer superminds will be smarter than anything our world has ever seen. And it's about how we can use these new kinds of collective intelligence to help solve some of our most important problems in business, government, and many other parts of society.

Introduction

In January 2009, Tim Gowers posted a blog entry that would make history. Gowers is a mathematics professor at Cambridge University, and he proves mathematical theorems for a living. If you're like most people, you probably haven't proved a theorem in your life, or at least not since high school geometry class. But the rigorous, logical thinking that is captured in mathematical proofs is at the heart of many of humanity's most important scientific and technological achievements.

Usually, proving theorems requires hours of solitary work, trying to figure out how to do just one piece of one subpart of a complex proof. In 2009, Gowers decided to try a different way of doing things. He wanted to see if a large group of people on the Internet could prove a theorem together.[1]

In a blog post titled "Is Massively Collaborative Mathematics Possible?" Gowers invited anyone on the Internet who was interested to collaborate in proving the theorem.[2] He speculated that this kind of large-scale collaboration might be useful for at least three reasons. First, in many kinds of problem solving (including mathematical proofs), luck often matters. Having many people working on a problem increases the chances that at least one of them will get lucky and have an important idea.

Second, different people know different things. So even if everyone just contributes ideas that seem obvious to them, the group as a whole can bring to bear much more knowledge than one or two individuals ever could alone.

Finally, different people think differently. Some are good at coming up with new things to try, others at finding the faults in someone else's ideas, still others at putting together lots of pieces into a coherent new picture. As Gowers summarized, "...if a large group of mathematicians could connect their brains efficiently, they could perhaps solve problems very efficiently as well."

The post went on to suggest ground rules to make the collaboration easier, such as keeping discussion respectful and making only bite-sized, focused contributions. In a subsequent post, he gave his group the task of proving the Hales-Jewett theorem, which is part of an esoteric branch of mathematics that has applications in computer science and other fields.

Other mathematicians quickly took up his challenge. Within seven hours after Gowers put up his blog post, the first comment was made by Jozsef Solymosi, a mathematician at the University of British Columbia. Fifteen minutes later, Jason Dyer, a high school mathematics teacher in Arizona, made the next comment. Three minutes after that, another comment came from Terence Tao of UCLA (a winner, like Gowers, of the Fields Medal, the equivalent of a Nobel Prize in mathematics).

By mid-March, the participants had solved the core of the problem. By the end of May, there had been over 1,500 comments in which 39 different people made substantive contributions. And in October, the group submitted the first of several articles describing their results, all of which were attributed to "D. H. J. Polymath," a pseudonym for the whole group.[3]

With all the famous mathematicians involved, you might wonder whether this was really a group project or whether the key work was done by a handful of the most prestigious contributors. It's true that some members of the group contributed much more than others, but a detailed analysis of the complete working record of the project shows that almost every one of the 39 substantive participants contributed influential content.[4]

In other words, the Polymath project made history as the first example of a real contribution to mathematics from a loosely organized group of dozens of people on the Internet, many of whom didn't even know each other before the project started.

WHAT'S OLD HERE?

The Polymath project was successful because it used new information technology (IT) to connect people in ways that would never have been possible before. We'll see many more such stories in this book: vast online groups creating an encyclopedia (Wikipedia), solving difficult scientific problems (Foldit), entertaining each other with gossip (Facebook), and responding to humanitarian disasters like hurricanes (Ushahidi).

But in a sense, these digital-age accomplishments are all just examples of one of the oldest stories in the history of humanity. The story goes like this: "There was a problem. Different people worked on different parts of it. Together, the group solved the problem better than any of the individuals could have solved it alone."

In fact, it's not too much of an exaggeration to say that almost *all* our important problems are solved by groups of people rather than by individuals alone. For instance, it may be a common shorthand to say that Steve Jobs created the iPhone, but of course the iPhone was really designed and made by thousands of people all over the world who in turn built upon a vast edifice of technological inventions that came before them. Even making the turkey sandwich I had for lunch today required hundreds of people to grow, transport, and prepare the meat, bread, lettuce, mustard, and other ingredients.

Compared to "simple" problems like these, trying to solve big societal problems like what to do about climate change, crime, war, poverty, health care, and education is far more complex and requires far more people.

One name for the ability to solve problems well is *intelligence*, and we usually think of intelligence as something that individuals have. But as all these examples make obvious, intelligence—in the sense of solving problems well—is something that groups can have, too.

We'll call the intelligence of groups *collective intelligence*, and this book is the story of that ubiquitous—but often invisible—kind of intelligence. We'll see that it was the collective intelligence of human groups, not the intelligence of individual humans, that first differentiated our human ancestors from all their animal relatives. We'll see that human progress has been mostly a story of what groups of people—not individuals—have accomplished. And we'll see that, over time, information technologies—like writing and the printing press—allowed groups to become dramatically larger and more intelligent.

Most important, we'll see that we are now in the early stages of another dramatic change in collective intelligence, this time enabled by new electronic information technologies. But before imagining the future of collective intelligence, it's useful to think briefly about its past.

A SHORT HISTORY OF COLLECTIVE INTELLIGENCE

Here's a thought experiment: Imagine that you've been transported by a time machine to an African rain forest in the year 45,000 BC. You know everything you know today, but you are all alone. It's hot, humid, and there are lots of strange sounds coming from all around you. If you're lucky, you might be able to survive on fruits, nuts, dead animals left behind by other carnivores, and maybe the occasional fish or grasshopper you manage to catch. But you will be somewhere in the middle of the food chain, living in constant fear of predators more powerful than you are.[5] If you stumble upon a hungry lion, for instance, you'll probably end up as his lunch, not the other way around.

That's the situation our distant human ancestors faced, with one major difference: ancient humans weren't alone; they lived in groups. In fact, their brains were hardwired to help them connect with each other. Relative to what a similar animal of their body size would need, humans have by far the largest brains in the animal kingdom. And much of that extra brain volume appears to be devoted to what you might call social intelligence.[6]

If you look at the whole range of primates, including monkeys, apes, and humans, the species whose brains have larger neocortex regions also form larger social groups.[7] And that ability to participate effectively in larger social groups was one of the most important evolutionary advantages of our bigger brains.

Perhaps the most important reason was that groups could protect themselves from predators much more effectively than individuals could.[8] A few people in a group can watch for lions while the others eat mangoes. A lion is also less likely to attack a large group of people in the first place, because he knows that even though he could easily overpower a single human, he would probably lose a fight with a dozen of them. Large groups can also be much more effective as predators themselves. For instance, a group of dozens of people could surround an entire herd of wild horses, chase them into a gorge, and then butcher them all.[9]

Along with their greater social intelligence, early humans also developed much richer ways of communicating than other animals. These human languages could be used not only to coordinate hunting but also to share innovative ideas like how to control fire, how to make bows and arrows, and how to build boats.

Even the Albert Einsteins of fire making—whoever they were—wouldn't have made much difference in the world if they had been unable to communicate their techniques to other people. Their innovations were powerful only because their ideas were shared with groups of humans who could apply and develop them further.

By around 30,000 to 70,000 years ago, our human ancestors had bodies and brains that would be indistinguishable from those of modern humans,[10] and they used their abilities to move up in the world. For instance, about 45,000 years ago, humans reached the shores of Australia. Within a few thousand years of their arrival, all but one of the other 24 largest animal species on the continent were extinct.[11]

We don't have any eyewitness reports of the slaughters, but somehow our hunting-and-gathering ancestors had finally reached the top of the food chain. And it was human *groups*—not individual humans—who had become the apex predators.

Agriculture

A similar story was repeated in each of the other two major stages of human development: the Agricultural Revolution and the Industrial Revolution. By about 12,000 years ago, humans began to systematically cultivate wheat, corn, cows, and many other plants and animals. This allowed humans to increase their global population from about 2 million to 600 million by 1700 and to further solidify their dominance over the rest of nature.[12]

But agriculture required much more coordination in large groups than hunting and gathering did. Farmers raised food, but they usually didn't build their own houses by themselves. The carpenters who built houses needed food from the farmers. So people traded what they had for what they needed in markets. As agricultural societies developed, crops and houses also needed protection from invaders and thieves. For this, they usually relied on governments ruled by kings and emperors.

None of these achievements could have been made by single humans alone; they all depended on the collective intelligence of human groups and their technologies. Information technologies such as writing were particularly important, since they allowed communication over time and distance that would have otherwise been impossible.

Industry

Starting in the 1700s, division of labor and more complex kinds of coordination went much further as humans developed the factories and machines of the Industrial Age. New technologies coupled with new ways of organizing work allowed vastly increased productivity. For instance, the Scottish economist Adam Smith famously used the example of a pin factory to illustrate the power of division of labor. In this factory, what was formerly the task of a single pin maker was divided into 18 separate tasks, like cutting wires and sharpening points, each done by a different specialized worker. Dividing up the work in this way, among a larger group of people, led to a vast increase in productivity.

In addition to larger versions of markets and governments, the Industrial Age also saw the rise of larger-scale communities—like the world scientific community—which enabled new kinds of interaction. These changes relied on further information technology developments, including the printing press and, eventually, all the forms of electronic communication we know today. The result of all this progress was that world population increased again, this time from 600 million to over 7 billion in only the last 300 years. And human domination over the planet has been so successful that humans themselves are now perhaps the greatest risk to our planet's future.

Once again, these developments weren't just the results of individual human intelligence. Probably no single human ever said, "I want human population to increase as much as possible so humans can rule over nature." Instead these outcomes—for better or for worse—are the result of collectively intelligent *groups* of people and their technologies.

WHO ARE THESE COLLECTIVE INTELLIGENCES?

Thinking about groups of people and computers as a kind of superorganism might seem like just a poetic metaphor. But we'll see many ways in which this view is quite concrete. It turns out that groups have scientifically measurable properties, just as individual humans do. We'll see research that shows how the same statistical techniques psychologists use to measure individual intelligence can also be used to measure the intelligence of groups. When we do this, we see that some groups are just smarter than others, and we get a much more precise understanding of why.

We'll also see research where a colleague and I took a method developed by neuroscientists to measure consciousness and used it to analyze the interaction patterns in groups of people and computers. We found that the groups who were most effective were also the ones whose interaction patterns more closely resembled those in conscious human brains. Does this mean that those groups were really "conscious"? No. But we'll see a number of reasons why it may not be silly to think of them that way.

And we'll see, time and again, how a group can have a will of its own that's different from that of the individuals in the group. It's no surprise, for instance, to say that companies often do what's good for their own profits even when that's not what's good for their employees. Democratic governments often make choices that many of their citizens don't like. And markets ruthlessly allocate food, houses, and all kinds of other resources to the people who can pay the most for them, even when that leaves others with almost nothing.

So in important senses, these collectively intelligent creatures do have lives of their own, beyond the individuals in them. We'll call these creatures superminds. By *super*, here, we don't necessarily mean "better"; we just mean "more inclusive." In other words, just as a superorganism (like an ant colony) includes other organisms (like individual ants), a supermind (like a company) includes other minds (like those of the people in the company).

Like individual plants and animals, superminds can be categorized into species. We'll get to know four important species especially well:

- *Hierarchies*, where people with authority make decisions others are required to follow. Found in businesses, nonprofit groups, and the operational parts of governments.
- *Democracies*, where decisions are made by voting. Found in governments, clubs, businesses, and many other groups.
- *Markets*, where decisions are made by mutual agreement among trading partners. Found wherever people trade money, goods, and services.
- *Communities*, where decisions are made by informal consensus or shared norms. Found throughout human life, from local neighborhoods to professional groups to national cultures.

All these different types of superminds are constantly interacting: sometimes cooperating, sometimes competing, sometimes destroying each other altogether. When you look at the world this way, you can see that today's news is mostly about the adventures of these different types of superminds.

Here are just a few examples: *Hierarchical* companies, like Apple and Samsung, fight for dominance in the world's smartphone *market*. Liberals and conservatives in the American *democracy* argue about whether health-care problems would be better solved by free *markets*, government *hierarchies*, or some combination of the two. The *hierarchical* government of China tries (and mostly fails) to control its stock *market* to prevent a dramatic fall in prices.[13] The US Supreme Court (a somewhat *democratic* part of a *hierarchical* government) rules on Citizens United, which helps large *hierarchical* corporations use their money to influence elections in *democracies*. Local *communities* resist attempts by *hierarchical* governments to control which restrooms transgender people can use.

All these dramas occur in the context of the final type of supermind, the one that encompasses all the rest:

• *Ecosystems,* where decisions are made based on who has the most power and the greatest ability to survive and reproduce. Found wherever there are no overall frameworks for cooperation, such as in the conflicts among the different types of superminds we've just seen.

Like ecosystems in nature, ecosystem superminds operate on the law of the jungle and survival of the fittest. They simply reward what works.

That means that, whether we like it or not, the kinds of individuals and superminds that are present in an ecosystem at any given time are those that were powerful and successful enough in the past to survive or reproduce. This drive for survival is, perhaps, the most important reason why superminds have wills of their own, independent of their members. But we'll also see how—surprisingly often—what's good for the supermind is also good for the individuals in it.

As individuals, we usually have to rely on various kinds of superminds to solve the big problems our world faces. But we can sometimes influence the superminds that already exist or create new superminds to work on problems that are important to us. When we do that, we should place our bets on the superminds that are best suited to the problem at hand. And to help do that, we'll examine some of the key advantages and disadvantages of the different species of superminds.

HOW CAN INFORMATION TECHNOLOGY MAKE SUPERMINDS SMARTER?

To think clearly about how IT will change the world, we need to understand the superminds that run the world today. But we also need to understand how new electronic information technologies will profoundly transform these superminds.

Many people today believe that the most important new kind of information technology will be *artificial intelligence* (AI), embodied in robots and other software programs that do smart things only humans could do before. It's certainly true that machines like Amazon's Alexa and Google's self-driving cars are getting smarter, and it's possible that someday, in the future, we will have artificially intelligent machines that are as smart and broadly adaptable as humans.

But most experts estimate that, if this happens, it probably won't be for at least several decades and quite possibly much longer. In the meantime, we will need to use AI in combination with humans who provide whatever skills and general intelligence the machines don't yet have themselves.

For the foreseeable future, therefore, there is another way of using IT that will be even more important than just creating better AI: creating groups of people and computers that, together, are far more *collectively intelligent* than was ever possible before.

While we often overestimate the potential of AI in doing this, I think we often underestimate the potential power of *hyperconnectivity* among the 7 billion or so amazingly powerful information processors called human brains that are already on our planet, not to mention the millions of other computers that don't include AI.

It's easy to overestimate the potential for AI because it's easy for us to imagine computers as smart as people. We already know what people are like, and our science fiction movies and books are full of stories about smart computers—like R2-D2 in *Star Wars* and the evil Terminator cyborg—who act like the kinds of good and bad people we already know. But it's much harder to create such machines than to imagine them.

On the other hand, we underestimate the potential for hyperconnectivity because it's probably easier to *create* massively connected groups of people and computers than to *imagine* what they could actually do. In fact, the main way we've really used computers so far is to connect people. With e-mail, mobile applications, the web in general, and sites like Facebook, Google, Wikipedia, Netflix, YouTube, Twitter, and many others, we've created the most massively connected groups the world has ever known.

But it's still hard for us to understand what these groups are doing today and even harder to imagine how they will change in the future. One goal of this book is to help you imagine these possibilities—and how they can help us solve our most important problems.

We'll see, for instance, how IT can help us create much larger groups, much more diverse groups, groups that are organized in radically new ways, and groups that combine human and machine intelligence to do things that would never have been possible before. In other words, we will ask one of the core questions of collective intelligence:

How can people and computers be connected so that—
collectively—they act more intelligently than any person, group, or
computer has ever done before?

HOW CAN SUPERMINDS HELP SOLVE OUR PROBLEMS?

For superminds to be useful, they need to solve problems we care about. To illustrate some of these possibilities, we'll see examples of how we could use superminds to solve problems in corporate strategic planning, in dealing with climate change, and in managing the risks of artificial intelligence.

We'll also see that there is an obvious end point for the growing collective intelligence on our planet. It is the "global mind"—the combination of all the people, computers, and other kinds of intelligence on the earth.[14] We'll see that, in some ways, the global mind already exists and is getting smarter all the time. And the book will conclude with some reflections on how we can use our global collective intelligence to make choices that are not just smart but also wise.

Part I

What Are Superminds?

Chapter 1

Would You Recognize a Supermind If You Saw It on the Street?

W hen Adam Smith wrote *The Wealth of Nations,* in 1776, he said that buyers and sellers in a market who do what's best for them-selves are often "led by [the] invisible hand" of the market to also do what's best for society. For instance, if you can make more profit for yourself by selling mustard ice cream instead of mocha from your ice cream truck, then that's also the way your business can contribute more economic value to society.[1]

Of course, there are certainly situations where maximizing your own profit isn't what's best for society. But Smith's profound realiza-tion was that the human interactions in a market can often lead to good overall outcomes that none of the individuals themselves are try-ing to achieve. Even if you are just selling mustard ice cream to make more money for yourself, you are also—unwittingly—helping to use all the milk, sugar, human labor, and other resources of your whole society in a way that makes more people happy. Smith called this almost mystical property of markets their "invisible hand."

But markets don't just *have* invisible hands; they *are* invisible minds. In fact, they're superminds. Superminds are all around us all the time, but to see them, you have to know how to look. Some superminds, like companies, are usually pretty easy to see. Others, like ecosystems, are much harder.

I sometimes play a little game with myself: How many superminds can I see while walking down the street? When I walk out of my MIT office building and turn left, toward Kendall Square, here are some of the things I might see: a construction crew, a bank, stores and restaurants, and a crowded sidewalk full of pedestrians who don't run into each other.

These are all superminds, but to see them as such, we need to look in a very particular way. And to look in that way, we need a definition of *superminds*. Here's the one we'll use throughout this book:

Supermind—a group of individuals acting together
in ways that seem intelligent.

We can also define *collective intelligence* as a property that any supermind has:[2]

Collective intelligence—the result of groups of individuals
acting together in ways that seem intelligent.

Every word of the definition of *supermind* is important, so let's take the definition apart, piece by piece.

A Group . . .

To see a supermind, we have to first identify a *group*. That's often easy. For instance, the construction crew remodeling a building near my office is clearly a group of people. So are the employees in the restaurant where I sometimes buy turkey sandwiches.

Some groups aren't quite so obvious. For instance, the people walking on the sidewalk aren't a group you would ordinarily think much about, but when they do their (mostly) unconscious dance to avoid running into each other, they become, for a fleeting moment, a kind of supermind.

Of Individuals . . .

Our definition says that the parts of a supermind are "individuals," but it doesn't specify exactly what kind of individuals. That means the individual parts of a supermind can be very small or very large, and they can include not just minds but also bodies and other resources the minds control.

For instance, we could say that my neighborhood Starbucks coffee shop is a supermind that includes all the individual employees in the shop as well as the tables, chairs, coffeemakers, and coffee beans. Alternatively, we could say that the whole coffee shop itself is an individual that is part of an even larger supermind: the market that includes all the vendors competing to sell coffee in my neighborhood. Or, at a lower level, we could say that a single Starbucks barista is a kind of supermind whose individual parts include all the neurons in the barista's brain—yes, each person's mind is a supermind on its own.

Acting Together . . .

So are all groups of individuals superminds? Not necessarily. First, a group is a supermind only if its individuals are *acting* in some way. For instance, you probably wouldn't say that a group of four empty coffee cups just lying on the ground is a supermind.

But just because a group is acting doesn't mean it's a supermind, either; the individuals must be acting *together*. In other words, their activities must be connected in some way. Two unrelated people in two different cities, each groggily making coffee on the same morning, are probably not a supermind. But two Starbucks baristas working together to fill all the customer orders in a single shop would be.

Now, here's an important point: even though the individuals' actions need to be connected, the individuals in a supermind do *not* need to cooperate with each other or have the same goals. A company called InnoCentive, for instance, has online contests where scientists and technologists compete to solve difficult problems, like how to synthesize a particular chemical compound. But even though the problem solvers are competing with each other—not cooperating—their actions are connected because they are all working on the same problem.

In Ways That Seem Intelligent

Finally, it's not enough just to have a group of individuals performing connected actions. To be a supermind, the group also has to be doing something that *seems intelligent*. You may be surprised to see the word *seem* in this definition because it sounds a little wishy-washy. But it is critical because there is an important sense in which superminds—like beauty—exist only in the eye of the beholder.

In fact, all the elements of a supermind—not just intelligence but also individuals, groups, actions, and connections—have to be identified by an observer.[3] And different observers can analyze the same situation in different ways. For instance, if you say that each Starbucks shop is itself a supermind, and I say that each one is part of a larger supermind, we can both be right, but we will get different insights about the situation.

The role of the observer is especially critical in judging *intelligence*, because this is always, to some degree, a subjective judgment. For instance, whether you think an entity is intelligent depends, crucially, on what goals you think the entity is trying to achieve. When students take multiple-choice intelligence tests, we assume they are trying to give the answers the test designers consider correct. But I can easily imagine a girl I knew in high school, who was very smart—and very rebellious—taking such a test and deciding to fill in the circles on the multiple-choice answer sheet in the pattern of a pretty flower. If she did that, the usual scoring method for the test wouldn't measure her high intelligence at all!

In order to assess an entity's intelligence, then, an observer always has to make assumptions about the entity's goals. And when evaluating a group's intelligence, it is often useful to consider overall goals for the group that are important to the observer, even if none of the individuals in the group has those goals.

For instance, each of the ice cream truck owners in a city has a different goal: most of them probably want to make as much money as possible for themselves and to have fewer permits issued to their competitors. But if your job for the city's parks department includes determining how many ice cream truck permits to issue for the city parks, you might want to survey park visitors about whether they feel there is enough good-tasting ice cream available at reasonable prices. These surveys would be one way of evaluating the overall intelligence of the supermind that includes all the ice cream trucks in the park.

Finally, it's important to note that we can consider a group a supermind if we observe the group *trying* to do something intelligent, even if it isn't succeeding. For instance, you might well consider a software start-up company a supermind, even if, after all the group's intelligent efforts, its product fails and the company goes out of business.

WHAT IS INTELLIGENCE?

But what do we mean by *intelligence* in the first place? This term is a notoriously slippery one, and different people have defined it in many different ways.[4] For example, the *Encyclopaedia Britannica* defines it as "the ability to adapt effectively to the environment." The cognitive psychologist Howard Gardner defines it as "the ability to solve problems, or to create products, that are valued within one or more cultural settings." And a group of 52 leading psychologists summarized the mainstream view within the field like this:

Intelligence is a very general mental capability that, among other things, involves the ability to reason, plan, solve problems, think abstractly, comprehend complex ideas, learn quickly and learn from experience. It is not merely book learning, a narrow academic skill, or test-taking smarts. Rather, it reflects a broader and deeper capability for comprehending our surroundings—"catching on," "making sense" of things, or "figuring out" what to do.[5]

For our purposes in this book, we will define two kinds of intelligence, each of which is useful for different purposes. The first kind is *specialized intelligence:*

> *Specialized intelligence—the ability to achieve specific goals effectively in a given environment.*

This definition is equivalent to the definitions above from the *Encyclopaedia Britannica* and Howard Gardner. Basically, it means that an intelligent entity will do whatever is most likely to help it achieve its goals, based on everything it knows. Stated even more simply, specialized intelligence is just "effectiveness" at achieving specific goals. In this sense, then, specialized collective intelligence is just "group effectiveness," and a supermind is an effective group.

Our second kind of intelligence is more broadly useful and often more interesting:

> *General intelligence—the ability to achieve a wide range of different goals effectively in different environments.*

This definition is similar to the definition above from the group of 52 psychologists, and this is the kind of intelligence that intelligence tests measure. Intelligence tests don't just measure your ability to do a few specific tasks effectively. The tasks on these tests are carefully selected so that they predict your ability to do a very wide range of other tasks beyond those you're being specifically tested on.

For instance, people who get high scores on intelligence tests are—on average—better than others at learning to read, write, do arithmetic, and solve many other kinds of problems. Of course, it's quite possible for someone who has been doing a specific task for a long time—like repairing Honda cars—to be much better at that task than someone who is more intelligent but has never opened the hood of a Honda. But in general, people who are more intelligent are better at learning new things quickly and adapting rapidly to new environments.

We'll see much more about this definition in the next chapter, but for now the key point is that the definition of general intelligence requires an intelligent actor to be not just good at a specific kind of task but also good at learning how to do a wide range of tasks. In short, this definition of intelligence means roughly the same thing as "versatility" or "adaptability." In this sense, then, general collective intelligence means "group versatility" or "group adaptability."

The difference between specialized intelligence and general intelligence helps clarify the difference between the abilities of today's computers and the abilities of people. Some of today's artificially intelligent computers are far smarter than people in terms of specialized intelligence. For instance, they can perform specific tasks, like playing chess or Jeopardy, better than humans. But no matter how good they are at these specific tasks, none of today's computers is anywhere close to having the level of general intelligence that any normal human five-year-old does. No single computer today, for example, can converse sensibly about the vast number of topics an ordinary five-year-old can, not to mention the fact that the same child can also walk, pick up weirdly shaped objects, and recognize when people are happy, sad, or angry.

So as I walk down the street near my office—or anywhere else—there are lots of superminds to be seen. To recognize them, I need to identify four things: (1) a group of individuals, (2) some actions these individuals are taking, (3) some interconnections between these actions, and (4) some goals with respect to which we can evaluate these actions.

Whenever I see a combination of these four things, I see a supermind. But it's important to realize that seeing a supermind is sometimes useful and sometimes not. For instance, I might say that the four legs on the table in my office constitute a group of individuals acting collectively to keep the top of the table from falling to the floor. This is true as far as it goes, and in this sense my table is an extremely simple kind of supermind. But applying the concept of superminds to my table in this way is probably not very useful because—as far as I can tell—it doesn't give us any new insights about how to use tables or do anything else.

Just as physicists need to learn how to artfully apply concepts like force, mass, and energy to get useful insights about real physical situations, so, too, do we need to learn how to artfully apply the concepts of superminds and collective intelligence to get useful insights about the real world.

Chapter 2

Can a Group Take
an Intelligence Test?

For perhaps as long as humans have existed, people have known informally that some humans seem to be smarter than others. Some people just figure things out faster, know more, and learn more quickly. But in the early 1900s, psychologists made a breakthrough in our understanding of this phenomenon: they developed a way to objectively measure something similar to what we have always called intelligence.

Can we do the same thing for groups? Can we objectively measure how smart a group (or supermind) is? If so, can we objectively say that some groups are smarter than others? Is there even a scientific sense in which we can say that a group is "intelligent" in the first place? Thanks to recent research my colleagues and I did, we now know that the answer to all these questions is yes. But to understand why, we first need to know a little more about individual intelligence and how it is tested.

MEASURING INDIVIDUAL INTELLIGENCE

The most important advance that made intelligence tests possible was the discovery of a surprising fact about human abilities. Imagine that you know John is good at math and Sue is good at reading. How would you guess each would perform at the other subject? If you're like many people, you might guess that John is probably average or worse at reading and Sue is similarly average or below in math. Based on our everyday experience, it seems like this might well be true in general.

But here's the surprising fact that we now know from hundreds of scientific studies: on average, people who are good at one kind of mental task are good at most others, too.[1] Those who are good at reading are usually better than average at math and vice versa. Those people who are good at math and reading also tend to have good memories, possess greater general knowledge about the world, and be better at logical reasoning, among many other qualities.[2] Of course, different people *develop* their skills more fully in some areas than others, but some people are just better than others at what we defined in the previous chapter as general intelligence—the ability to do a wide range of mental tasks well.

Here's a more scientific way of saying this: if you ask lots of people to do lots of different mental tasks, and if you analyze the results statistically, you'll find that their scores on each task are positively correlated with their scores on most of the other tasks.

Then, with that data set, you can use a statistical technique called factor analysis to see the underlying structure of how the different scores are related. If you want to use factor analysis to analyze the structure of people's political attitudes, for instance, you could ask their opinions on lots of issues (like abortion, taxes, gay marriage, and universal health care). And the analysis would tell you whether a single underlying dimension (like liberal versus conservative) explains most of their answers or whether multiple dimensions (like for social issues and economic issues) are necessary.

When psychologists use this technique to analyze people's scores on different mental tasks, they usually find that a single statistical factor predicts about 30–60 percent of the variation in people's performance on all the tasks. No other single factor predicts more than about half this much variation.[3] The statistical technique calculates a score on this factor for each individual, and the people with high scores do better on most of the tasks than those whose scores are low. This statistical factor corresponds well with what we intuitively call intelligence, and all modern intelligence tests are designed to include the kinds of tasks that measure this factor.

It is important to realize that this result wasn't preordained. There are other characteristics of people, like personality, for which there is no single factor that predicts others. For instance, if you know that someone is an introvert, that doesn't predict either way whether he or she will be conscientious or agreeable.[4] But it turns out to be a very well-established scientific fact that different people have different amounts of general intelligence for doing mental tasks.

Of course, this result is scientifically interesting, but it also has significant practical importance. With any standard intelligence test, you can predict how well someone will do on lots of other tasks without taking months or years to observe them all individually. If you want to predict how well someone will do in school, for instance, or how successful he or she will be in many jobs, you can do so pretty well with just the results of a short paper-and-pencil intelligence test.[5] It even turns out that, statistically speaking, people who are more intelligent live longer. Being able to predict these important life outcomes based on an objective measure has lots of very important practical consequences, including, among many others, the growth of the multibillion-dollar educational testing industry, which uses tests very similar to intelligence tests.

But it's important to remember that these intelligence tests are far from a magic bullet for predicting everything about a person's future. There are many other important kinds of abilities that are not measured by standard intelligence tests. For example, Howard Gardner includes musical ability, physical ability, and interpersonal ability as different kinds of intelligence.[6] And there are many other factors besides intelligence that affect success in school and life, including—to name just a few—how hard you work, how much help you receive from your family and friends, and—of course—how lucky you are.

Some people have—rightly—criticized our excessive reliance on standardized intelligence and other tests. (SATs and other similar educational tests aren't intentionally designed as intelligence tests, but their results are highly correlated with those of intelligence tests.) But the problem is not that the tests have no value; it's that we sometimes expect too much from them. We often assume that the tests are even better predictors than they actually are, and we place too much emphasis on the qualities the tests measure and not enough on other things that also matter.

But this shouldn't cause us to lose sight of the fact that intelligence tests are often the best single predictors we have of how well people will perform on things that matter to us. For instance, in one very comprehensive study, intelligence tests were the most accurate single predictor of job success, proving more accurate than job tryouts, reference checking, interviews, and academic achievement.[7] So even though they're certainly not perfect predictors of all life outcomes, it's fair to say that the development of individual intelligence testing is one of the most important achievements in the field of psychology in the 20th century.

AN INTELLIGENCE TEST FOR GROUPS

But what do all these results about *individual* intelligence mean for *collective* intelligence? Can groups be intelligent in the same way individuals are? Is there any objective way to say that some groups are smarter than others? In other words, is there a single statistical factor for a group—like there is for an individual—that predicts how well the group will perform on a wide range of very different tasks?

As far as my colleagues and I could tell, no one had ever asked this obvious question before. So we set out to answer it. My colleague Anita Woolley played a key role in all this work and was the first author on the paper in which we reported our original results.[8] Christopher Chabris and a number of others (named in the notes for this chapter) were also involved in parts of the work.

To create an intelligence test for groups, the first thing we needed to do was to select a set of tasks for the groups to do. We could have just asked groups to work together to answer the questions on a standard individual intelligence test. That would have included a variety of *mental* tasks, but it wouldn't necessarily have included a variety of tasks on which groups work together. So we used a well-known framework created by social psychologist Joseph McGrath for classifying group tasks,[9] and we selected tasks from each of the main categories in his framework: generating, choosing, negotiating, and executing.

For tasks involving *generating* something new, for instance, we asked groups to brainstorm various uses for a brick. For tasks involving *choosing* from among specified alternatives, we asked groups to solve visual puzzles from a standard individual intelligence test called Raven's Matrices. For *negotiating* tasks, we asked members of groups to pretend that they all lived in the same house and then to plan a shopping trip subject to various constraints on travel time, costs, and perishability of the items they needed to buy. Finally, for *executing* tasks, we asked them to type a long text passage into a shared online text-editing system. We also asked them to perform other tasks like word-completion problems, spatial puzzles, and estimation problems. Overall, we used these tasks to represent the wide range of tasks that groups might perform in the real world.

The next thing we needed to do was recruit groups to take our test. It would have been easy to recruit college undergraduates like those who surround us on the campuses of MIT and Carnegie Mellon University, the two universities where we carried out these studies. But we thought that—especially for a study of group intelligence—our results might be skewed if all our subjects were the kind of highly intelligent and academically accomplished students who study at our universities. So instead we recruited our test subjects from the general public in our cities using a variety of channels, including public websites like Craigslist, because we wanted the groups to be representative of a broad cross-section of our communities. And according to the short individual intelligence tests we gave our subjects, their intelligence distribution was very similar to that of the general US population.

In our two original studies, we had a total of 699 people in 192 groups of two to five people each. Unlike most groups in businesses and other organizations, our groups had no assigned leaders, and people weren't selected for the groups based on any special skills. But in all cases, the groups worked together on their assigned tasks as a group, not as individuals.

DOES THE TEST WORK?

After we had given all the groups a chance to perform all the tasks, we analyzed the correlations among them. This was a key moment of suspense in our research. Would there be a single factor that explained how well groups performed a wide range of tasks, as there is for individuals? Or would there be some more complicated factor structure where, for example, some groups were good at mathematical tasks and others were good at verbal tasks?

The answer was: groups are like individuals. It turned out that there is a single statistical factor for a group—just as there is for an individual—that predicts how well the group will do on a wide range of tasks. As we saw above, for individuals this factor predicts about 30–60 percent of the variation on different tasks. For the groups in our studies, it was in the middle of that range—about 45 percent. Because this factor is called intelligence for individuals, we called our new factor for groups collective intelligence.

In other words, we found that groups have a form of general intelligence, just as individuals do. This means that, just as with individual intelligence, we may be able to use collective intelligence to understand much more about what makes groups effective on a wide range of tasks.

To begin this process, our original studies included a check to see whether the collective intelligence factor we measured predicted performance on tasks not used to calculate it. To do this, we also asked the groups to perform more complex tasks that required a combination of different kinds of abilities. In one study, for instance, the groups played checkers against a computer. In another study, they built structures using building blocks, subject to a set of rules about what to build.

We found that the collective intelligence scores did indeed significantly predict performance on these more complex tasks. In fact, a group's collective intelligence score was a much better predictor of how well the group did on these more complex tasks than either the average or the maximum individual intelligence of the group members.

WHAT MAKES A GROUP SMART?

Before we conducted our studies, we thought we might find a single *collective* intelligence factor for groups that was mostly predicted by the average *individual* intelligence of the group members—that is to say, the smarter the members, the smarter the group. But what we found was much more interesting.

First, we did find that the average and maximum intelligence of the group members was correlated with the group's collective intelligence, but this correlation was only moderately strong. In other words, just putting a bunch of smart people together doesn't guarantee that you'll have a smart group. You might guess this from your own experience: most of us have seen plenty of groups of smart people who couldn't get anything useful done. But if just having a bunch of smart people in a group isn't enough to make the group smart, what is?

We looked at a number of factors that previous research suggested might have predicted how effective a group would be, such as how satisfied the group members were with their group, how motivated they were to help the group perform well, and how comfortable they felt in the group. None of these factors was significantly correlated with the group's collective intelligence.

But we did find three factors that were significant. The first was the average *social perceptiveness* of the group members. We measured this using a test called Reading the Mind in the Eyes, in which people looked at pictures of other people's eyes and tried to guess the mental state of the person in the picture (see below).[10] This test was originally developed as a measure of autism—people with autism and related conditions do very poorly on the test—but it turns out that even among "normal" adults, there is a significant range of people's abilities to do this task well.

You might call this a measure of a person's social intelligence, and we found that the groups in which many of the members were high on this measure were, on average, more collectively intelligent than other groups.

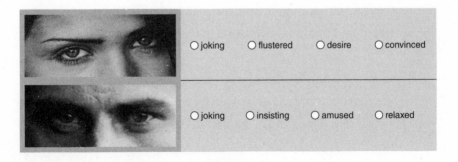

The second important factor we found was the degree to which group members *participated about equally* in conversation. When one or two people dominated the conversation, the group was, on average, less intelligent than when participation was more evenly distributed.

Finally, we found that a group's collective intelligence was significantly correlated with the *proportion of women* in the group. Groups with a higher proportion of women were more intelligent. But this result was mostly explained statistically by the measure of social perceptiveness.

It was already known before we started our research that women, on average, score higher on this test of social perceptiveness than men. So one possible interpretation of our result is that what matters in making a group collectively intelligent is the social perceptiveness of the group members, not their gender. In other words, if you have enough people in a group who are high on social perceptiveness, that may be enough to make the group smart, regardless of whether those people are men or women. But if you're choosing people to be in a group, and you know nothing about a person except his or her gender, you are a little more likely to find social perceptiveness in women than in men.

Interestingly, our result didn't match up with typical assumptions about diversity. Most people would think that the most intelligent groups should be the ones that have about half men and half women. But in our data, the groups with an equal number of men and women were among the least intelligent. As the following graph shows, our data suggests that the collective intelligence of the group may continue to increase along with the percentage of women.[11]

It's also important to realize that, since the points on the graph don't follow any smooth line, there is probably a fair amount of "noise" in the data (for instance, the vertical lines extending from the data points show what statisticians call the standard error of the points). We expect that future research will shed more light on the complexities

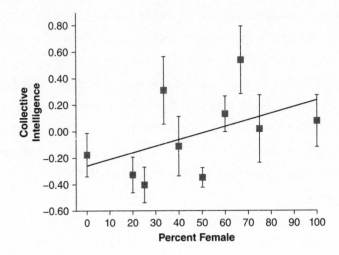

of what is happening here. But at a minimum, our results already provide intriguing suggestions about the role that the proportion of men and women in a group might play in determining the group's collective intelligence.

SOCIAL INTELLIGENCE IS A KEY TO COLLECTIVE INTELLIGENCE

An important clue to what's going on comes from the fact that when we tried to predict collective intelligence using all three factors at the same time (social perceptiveness, distribution of speaking turns, and percentage of females), we found that the only factor that was statistically significant was social perceptiveness. This doesn't mean that the other two factors were unimportant. It just suggests that the underlying mechanism at work in both of the other cases may be social perceptiveness. We saw above, for instance, that social perceptiveness might be what causes the effect of gender and that perhaps socially perceptive people are more likely to take turns speaking, too.

A striking demonstration of how powerful this social perceptiveness factor can be comes from a later study we did with online groups.

In this study, we randomly assigned people to one of two kinds of groups.[12] The *face-to-face groups* sat around a table talking to one another while they took a version of the collective intelligence test on laptop computers. The *online groups* took the same test, but they couldn't see each other at all, and they could only communicate by typing text messages to one another. We found that the social perceptiveness of the group members was equally good at predicting collective intelligence in both kinds of groups. In other words, people who were good at reading emotions in other people's eyes were also good at working together, even when they were doing so online and couldn't see each other's eyes at all!

This suggests that social perceptiveness must actually be correlated with a much broader range of interpersonal skills that are just as useful online as face-to-face. For instance, the kind of social intelligence that lets you read emotions in people's faces might also help you guess what other people are feeling based on what they type and help you predict how they will react to various things you might type back.

In other words, the social skills and social intelligence that are so important in a face-to-face world may be at least as important in the increasingly online world of our future.

COGNITIVE DIVERSITY MATTERS, TOO

In another study,[13] we looked at diversity of *cognitive style*—differences in how people habitually think about the world. Based on previous research on this topic, we considered people with three different cognitive styles: *verbalizers, object visualizers,* and *spatial visualizers.*[14] Verbalizers are good at reasoning with words; object visualizers are good at dealing with the overall properties of images (like paintings); spatial visualizers are good at analyzing images part by part (as in an architectural blueprint). Loosely speaking, these three cognitive styles are typical of students in the humanities, the visual arts, and engineering, respectively.

When we analyzed the collective intelligence of groups with various mixes of these cognitive styles, we found that the most collectively intelligent groups were those with an *intermediate* level of cognitive diversity. In other words, groups where the members had very different cognitive styles weren't as smart, perhaps because they couldn't communicate effectively with one another. And groups where all the members had the same cognitive style weren't as smart, either, perhaps because they didn't have the range of skills needed to do the different tasks. The best combination seemed to be groups in the middle, perhaps because there was enough commonality to communicate effectively and enough diversity to solve a range of different problems.

DO COLLECTIVELY INTELLIGENT GROUPS LEARN FASTER?

One of the most important characteristics of individual intelligence is that it predicts not just what people can already do but also how quickly they can learn new things. Is the same true for collective intelligence? Does a group's collective intelligence predict how fast the group will learn?

As a first step in answering this question, we gave some of the groups in our original studies another task after they had completed the collective intelligence test. We asked them to play a game that the game's developers called the minimum-effort tacit coordination game.[15] In each round of this game, each player had to pick one of five numbers. The number of points players earned was determined by the number they chose as well as by the numbers the other members of their group chose. In order to help them make a choice, the players could each see a "payoff matrix" (see chart) showing how many points they would receive individually based on the number they chose and the minimum number chosen by anyone in the group.[16]

Somewhat like the well-known prisoner's dilemma game, the minimum-effort tacit coordination game requires players to make

Minimum of All Group Member Choices

		0	10	20	30	40
	0	2,400				
	10	2,200	2,800			
Individual's Choice	**20**	1,600	2,600	3,200		
	30	600	2,000	3,000	3,600	
	40	–800	1,000	2,400	3,400	4,000

their moves simultaneously and independently. They weren't allowed to talk to one another about their choices, and the only way they could coordinate was by watching what the other members of the group had done in previous rounds. But unlike prisoner's dilemma, this game strongly rewards players for cooperating, not competing. Their individual rewards were maximized if, over the 10 rounds of the game, they all picked the same choice (the number 40). But this choice was a risky one, because if you picked 40 and someone else in the group picked 0, you lost points. With all the other choices, you could never lose points, regardless of what the other group members did.

Most groups didn't do very well in this game for the first few rounds, but we found that, over the 10 rounds of the game, the groups with higher collective intelligence learned more rapidly how to implicitly coordinate with each other based on what they had done in the previous rounds, and their point totals were significantly greater than those for the other groups. So at least by this measure, groups that are more collectively intelligent also—as we hoped—learn faster.

WHAT ELSE DOES COLLECTIVE INTELLIGENCE PREDICT?

In another set of studies, we translated our collective intelligence test into German and Japanese, and we studied groups taking it in their respective languages in the United States, Germany, and Japan. As further confirmation of our original results, we found that the same kind of collective intelligence factor as in our original study emerged across all three countries and across various group communication modes: face-to-face, voice, video, and text.

We also found that scores on our collective intelligence tests predicted how well student groups performed on a class project and how well laboratory groups performed on a task where they had to select items that would be most important to their survival if they crash-landed in the desert.[17]

Perhaps an even more important question is whether collective intelligence predicts how well groups will perform on tasks whose outcomes matter in the real world, not just in the laboratory or the classroom. As a first step in this direction, we found some intriguing results in the world of video games. We studied teams in one of the most popular online video games in the world: League of Legends. In this game, players typically form teams of five that work together to capture the opposing team's base, killing monsters and meeting other challenges along the way. Even though this is a simulated combat environment, team members have to cooperate, much as they would in a real-life military setting.

Many of the teams consist of people who play together repeatedly over an extended period of time, and the game gives rankings to these teams—similar to the rankings of expert chess players—based on how well they have fared in their matches.

In cooperation with the game's developers, Riot Games, over 200 of these teams took our collective intelligence test online. As we hoped, we found that the teams' collective intelligence scores were significant predictors of their performance in the game, both at the time they took the test as well as six months later, which indicates that the effect is fairly long-lasting.[18] So just as individual intelligence predicts many kinds of real-world performance for individuals, collective intelligence predicts this kind of real-world performance for groups.

MEASURING COLLECTIVE INTELLIGENCE

Before proceeding, it's worth pausing for a moment to reflect on what we have just seen. The combination of all these studies provides a strong basis for concluding that:

1. Human groups have a kind of collective intelligence that is directly analogous to what is measured by individual intelligence tests.
2. This kind of collective intelligence is what we called general intelligence in chapter 1: the ability to perform well on a wide range of very different tasks.
3. This kind of collective intelligence is affected by
    o   the individual intelligence of the group members,
    o   the ability of the group members to work well with others (as measured by their social perceptiveness), and
    o   the cognitive diversity of the group members.
4. The test my colleagues and I developed for measuring this kind of collective intelligence predicts how well groups will perform
    o   on a variety of tasks in laboratories, classrooms, and online games;
    o   using face-to-face and online forms of communication; and
    o   across different languages and cultures.

These results raise some interesting questions about how collective intelligence tests can be applied. Could we give a short test like ours to a sales team to predict how effective their efforts will be over the coming months? Would the scores of a top management team or a board of directors predict how well they will meet the challenges they face? We don't know the answers to these questions for sure yet, but we expect that they will be yes.

Another interesting possibility involves *increasing* the collective intelligence of a group—making it a more intelligent supermind. We know that individual intelligence is hard to change after a young age, but it seems quite possible to change the intelligence of a group. At a minimum, it certainly seems possible to change a group's intelligence by replacing enough of its members. And in later chapters of this book, we'll see many other ways to increase a group's intelligence.

HOW ELSE COULD WE MEASURE COLLECTIVE INTELLIGENCE?

Though we were pleased with its results, the method my colleagues and I developed for systematically measuring the intelligence of a group has its limits. For one thing, this test is designed for relatively small groups. We are using a version of it as I write this for groups of up to 40 people, and we are very interested in pushing the limits to see how large a group we can test with this method. But we expect that when groups get large enough, some other method of testing will be necessary.

On an even more basic level, in order to use the test we developed, we have to *intervene* in a group, getting its members to do something they wouldn't otherwise do: take the test. For many groups in the real world—such as large companies, markets, and democracies—it would be very difficult indeed to convince everyone in the group to take the time to spend even a few minutes on a special test like this. It would be ideal if instead we could just *observe* a group doing what it ordinarily does and use those observations to accurately estimate the group's intelligence.

Fortunately, there are a number of ways to measure a group's collective intelligence by either intervening or observing and by using either of the definitions of intelligence in chapter 1.

You Can Observe a Lot by Watching

One way to measure a group's specialized intelligence is just to pick a goal and then observe how well a group achieves that goal. For instance, you can measure how well a business achieves its financial goals by using metrics like profit, productivity, and return on investment. Or you can measure other aspects of a business's performance with metrics like the percentage of revenue that comes from products introduced in the previous five years (a measure of product innovation), how many jobs it creates, how well employees rate it as a place to work, and how often executives at other companies express admiration for it.

You can measure the performance of a society as a whole by using economic metrics like gross domestic product (GDP) or social metrics like crime rates, literacy rates, and quality-of-life surveys. And you might measure the performance of markets with metrics like how liquid the market is, how volatile it is, and how rapidly it adjusts prices based on new information.

In some cases, you can also observe a group's collective general intelligence. To do this, you need to be able to observe the group in enough different situations to see how flexible or adaptable it is.

For example, we often think of the inventor Thomas Edison as a genius, but in an important sense, the company he helped create, General Electric (GE), may have been even more of a genius as an organization. GE is the only company included in the original 1896 Dow Jones Industrial Average that is still included today.[19] To survive and prosper for over a century, in many different industries and many economic environments, GE had to have been extremely flexible and adaptable. Of course, it may well have benefited from good luck and other factors, too, but it certainly seems reasonable to say that GE has had a high level of collective general intelligence.

More recently, Apple has revolutionized at least three whole industries: personal computing, music, and mobile telephones. Many people would attribute much of this success to a single individual, Steve Jobs, but even since Jobs's death, the company has continued to prosper. Whatever the causes of its success in all these industries, I think it's fair to say that Apple has exhibited a great deal of collective general intelligence.

In general, economists have found that there is often a surprising amount of persistence in the performance of companies—high performers tend to stay successful and low performers tend to linger at the bottom of the pack.[20] For example, one study of manufacturing plants in the United States found that 61 percent of plants that were in the top fifth of all plants in terms of productivity in 1972 were still there five years later, and 42 percent were still there after 10 years. At the bottom end of the scale, 38 percent of the plants in the bottom fifth were still there 10 years later.[21] Whole fields of management and economics are attempting to determine what causes these differences, but this stability of performance over time suggests a kind of collective intelligence in these plants, high in some and low in others.

In addition to measuring the same variables over an extended period of time, it is also possible to measure the general intelligence of a group by observing many different variables at once. For instance, the country of Bhutan focuses a great deal of attention on what they call gross national happiness, a measure of societal well-being that combines a wide variety of indicators, such as health, living standards, education, and psychological well-being. If a society does well on all these different measures, then we could say the society has more collective *general* intelligence than if it just does well on one or two.

Sometimes You Have to Do Something

To measure the collective intelligence of a group by intervening, you need to pick some aspect of the group's performance that you can test by seeing how the group responds to your actions. This is often difficult with large groups because you either have to convince everyone in the group to participate in the intervention or you have to have enough resources to change the group's environment.

For instance, if you had huge resources, you could intervene in an organization's environment by putting the organization in all kinds of different situations—maybe starting a competing organization or giving it greatly discounted prices on some of the raw materials it needs. Watching how the organization responds to such drastic actions could certainly tell you interesting things about the organization's intelligence. But, of course, there are limits to doing such large-scale experiments.

Small-scale interventions can also be useful, however. For instance, many businesses use "mystery shoppers" to evaluate the performance of employees who deal with the public in retail stores, restaurants, and customer-service call centers. The mystery shoppers use an organization's services just as any customer would—eating a hamburger, buying clothes, or calling a telephone help line. The employees of the organization being evaluated think the mystery shoppers are just ordinary customers and presumably treat them as they would anyone else. But unlike typical customers, these mystery shoppers are paid to carefully note and report what kind of service they receive.

Using mystery shoppers is often a good way of evaluating an organization's specialized intelligence for achieving goals, like promptly greeting and politely serving customers. And if interacting with the mystery shoppers requires employees to perform many different kinds of tasks, this could be a (partial) way of measuring the organization's collective general intelligence.

For instance, you could recruit a broad range of mystery shoppers—old and young, male and female, well educated and not, angry and polite—and ask them to call smartphone vendors' customer-service lines with a broad range of problems—hardware problems, software problems, and simple failures to understand the product. If some companies perform consistently well, you could say their customer-service operations are high on collective intelligence, and if others do badly, you could say their collective intelligence is lacking.

It would be interesting to see whether a statistical analysis of these results would reveal a single factor that predicts a substantial amount of the variation in performance across all the types of problems—

similar to what we found in our small working groups. I wouldn't be surprised if that were the case.

So what does all this mean? We now know that applying the concept of intelligence to groups is not just a poetic metaphor. For *general intelligence*—good performance across a wide range of goals—we've seen that intelligence emerges statistically for groups of people just as it does for individuals. And *specialized intelligence*—effective performance on a specific goal—provides a useful way of comparing group performance on a single goal across many different groups.

We also learned some tantalizing hints of what makes some groups smarter than others: just having smart individuals isn't enough. The individuals also need to be able to work together effectively.

Part II

How Can Computers Help Make Superminds Smarter?

Chapter 3

How Will People Work with Computers?

Many people think the future of computing is artificial intelligence (AI). And depending on how you define *artificial intelligence*, Google's online search engine is almost certainly the most widely used example of AI in the world today. Over 2.3 million times every second, someone in the world types keywords into the Google search bar and sees, in return, a listing of web pages related to that search. In fact, more than one in every seven people in the world does a Google search every month, and on average, they do about three searches per day.[1]

But Google isn't like R2-D2, C-3PO, the Terminator, or most other artificially intelligent robots we know from science fiction. Instead:

- it is more of a tool or assistant than a peer,
- it doesn't look or act like a human, and
- it doesn't usually communicate with people in conversational sentences.

I think that the vast majority of ways people will use computers in the next few decades—and perhaps for much longer—are likely to be more like Google than the imaginary robots of popular fiction. In this chapter, we'll see why each of these popular images is probably wrong and what the future is more likely to be instead.

WHAT ROLES WILL COMPUTERS PLAY RELATIVE TO HUMANS?

The first thing to notice about real uses of computers in the world is that people are *always* involved somehow. Even if a computer can do a complete task all by itself, people are always involved in developing the software in the first place and usually modifying it over time. People decide when to use different programs in different situations and what to do when things go wrong. And, in many cases, people are involved all along in doing the parts of the work that machines can't do.

One useful way of thinking about how people and computers will work together is to consider what roles the computers can play relative to the people. People have the most control when machines act only as *tools*, and machines have successively more control as their roles expand to *assistants*, *peers*, and, finally, *managers*.

Tools

A physical tool, like a hammer or lawn mower, provides some capability that a human doesn't have alone, but the human user is directly in control at all times, guiding the actions of the tool and monitoring its progress. Information tools are similar. When you use a word processor or a spreadsheet or an online calendar, the machine is doing what you tell it to do (even when that's not always what you really *want* it to do).

In many cases, automated tools can substantially increase the specialized intelligence of the humans who use them. A financial analyst who uses a spreadsheet, for instance, can do many more calculations much faster and much more accurately than one who tries to do arithmetic in his or her head. An architect working with a computer-aided design tool can create, modify, and measure designs much faster and more accurately than one working only with paper and pencil.

Many of the most important uses of automated tools in the future, however, won't be to increase the specialized intelligence of individual users but instead to increase the *collective* intelligence of a group by helping humans communicate more effectively with each other. In fact, as we saw in chapter 1, the vast majority of uses for computers today are essentially as tools to help humans communicate with each other: e-mail, word processing, texting, and most uses of the web or mobile apps such as Wikipedia, Facebook, Twitter, YouTube, and others. In all these cases, computers are not doing much "intelligent" processing; they are primarily just transferring information created by humans to other humans.

I think that point is obvious if you look at how we actually use computers today, but most people still think computers are primarily machines for, well, computing things. Perhaps it's because the first uses of computers did actually emphasize calculating. Perhaps it's just etymology, since *computer* is derived from the verb *compute*. Perhaps it's because we've long thought of computers as "electronic brains."

Whatever the reason for that inaccurate perception, it's clear that computers have mostly been used, so far, to help humans communicate. And I don't think this primary way of using computers is going to change anytime soon. For at least the next decade or two, and perhaps much longer, I think the most common uses of computers will still be as sophisticated tools to help humans communicate with each other.

Assistants

A human assistant, unlike a tool, can work without your direct attention and often takes more initiative in trying to achieve the general goals you have specified. Automated assistants are similar, but the boundary between tools and assistants is not always a sharp one. Text-message platforms, for instance, are mostly tools, but they sometimes take the initiative to do automatic spelling correction without your telling them to (occasionally with hilarious results[2]).

Google's search engine is also a tool: when you type in keywords, it shows you websites with those keywords. But to make this work almost instantaneously, the Google algorithms are constantly working in the background, continuously updating a massive index of essentially all the pages on the web. And Google's search algorithms also exercise a fair amount of discretion about the order in which they show you the search results. Because they do all these other tasks without any attention from you, they are really some combination of tools and assistants.

As we move further along the continuum toward greater machine control, Google Assistant and Amazon's Alexa are examples of automated systems that strive to be assistants rather than just tools, especially when they do things like volunteering information you never asked for—such as reminding you that you need to leave for the airport now to make your flight. Similarly, a fully self-driving car would be a clear example of an assistant. Like a human taxi (or Uber) driver, this automated assistant will take a great deal of initiative to navigate through traffic to the destination you specify.

Another example of an automated assistant is the software used by the online clothing retailer Stitch Fix to help its human stylists recommend items to customers.[3] Stitch Fix customers first fill out detailed questionnaires about their style, size, and price preferences. Then all that information is digested by machine-learning algorithms that select promising items of clothing for the stylists to consider. But it is the stylists who make the final selection of five items to send to the customer in each shipment. Customers pay only for the items they want and return the rest.

The algorithmic assistant in this partnership is able to take into account far more information than the human stylists could. For instance, stylish jeans are often notoriously hard to fit, but inseam measurement is a good indicator of fit, and the algorithms are able to select for each customer a variety of jeans that other customers with the same inseam measurement decided to keep.

The human stylists, however, are also able to take into account information the machine can't—like whether the customer wants an outfit for a baby shower or a business meeting. And, of course, the human stylists can relate to the human customers in a more personal way than the machine does. So the combination of people and computers together can provide better service than either could alone.

In a very different industry, the WatsonPaths software that IBM is developing in collaboration with Cleveland Clinic[4] is also an automated assistant. Building on the same basic technology used in the version of Watson that beat the human champions of the TV game show *Jeopardy!*, WatsonPaths uses knowledge it has culled from the medical literature to identify multiple possible diagnoses that are consistent with a patient's symptoms and medical history.

Then, like the Stitch Fix software, the Watson system shows a number of plausible diagnoses to the doctors. It also shows the doctors the chain of reasoning it used and the degree of confidence it has for each of these different diagnoses. Human doctors make the final decisions about how to treat the patient, but their automated medical assistant helps them take into account vast amounts of medical literature and come up with diagnoses they might never have even considered.

Peers

Some of the most intriguing uses of computers will involve roles where the machines operate as peers of the humans more than as assistants or tools, even in cases where there isn't much actual artificial intelligence being used.

In many cases, this will happen because a program that acts as an assistant for one human acts as a peer of another. For example, if you are riding in a self-driving car, and I am driving myself on the same road, then your driving *assistant* is my driving *peer.* If you are a stock trader, you may already be transacting with someone else's automated program trading system without even knowing it. And if you are bidding in an eBay auction, you may be competing with someone else who uses an automated "sniping" assistant that is programmed to outbid you in the last few seconds of an auction.

Sometimes automated peers aren't operating to represent the interests of a specific person; they are advancing the interests of a whole group. For instance, if your job is dealing with claims for the Lemonade insurance company, you have an automated peer named AI Jim.[5] AI Jim is an online "bot," and when customers file a claim, they do so by exchanging text messages with AI Jim. If their claim meets certain parameters, the bot pays the claim automatically and almost instantly. If not, the claim is referred to a person who does whatever additional processing is needed.

Wikipedia also has a number of bots that automatically make certain kinds of edits themselves and notify humans about others that might need to be done.[6] One bot, for example, uses machine-learning algorithms to automatically undo changes to articles that are very likely just vandalism (such as adding obscene words). Another bot automatically checks new pages to see whether they contain large portions of text that also appear elsewhere on the web. If they do, the bot flags them as potential copyright violations that require human attention.

In other words, the human editors of Wikipedia and the computer bots are acting as peers, all editing the same articles. The bots are all managed by humans, so in some sense, the bots are just assistants to their human owners. But if you are a human vandal trying to deface a Wikipedia page, the bot that undoes your malicious changes is performing the same task that a human peer would. And the overall effect on the content of Wikipedia is almost certainly better than if there were no computers acting as peers to the humans.

Managers

Human managers delegate tasks, give directions, evaluate work, and coordinate the efforts of others. Machines can do all these things, too, and when they do, they are performing as automated managers. Even though some people find the idea of a machine as a manager threatening, we already live with them every day. Think about a traffic light, for instance. Instead of a human police officer in the intersection directing traffic, a machine plays that role. Or think about the workers in a telephone call center. A machine automatically routes calls to them—a task that could be performed by a human manager. But most people don't find either of these situations threatening or problematic.

I think it's likely that there will be many more examples of machines playing the role of managers in the future. For instance, the Crowd-Forge system, developed by my friends Aniket Kittur, Robert Kraut, and their colleagues at Carnegie Mellon University, uses online workers to write documents like encyclopedia articles.[7] We'll call the online workers Turkers because they are recruited from an Amazon service called Mechanical Turk, which we'll see in more detail later.

The process begins with the system asking Turkers to come up with an outline for a document—say, an encyclopedia article about New York City. An outline for such an article might, for example, include sections for attractions, a brief history, and so forth (see the following chart).[8] For each section in the outline, the system then asks other Turkers to find facts that might be relevant for that section. Next, the system collects the facts for each section and sends them to still other Turkers, who write a paragraph for the section based on the provided facts. Finally, the system puts all the paragraphs in order to create a complete encyclopedia article. The average article produced in this way requires 36 separate subtasks, presumably done by 36 different people, and costs only $3.26 to produce.

When the researchers had other Turkers evaluate these articles, the articles were judged to be significantly better than similar articles

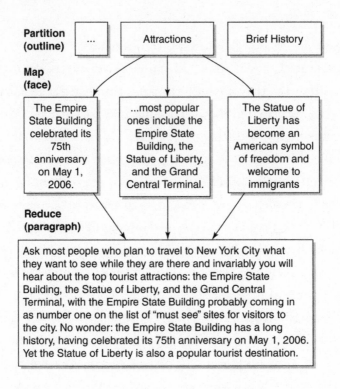

written by a single person for the same amount of money, and the articles were approximately equivalent in quality to those in the "simple English" version of Wikipedia.[9]

In other words, here's a case where the researchers created an automated assistant for themselves to help manage a group of Turk workers by delegating tasks to them and coordinating the interdependencies among the tasks. For the Turk workers, this was no different from doing tasks given to them by a human manager, but the automated system allowed the process to be scaled over huge groups of contributors.

I think it's likely that this form of what you might call industrialized writing will become much more common in the future. In today's world, for instance, almost all the furniture and clothing we use is produced in factories where many people (and usually many machines) are involved in the production of each item. We still occasionally buy handmade things like sweaters or chairs, but these are certainly the exceptions rather than the rule. In the same way, I suspect that much of the written material we see in the not-too-distant future may be produced by something like the industrialized writing process that CrowdForge exemplifies. And, as we'll see in later chapters, an increasing amount of the actual writing may be done by machines, not people. It's not as if we'll never again read long textual documents written by a single person, but they may someday become as rare as handmade sweaters are today.

WHAT WILL ARTIFICIALLY INTELLIGENT MACHINES LOOK LIKE? (HINT: NOTHING)

As philosopher Marshall McLuhan noted, we often first understand new technologies by comparing them to old ones.[10] For instance, the first cars were called horseless carriages, and that's what they looked like, too. They were designed like traditional carriages, with running boards and all, just without any horses in front. Over time, of course, the unique requirements and possibilities of the new technologies were reflected in automobile designs. Because cars traveled much faster than carriages, for instance, they acquired smooth, aerodynamic shapes and windows that sealed the passenger compartments to be airtight.

In the same way, many people imagine that artificially intelligent machines will look and act more or less like people. With the exception of a few cuddly ones, like R2-D2, most fictional robots have two arms, two legs, and a face with a pair of eyes, a nose, and a mouth. But the real artificial intelligence we use today rarely looks like the robots of science fiction. Google's search functions, Alexa, and the hundreds of credit-approval algorithms used by banks don't look like anything. To the humans who interact with them, they are just disembodied intelligences, existing somewhere in the vague world of cyberspace, or "the cloud."

Even the robots doing physical tasks usually don't look anything like the humans who might previously have done those tasks. The robots that move items around in Amazon's warehouses, for example, don't look like people carrying boxes. They are little orange boxes about eight inches tall and about one foot square with small wheels mostly hidden on the bottom. They travel around a warehouse, insert themselves underneath a shelving unit, then lift and move the shelves (and everything they hold) to another location.

Google's newest driverless cars also don't look like traditional cars with robots sitting in the drivers' seats. Instead the steering wheels, brake pedals, and accelerators are gone completely. All the intelligence is hidden, along with the engine and other mechanical parts of the car, out of the passengers' view altogether.

By the time you read these words, the examples I've just used may already sound old-fashioned, but I think it's very likely that most future uses of artificial intelligence will evolve into unique forms that fit the actual requirements of their intended tasks rather than the humanoid shapes of science-fiction robots. Various forms of intelligence will be embedded in different ways in different societal processes.

The supply chains for manufacturing and delivery of physical products, for instance, will include all kinds of machines to create, combine, and transport physical objects, but each of those machines will have its own unique shape to match its purpose. The intelligence that controls them will sometimes be in the machines themselves and sometimes on the other side of the planet. The same will be true for all the machines involved in diagnosing and treating you when you're sick, keeping your home clean and comfortable, and generating the energy needed to power all these other activities.

The Exceptions: Where Will We Want Robots That Look Like Humans?

There are two important exceptions to this general prediction of mostly invisible intelligence. First, some physical tasks need to be done in physical environments designed for humans, and for robots to navigate successfully in human environments, they may need to have something like human forms. For instance, if you want a robot to serve you meals, make your bed, and carry other things around in your house, you need it to be able to fit through your doorways and climb your stairs. That robot may look quite a bit like a person.

Second, we may create robots that look like people just to satisfy our human desire to interact with humanlike creatures. For instance, Baxter is an industrial robot from Rethink Robotics designed to do the kind of physical tasks in factories that human workers do today. And it's probably no accident that Baxter has a humanlike face mounted on its body between its humanlike arms, right where a human head would be. There's no technical reason why a face or head is needed there, but presumably the designers of Baxter thought the humans in a factory would be more comfortable around a robot that sort of looked like a person.

And if the future of AI is anything like the history of other information technologies, it will almost certainly be used for erotic purposes, too. Some of the earliest uses of CDs, DVDs, and the Internet were for pornography, and it seems very likely that there will be artificially intelligent sex robots in the future.

HOW WILL WE COMMUNICATE WITH COMPUTERS?

Over hundreds of thousands of years of biological and cultural evolution, humans have developed a multitude of ways of communicating with each other. Perhaps the most important way is by talking, using words in languages like English, Chinese, or Swahili. And it's hard to overstate the importance of the invention of written versions of these languages. But humans also communicate in many other ways: They use facial expressions and gestures. They touch each other. They sing to each other. They create art.

Since we humans have so many years of practice communicating in all these ways, it comes very naturally to us, and it's only natural that we will want to communicate with our machines in the same ways. For instance, systems like Amazon's Alexa and Apple's Siri can already use ordinary human languages like English in limited ways, and over time, our machines will become increasingly capable of using human languages to communicate with us. That means there will be many more examples of computer systems that interact with us for specialized tasks using voice or text. But as we'll see in the next chapter, it will probably require decades of hard technical work before our machines will be able to speak and understand ordinary human language as broadly and flexibly as people do.

And even if we can technically achieve that goal, there is a very important reason why we won't always want to communicate with our machines in the same ways we do with other people. That is that our machines have far superior capabilities for communication than people have, at least for some purposes. The most obvious of these capabilities is that machines can generate extremely rich visual images instantly in ways that humans will never be able to do by themselves.

For instance, if a human with no other tools were giving you directions to a store across town, the best he or she could do would be a sequence of spoken directions for landmarks and turns. But even today's computers can already do something much better by instantly giving you a detailed visual map showing the complete route.

And imagine trying to edit a letter by telling someone over the phone what changes to make. You would have to say things like: "Go to the third sentence in the second paragraph. Take out the word 'Susan' and replace it with 'John comma, Mary comma,' then the word 'and.'" Think about how much easier it is to do this when you can just point, click, and type, the way you do with today's computers.

My colleague Hiroshi Ishii, in the MIT Media Lab, is taking this idea of nonverbal interaction with computers several steps further, using the ideas of "tangible bits" and "radical atoms." Many years ago, I worked with Hiroshi on a project in which we let people experiment with different configurations for a company's supply chain by moving small objects around on a special table that sensed their positions.[11] Some objects represented factories, for example, and others represented warehouses. By moving and rotating the objects, people could see what would happen to, say, the capacities and lead times of their supply chains if they removed a warehouse or increased the throughput of a factory. In other words, instead of telling the computer in words what configurations they wanted to evaluate, people directly manipulated physical objects.

More recently, Hiroshi and his colleagues have been experimenting with even more radical ways for humans to communicate with computers. In these experiments, they use three-dimensional materials that can be manipulated by both the people and the computers. For instance, in one project, called SoundFORMS, users can compose music using a shape-shifting display that represents the sound waves of the music being composed (see the image below). Users can touch the display and change the actual shapes of the sound waves with their hands.[12]

Or think about the Baxter factory robot. Most robots today require very detailed programming to do new tasks, but you can program Baxter to do something new by simply moving its arms the way you want them to move.[13]

In the long run, perhaps the ultimate way for people to communicate with machines will be with a kind of mind-meld: direct neural connections that go straight from the machines to different neurons in a person's brain. Of course, it will be some time before we are able to do this in any substantial way, but the results of some of the early experiments seem very promising. For instance, a team of researchers led by Richard Andersen at California Institute of Technology recently connected a robotic arm to silicon chips implanted in the brain of a man who had been paralyzed from the neck down for 13 years.[14] With practice, the man was able to move the arm just by thinking about it, managing to give himself a drink from a bottle of beer, among other things.

We don't know for sure how rapid progress will be with this technology, but I am optimistic enough to joke with my friends that I want to be the first 90-year-old who has a neural implant. At the current rate of progress, it certainly seems possible that we may have very capable neural interfaces before we have machines that can speak and understand ordinary human languages like English as well as humans can.

We saw in the previous chapter that for a human group to be smart, it needs people who can work well together. In the same way, when human groups include computers, they need people and computers that can work well together. Sometimes the best way for this to happen is for the people to learn better how to work with computers. But often the best way will be to design computers that can work well with people. As we've seen in this chapter, there are some promising possibilities for how this is likely to happen. But a key question that arises when we consider many of these possibilities is: How much intelligence—particularly how much *general* intelligence—will computers have in the future?

CHAPTER 4

How Much General Intelligence Will Computers Have?

Like many important concepts, the term *artificial intelligence* is diffi-cult to define.[1] Some people use it to mean "machines that are able to think or act like humans do." For instance, the famous Turing test[2] says that a computer can be considered "intelligent" if a person who asks the computer questions cannot tell whether the answers come from a human or a machine. Another definition of AI is "machines that act rationally," even if they do this in some way that is different from—perhaps better than—humans. For instance, the Google search algo-rithm almost certainly doesn't "remember" web pages in the same way humans remember things, but it does a very good job of finding pages that Google users are looking for.

Perhaps the simplest way of defining AI is as "intelligence exhib-ited by machines."[3] Then we can use our definitions of intelligence from chapter 1 to say that AI can be specialized or general, just like human intelligence.

One of the most important things most people don't realize about AI today is that it is *all* very specialized.[4] The Google search engine is great at retrieving news articles about baseball games, but it can't write its own article about your son's Little League game. IBM's Watson[5] is better than the best humans at playing Jeopardy, but the version of the program that played Jeopardy can't even play tic-tac-toe, much less chess. Tesla's self-driving cars are great at keeping a car moving with traffic in well-marked lanes, but they can't pick a box from a warehouse shelf and take it to a packing station.

Of course, there are computer systems that can do these other things as well. But the point is that these are all different specialized programs, not a single general AI that can figure out what to do in each specific situation. In each case, humans—with their general intelligence—have to write programs that contain rules for solving different specific problems, and they have to decide which programs to run in a given situation.

WHEN (IF EVER) WILL MACHINES REALLY HAVE GENERAL INTELLIGENCE?

How soon—if ever—will this change? Some people argue that machines will *never* be able to do all the subtle, intelligent things humans do. In other words, they say, machines will never have general intelligence.[6]

In some cases, this argument is made on philosophical grounds: even if a machine could do everything humans can, the machine still wouldn't really be intelligent because only humans can be intelligent.[7] I confess I don't have a lot of patience with this argument. To me, this is like asking, as computer scientist Edsger Dijkstra did, "Can a submarine swim?"[8] Both fish and submarines move through water using their own power, so which word you use to describe that phenomenon is purely a matter of semantics. In English, it sounds strange to use the word *swim* about a submarine, but in Russian, for example, this sounds perfectly natural.[9] In other words, this isn't a debate about the facts; it's just a debate about how we want to define the words we use to describe those facts.

In the same way, the philosophical question of whether, in principle, machines can be intelligent is really just a debate about how we want to define the word *intelligence*. It seems to me perfectly reasonable to define it—as we did in chapter 1—in a way that can include machines.

Others argue that machines will never have general intelligence because the practical problems of achieving this are just so hard we will never solve them, or if we do, it will be far beyond the lifetimes of anyone alive today. Here there is clearly room for differing viewpoints. Some people, like my former student and now colleague Erik Brynjolfsson and his coauthor Andrew McAfee, suggest that continuing advances in computer hardware together with the surprisingly rapid progress in artificial intelligence make it likely that machines may possess general intelligence soon.[10] Others, like artificial intelligence expert Rodney Brooks, say that it may take hundreds of years.[11]

In fact, progress in the field of artificial intelligence has been notoriously difficult to predict ever since its early days, in the 1950s. For instance, one study by researchers Stuart Armstrong and Kaj Sotala analyzed 95 predictions—made between 1950 and 2012—about when general AI would be achieved.[12] They found a strong tendency for both experts and nonexperts to predict that general AI would be achieved between 15 and 25 years in the future...regardless of when the predictions were made! In other words, general AI has seemed about 20 years away for the last 60 years.

More recent surveys and interviews tend to be consistent with this long-term pattern: people still predict that general AI will be here in about 15 to 25 years.[13] So while we certainly don't know for sure, there is at least good reason to be skeptical of confident predictions that general AI will appear in "the next few decades." My own view is that, barring some major societal disasters, it is very likely that general AI will appear *someday*, but likely not until quite a few decades in the future.

WHAT'S SO HARD ABOUT PROGRAMMING COMPUTERS?

To understand why general AI is so hard to achieve, you need to understand what's hard about programming computers in the first place. If you've ever done any nontrivial computer programming yourself, you've directly experienced the challenges. But if you haven't, I'm going to try to give you a basic understanding very quickly.

The basic problem is that at the heart of all modern digital computers are "processors" that are, in a sense, very stupid. When I teach basic information technology courses to MBA students, I use an analogy that my MIT colleague Stuart Madnick developed for helping people understand what these processors can do. He describes an imaginary computer called the Little Man Computer.[14] This fictional computer consists of a little man who works in a little room (see the illustration below). But the little man is very stupid: he can do only about 10 very simple things. He has an inbox and an outbox in the wall of his room through which he can communicate with the outside world using pieces of paper that contain one three-digit number each. There is a blackboard in the room with 100 numbered locations where he can read and write the three-digit numbers. He also has a calculator with which he can add and subtract these three-digit numbers.

And whenever the little man has finished doing one thing, he decides what to do next by looking at a number that he has previously written in one of the locations on the blackboard and interpreting that number as an "instruction" for him. For instance, if the instruction is "901," he knows that is a code that means he should type whatever number is in the inbox into the calculator. If the instruction starts with a 1, he knows that means "add." If the instruction is 145, for example, that means he should add whatever number is in location 45 on the blackboard to whatever is in the calculator.

He has about 10 of these instructions, each with a different code, for things like inputting and outputting numbers, adding and subtracting, and moving numbers to and from the blackboard. Usually he follows the instructions in the order they are written on his blackboard. But sometimes he has to decide what to do next. To do this, he has a couple of additional instructions that let him decide where to look for his next instruction depending on whether the number in the calculator is 0 or greater than 0.

To see how this could work, imagine that the little man needs to add 10 numbers. To do this, he will need to not only add the numbers; he will also need to keep track of how many numbers he has added so far. He might use one location on the blackboard for the *total* of all the numbers so far and a different location for the *count* of how many numbers he has added. Each time he adds another number to the total, he would also add 1 to the count. And to see whether he is through adding, he could then subtract the count from 10. If the result is greater than 0, that would mean he hasn't added all 10 numbers yet, so he would do the instructions for adding another number again. But if the result is 0, he would look in a different location on the blackboard for a set of instructions that might, for example, tell him to put the total in the outbox.

And that's it. That's all the little man can do. He just follows various combinations of the same set of 10 or so simple instructions. Part of his blackboard contains the instructions that tell him what to do. These instructions constitute the "program" the little man is running. The rest of the numbers on his blackboard are the "data" he is processing. He can't do anything at all without a program to tell him what to do. And the programs he uses have to break everything he ever does down into tiny steps.

Now, here's the amazing thing: whenever a modern computer does anything—whether it's sending your most recent selfie to all your Facebook friends or deciding when to slow down your self-driving car—all it is really doing is following a very large number of very simple instructions that basically consist of the same things the little man can do! Of course, modern computers have access to millions of locations on the blackboard (memory locations)—far more than the little man has. These locations store numbers in binary format (1s and 0s) rather than the decimal numbers we generally use. And modern computers can carry out many millions of instructions per second—far faster than any real person could. Still, all the things they do are really just very complicated combinations of very simple instructions like the little man's.

Here's the hard part: to get a computer to do anything at all, a person has to write it a set of instructions. Figuring out how to get computers to do complex things using only the simple instructions computers really understand can be extremely difficult.

This is what software developers do all day long, and they've figured out all kinds of techniques to do it better and faster. For instance, many decades ago, software developers figured out how to write programs in "high-level programming languages" (like today's Java and C) and then let other programs (called compilers) do all the painstakingly detailed dirty work of translating these programs into the specific ("machine language") instructions that the computers actually need.

But even with powerful techniques like these, writing the detailed instructions that computers need to do their work—also called programs or code or algorithms or rules—means a lot of labor for human programmers. This is true even for relatively simple programs like accounting systems, and it is certainly true for complex AI programs. To give you a rough sense of how complicated these programs can be, Google estimates that there are about 2 *billion* lines of code in the high-level-language versions of the software they use for all their services.[15]

WHAT PATHS MIGHT LEAD TO GENERAL AI?

So is there any hope for general AI? Of course, there is. In spite of the difficulties of writing computer programs, we have already come a long way in creating computers with all kinds of capabilities, including many kinds of specialized AI. And we already know of a number of other kinds of programming techniques and computer architectures that might get us closer to general AI. Let's look at a few of these possibilities.

Commonsense Knowledge

Think about what you need to know to understand the following snippet of conversation:

PERSON A: I have a headache.
PERSON B: The drugstore on the corner closes at 6:00 p.m.

Of course, you need to know the meanings of the words used. But you also need to know lots of other facts about the world, including, to name just a few:

- Headaches are a kind of illness.
- Illnesses are usually unpleasant for the people who have them.
- People usually try to avoid unpleasant things.
- One way to avoid the unpleasantness of an illness is by taking drugs.

- One way to get drugs is to buy them in stores.
- You can only buy things in stores when the stores are open.

For a computer to "understand" that bit of conversation in anything like the way a human understands it, therefore, the computer has to know all these facts. Now, it wouldn't be too hard to write a program with these few specific facts encoded in a format that would enable a computer to do some reasoning about them. But that's just a tiny sliver of the millions of facts that are needed to have anything even remotely approaching general intelligence about our world. Of course, we humans learn these things as children, and now that we know them, they seem completely obvious to us. We just think of them as common sense.

But computers have to somehow acquire millions of these facts. The most obvious way for that to happen is for human programmers to write programs that encode this knowledge in a format machines can use.

Perhaps the most ambitious attempt to do this is the Cyc project, started and led since 1984 by the computer scientist Doug Lenat.[16] Doug and his colleagues have spent the time since then painstakingly programming millions of facts—about topics from diseases to weather to politics—in a huge commonsense knowledge base for computers to use.

The jury is still out on how far this approach will go toward creating general AI, but in the meantime, it is already being used for projects like helping doctors at Cleveland Clinic find patients for clinical studies who have certain combinations of characteristics, such as a history of "bacteria after a pericardial window."[17]

Big Data

In recent years, significant progress toward developing effective AI has sometimes come from having massive amounts of data available in a far more accessible form than ever before.

For example, machine translation of human languages (like English and Spanish) has long been one of the holy grails of AI research. For decades, researchers were consistently disappointed by how slow progress toward this goal was. But language-translation programs have recently become much better, in part because of the availability of vast amounts of translated documents. Google Translate, for instance, uses United Nations documents—which are usually translated by UN translators into at least six languages—to tally how often a phrase in one language corresponds to different phrases in other languages. For example, the Spanish phrase *darse cuenta* is usually translated into English as "realize" (instead of the more literal translation of "give account"), so that is how Google Translate has learned to translate it. The key to this approach is that it doesn't require human programmers to learn all the complex rules and idioms of languages; it just depends on having vast amounts of translated text available that a simpler set of rules can then analyze.[18]

Machine Learning

A related approach to making computers more intelligent is to focus on developing ways for computers to learn. With this approach, instead of having human programmers write very detailed rules telling computers how to do every little thing they need to do, the programmers just write general rules that tell computers how to learn things, then let the computers figure out how to do everything else based on their own experience. This promising approach is called machine learning, and it is inspired by how humans learn. Humans are born with the ability to learn built into their brains, and they learn specific abilities without anyone ever "programming" them in the detailed way today's computers need.

Of course, no one really knows yet exactly how humans do this, and programming a machine to learn in the way humans do is even harder than it sounds, but researchers have made important progress in this direction. In some cases, they use what is called supervised learning, where a program learns things by being told when it is right and wrong. For instance, if you want to train a program to recognize whether there is a human face in a picture, you could show it thousands of pictures and tell it which depict faces and which do not. Then the program could adjust its statistical parameters over time to get better and better at predicting which pictures have faces based on the weights it gives to various combinations of lower-level features, like where the circles and lines are in the picture.

An even harder problem is how to do what is called unsupervised learning. The idea is that you give a computer many examples, but you don't tell it anything about what you want it to learn from these examples. If you think about it, this is how we humans learn most of what we know about the world. For instance, most babies learn how gravity works without anyone ever explicitly explaining it.

One of the most impressive recent examples of a computer doing unsupervised learning was when a group of Stanford University and Google researchers gave a computer system 10 million digital images from YouTube videos and let the system look for patterns. Without the researchers ever telling the system what to look for, it learned to identify 20,000 categories of objects, including human faces, human bodies, and...cat faces.[19] This system used a particularly promising approach to machine learning called deep learning, which loosely simulates the way the different layers of neurons in a brain are connected to one another.

Neuromorphic Computing

Still another intriguing approach to creating more intelligent computers is to create new kinds of computer hardware that more closely resemble the structure of a human brain. The Little Man Computer represents digital computers that do only one instruction at a time, and until recently, almost all widely used computers were designed in this way. In the last few years, however, an increasing number of computers are built with multicore processors, where the equivalent of several little men are working in parallel in the same computer.

The human brain, however, has a very different architecture. Instead of having only one—or even a few—processors working in parallel, the human brain has something like 80 to 100 billion processors, called neurons.[20] The neurons are connected to one another in very complex ways, and all, in a sense, are working in parallel. While it would be possible in principle to simulate all this complexity on a conventional digital computer, it might be much more feasible in practice to create computers that actually, physically, have billions of processors working in parallel. It might then be much easier to program these more brainlike computers to operate in ways more like human brains. Doing this will require a very different approach to designing computer hardware from the one we've used in the past, and that is the goal being pursued by a number of research groups today, including at IBM, HRL Laboratories, and elsewhere.[21]

WILL GENERAL AI BE A FORM OF COLLECTIVE INTELLIGENCE?

This last example raises an intriguing possibility. We know that the human brain is itself a form of collective intelligence. It is made up of a group of billions of individual neurons that—when working as a group—act in ways that seem intelligent.

Perhaps one of the best ways to create a real general AI, therefore, is to create a collective intelligence that combines, inside a single system, many different kinds of artificial intelligence, like all those we've just seen. In fact, Marvin Minsky, one of the fathers of AI, suggested as much in his writings about a "society of mind." In Minsky's view, a society of mind emerges from the interactions of many smaller "agents," none of which is very intelligent as an individual but all of which, together, create an overall system that *is* intelligent.[22]

A hint of what this might look like comes from IBM's Watson system. When Watson plays Jeopardy, the system makes use of thousands of smaller agents, many of which work in parallel on different processors.[23] Each of these agents is more complex than a single human neuron, but none of them alone is nearly smart enough to be a competitive Jeopardy player.

For instance, one of the questions Watson answered was "President under whom the U.S. gave full recognition to Communist China." To answer this question, some of Watson's agents went to work proposing the names of US presidents as possible answers. Other agents started looking in encyclopedias and similar resources for information about "US," "recognition," and "Communist China." Using a special encoding of this reference information together with commonsense knowledge, these agents proposed more answers to the question, probably including the names of Chinese and American officials involved in the announcement. Eventually, based on many different agents evaluating many different kinds of evidence, and each "voting" for the answers it thought were most plausible, Watson's society of agents concluded that the answer with the highest confidence level was "Jimmy Carter," which was, in fact, correct.

HOW CAN AI HELP MAKE GROUPS SMARTER?

In the long run, it seems to me very likely that—whenever it happens—real general AI will include something like Minsky's society of mind: a combination of many different specialized forms of reasoning and intelligence that, together, produce general intelligence.

But what can we do in the meantime? Here's the surprisingly important idea that many people still don't really appreciate: *Long before we have general AI, we can create more and more collectively intelligent systems by building societies of mind that include both human and machine agents.* In other words, instead of having computer agents like those in Watson try to solve a whole problem by themselves, we can create cyber-human systems where human and machine agents work together on the same problem. In some cases, the human agents may not even know—or care—whether they are interacting with another human or another machine.

In this way, humans can supply the general intelligence and other specialized skills that machines don't have. The machines can supply the knowledge and other specialized capabilities that people don't have. And the groups of people and computers together can act more intelligently than any person, group, or computer has ever done before.

How is this different from the ways people are thinking about AI today? Many people assume that computers will eventually do most things by themselves and that we should put "humans in the loop" in situations where they're still needed.[24] But I think it's more useful to realize that most things now are done by groups of people, and we should put computers into these groups in situations where that's helpful. In other words, we should move from thinking about *putting humans in the loop* to *putting computers in the group.*

But how can we do that? That's the main focus of the rest of this book.

Chapter 5

How Can Groups of People and Computers Think More Intelligently?

If you want to create a smarter computer, there's an obvious place to look for ideas: look at what humans do. That's what the AI field has done ever since its inception in the 1950s; it has tried to make computers as smart as people.

But if you want to create a smarter *group*—one that includes both people and computers—it's not so clear where to look for ideas. A really smart group is already smarter than any of the individual people or computers in it. So where can you look for more ideas?

Here's a simple possibility: you can imagine a group that is *perfectly intelligent*. Of course, no real group will ever achieve perfect intelligence all the time. But if you want to make your company—or your nonprofit organization or your government or any other kind of group—more intelligent, you can start by imagining what a perfectly intelligent group would do in the same situation and then try to come close to those actions.

PERFECT COLLECTIVE INTELLIGENCE

A perfect intelligence is not one that always gets perfectly correct answers, because there are many situations in the real world where no amount of intelligence can do that. Instead, a perfect intelligence does the best job possible given the information and other resources available to it. Not just the best job *humanly* possible, or even the best job *mechanically* possible, but the best job *logically* possible.

It's already possible to create perfect intelligences for simple problems like playing tic-tac-toe. A computer program, or even a person who knows the simple rules, can play this game perfectly. Modern computers can also perfectly remember vast amounts of information and perfectly calculate the answers to many complex logical and mathematical problems.

But for most real problems, there aren't perfect answers: Which new product should we launch? What should be the US policy toward Russia? How should I treat this patient? What should we do about climate change? Whom should I marry?

No human or computer can always answer questions like these perfectly, and neither can groups of people and computers. But when they are connected in the right ways, groups of people and computers together can often get closer to perfect intelligence than either could alone.

To visualize how a perfectly intelligent supermind might approach real-world problems like these, let's imagine a group of people and computers—what's sometimes called a *cyber-human system*—that is perfectly intelligent given the resources it has. To be more specific, let's imagine this system is a company that makes and sells T-shirts. We'll call this genius company Alberts Corp. in memory of an individual human genius whose last name was Einstein.

A Perfectly Intelligent Company

Alberts is not omniscient or omnipotent. It only knows things based on information it has access to. But that's still a *huge* amount of knowledge. For instance, it knows all the work-related knowledge in the minds of all its employees, all the information in its computers, all the publicly available knowledge in all the books, magazines, and public websites in the world, and all the nonpublic information that other people would tell Alberts if they were asked.

Now, here's the main thing: Alberts doesn't just know all these things; it can also make *perfectly intelligent* use of all this knowledge. It never forgets anything, and it uses everything it knows to make every new decision.

For example, when the people and computers in Alberts decide what features to put in their new T-shirts, they consider everything that any customer has ever told them. They also consider all the kinds of T-shirts available anywhere in the world, including their features and, whenever available, their sales histories. And they consider all the scientific literature about new technologies that might be useful in making T-shirts.

But Alberts doesn't stop there. It also figures out lots of other things that are knowable from the knowledge it already has. Of course, there might be an infinite number of things Alberts could potentially figure out, so it only figures out the most useful things possible, given the limits of its own reasoning powers.[1]

For instance, suppose a materials-science professor in Italy has developed a new low-cost photoluminescent fiber. Some combination of people and computers in Alberts might see this research published on the web and quickly realize that it could potentially be used to display interactive designs on T-shirts.

They might make very rough projections of how profitable a new product based on this technology might be and conclude that it is a promising technology to explore. Finally, they might notice from public information on the web that one of Alberts's competitors has recently hired a former graduate student of the Italian professor and that there is another student about to graduate who might be a candidate for Alberts to recruit.

Alberts would also do similar analyses of hundreds of other new technologies and identify the most promising next steps to take given all these possibilities. And let's assume, for the sake of our story, that the luminescent T-shirts emerged from this process as the most promising new product possibility, that the Alberts supermind used all its other capabilities to launch the new product, and that the product was a huge success.

Now, of course, no real company can come close to being as smart as Alberts, but just thinking about extreme possibilities like these can often help us come up with ideas that we might actually be able to turn into reality.

For instance, I once asked a partner from a major accounting and consulting firm to imagine a perfectly intelligent cyber-human "creature" that could do all the things her firm currently does and then to think about what *else* she would want it to do. She immediately began to think about more things she could do for her corporate clients that would provide even more value for them. For instance, if the basic preparation of corporate tax returns were already taken care of, she quickly thought of how she could provide much more creative advice about new legal forms for joint ventures or other ways her clients could work with their suppliers while minimizing their tax bills. And these were things that she could potentially focus on today.

In the rest of this book, we'll see lots of possibilities—some of them extreme—for how superminds might use new technologies to go far beyond what groups do today. For instance, we'll see how democracies might reflect the desires of voters much more accurately than they do now, how people and computers might make more accurate predictions of future events than is possible now, and how specialists from all over the world could improve the ways they create things, like corporate strategies, news stories, and plans for dealing with global climate change.

But to do that, we need to better understand how any system—whether it's a single human brain or a vast collection of people and computers in a company—can act intelligently. One of the best ways to do that is by thinking about what psychologists call the basic cognitive processes involved in intelligent behavior.

WHAT ARE THE COGNITIVE PROCESSES NEEDED IN AN INTELLIGENT SYSTEM?

I'm not much of a baseball player, but I played Little League baseball as a kid, and one of the things I learned was that to play baseball, you need to be able to: catch the ball, throw the ball, hit the ball with a bat, and run around the bases. If you can't do all four of these things with at least minimum competence, you can't really play baseball. Good players are good at all four, and the best players can do at least one or two of these things really, really well.

In a way, intelligence is similar to baseball. To act intelligently, there are five basic things you need to do. Here they are, working backward from the action (see the following diagram):

- In order to act at all, you have to *decide* what actions to take, even if that decision is made unconsciously.
- Before you *decide* on an action, you need to *create* possibilities for one or more courses of action. But good options for action don't happen in a vacuum. To identify and choose good actions, you almost always need information about the world you're acting in. To get this information, you can
  o *sense* the world around you or
  o *remember* things from the past.

- Finally, at the heart of intelligence is your ability to *learn* from experience, to observe patterns in the environment, and to improve your own actions over time.

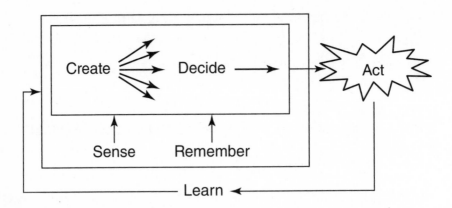

Together, these five *cognitive processes* are the building blocks of intelligent behavior, whether it occurs in individuals or in groups. Some systems with only specialized intelligence can get by with doing only one or two of these processes, but any system with general intelligence must do them all reasonably well. And being able to do some of these things really well can make a system with general intelligence even smarter.

In the next three parts of this book, we'll see how groups of people can do each of these things and how information technology can help do them better.

Part III

How Can Superminds Make Smarter Decisions?

CHAPTER 6

Smarter Hierarchies

Perhaps the most obvious way for groups to make decisions is to use the type of supermind we call a *hierarchy*. Hierarchies are everywhere in the modern world. Almost all businesses—from Apple and ExxonMobil to your local dry cleaner and grocery store—have a hierarchy at their core. So do most nonprofit organizations—from the Red Cross to the National Rifle Association. And the operational parts of governments—from the Internal Revenue Service to the Chinese army—are largely hierarchies, too.

In its pure form, we define a hierarchy as *a supermind where people in authority make decisions that their subordinates are required to follow.* Of course, hierarchies differ in many ways: there are variations in what kinds of decisions those in authority can make, how orders are communicated, and how they are enforced. As we'll see, many hierarchies are combined with other species of superminds, too, but the essence of a hierarchy is that those below follow the decisions of those above.

Many animal species use rudimentary forms of hierarchy to make decisions about access to food, territory, and mating opportunities—from pecking orders in chickens to dominance hierarchies in baboons.[1] But humans have developed the hierarchical form far beyond its use anywhere else in the animal kingdom. Over many millennia, we have created vast hierarchies that include thousands of people with many different levels and subgroups, and—in many cases—strict bureaucratic rules about the kinds of decisions people at different levels can make. And human hierarchies have been critical to our remarkable dominance over the other life forms on our planet.[2]

Of all the types of superminds, hierarchies are the easiest to recognize. A human hierarchy usually has a single person at its top, and that person speaks on behalf of the whole group.[3] When Tim Cook at Apple says something publicly, he is speaking for the whole organization in a way that isn't possible in any other form of supermind. Since a few people in a hierarchy usually make the most important decisions for the supermind as a whole, their individual human emotions, values, and limitations play a more influential role than in other types of superminds.

In fact, you can view a hierarchy as a supermind that mobilizes large numbers of individuals to achieve the goals of whoever controls the hierarchy. In some cases, like a business with a single owner, one person may control the whole hierarchy. In other cases, the hierarchy may be controlled by other superminds. For instance, at least in theory, voters control democratic governments, and stockholders control publicly held companies. But sometimes the politicians in a government, the managers in a company, or the workers in either kind of bureaucracy are able to get a lot of what they want even when it's not what the voters or stockholders really want.

HOW CAN INFORMATION TECHNOLOGY MAKE HIERARCHIES SMARTER?

In traditional hierarchies, like those in manufacturing companies, some parts of the work are automated (such as by machines on assembly lines), but humans are involved at every step of the way to manage the machines and do the things the machines can't do (such as driving on highways). But what if the machines can do almost everything that's needed to produce what the company sells?

Mostly Automated Hierarchies

Think about Google's search engine, for instance. When you type a question into the Google search bar, you see the results of your search almost instantly. No human is directly involved in producing the answer to your query; all the production is done by machines. The role of the humans is, instead, to manage the machines. Most important, the humans write the software the machines run. You could think of this as analogous to training the workforce. The humans also make sure the machines are actually running, and they deal with software bugs and other kinds of exceptions as they arise.

For example, my former postdoctoral associate David Engel now works at Google, doing what they call site reliability engineering. His job is to fix the problems that arise when the machines don't work the way the humans expect them to. For instance, if a program fails because there isn't enough computer memory available for it to run, David needs to figure out why the program ran out of memory and how to keep that from happening again.

As he explained it to me, "If there is something you have to do more than once, then why didn't you write a [program] to do that?" In other words, his job is not just to fix the unusual problems that arise but also to retrain the automated workers so those problems don't happen again.

So from that angle, Google is a highly automated hierarchy where the vast Google "server farms" are like giant factories in which a few humans manage thousands of machines that churn out search results all day long.

But it's worth noting that not everything Google does is automated. Even though the bottom layer of the Google hierarchy is filled with machines, the top layers are all made up of people. The people use their general intelligence to decide what the machines should do in the first place, and they manage the situations the machines can't manage themselves. For instance, even though companies can buy ad space directly from Google's automated selling agents through a service called AdWords, Google also has a whole division of humans in offices all over the world who do the high-touch work involved in managing relationships with Google's major corporate advertisers.

This is what hierarchies will look like as more tasks become automated: over time, the boundaries between what people do and what machines do will keep changing, but at any given time, humans will do the things the machines can't. For instance, there will usually be at least a few humans at the top of these hierarchies using their general intelligence to direct the organization's overall strategy and manage special-case exceptions.

There will also be humans in other places to do things that, for whatever reason, still elude the machines—like dealing with other humans in a very personal way. In some cases, lower-level humans may be "managed," at least in part, by software systems such as automated schedulers and workflow managers that act as assistants to the higher-level human managers.

Many people worry that this means human jobs will go away. Some version of this will almost certainly happen, no matter how fast (or how slowly) the AI capabilities of machines improve. Machines already do many things that used to be done by people. In the future, they will do more. The main uncertainty is just where and how fast the changes will occur. But as we'll see, when machines are doing the routine work that used to be done by people, people will often do new things that were never done before.

Decentralization

Aside from its ability to *automate* work, it's also clear that technology can act as a tool to help people *communicate* with each other and their machines. This means that new technologies can help *centralize* some decisions that might previously have been made much lower down in a hierarchy. The potential for this is illustrated by the famous photograph of Barack Obama and his top advisers watching live videos in the White House of the raid in Pakistan that killed Osama bin Laden. As far as we know, Obama didn't issue any new orders while watching the raid, but in principle, such detailed information from anywhere on the planet makes it possible for the US president as well as senior executives of other large organizations to exercise an unprecedented amount of detailed control over decisions far down in their organizations' hierarchies. In other words, they can now intervene in low-level decision making in ways they never could have before.

On the other hand, as I argued in my 2004 book, *The Future of Work*, it will probably be even more common for cheap communication to help *decentralize* decision making in many parts of our economy.[4] Here's why: New information technologies allow much cheaper communication. Cheaper communication means it's economically feasible for many more people to have much more information than in the past. That, in turn, means that many more people can have enough information to make sensible decisions for themselves instead of just following orders from someone above them in a hierarchy. And people who make decisions for themselves are often more highly *motivated*, more *creative*, and more *flexible* than those who just follow orders.

These benefits of decentralized decision making aren't important everywhere. But in our increasingly knowledge-based and innovation-driven economy, the critical factors in business success are often precisely the same as the advantages of decentralized decision making: motivation, creativity, and flexibility. That's why I think we're likely to see more and more decentralization of decision making over the coming decades.

In the years since *The Future of Work* was published, many of the things it predicted have become more common: Highly decentralized online groups like Wikipedia and open-source software are much more prominent. Decentralized markets for things like taxi services (Lyft) and hotel services (Airbnb) have captured our national attention. Even our largest corporations—like IBM, Google, and General Motors—have less of the rigid, centralized hierarchies that were common in the corporations of the past (think three-piece suits) and more of the loose, decentralized structures that used to be confined to a few cutting-edge sectors of the economy (think jeans and T-shirts).

In fact, this decentralized way of organizing people is likely to be particularly desirable in highly automated organizations. If machines are doing most of the routine work, then by definition, human employees will be doing nonroutine work where creativity, innovation, and flexibility are often key.

Furthermore, centralized hierarchies are usually *not* the best way to organize nonroutine work. Instead, as consulting firms and research organizations illustrate, it's often better to have lots of temporary project teams, constantly changing as new problems and projects arise. The bulk of the decisions need to be made by the people on these teams who are actually doing the work, not by higher-level managers. One good word for these loose, flexible hierarchies is *adhocracies*.[5]

Example: Valve Corporation

An intriguing look into the future of decentralized organization comes from Valve, a video-game developer. The most unusual thing about Valve is how much freedom it gives the software developers, animators, and other creators of its video games. Take a look at this excerpt from their handbook for new employees:[6]

> ...nobody "reports to" anybody else. We do have a founder/ president, but even he isn't your manager. This company is yours to steer—toward opportunities and away from risks. You have the power to green-light projects. You have the power to ship products.

To illustrate this, the handbook also includes whimsical organizational charts for the company (below). In diagram 1, everyone in the company is on the same level except for "gabe"—Gabe Newell, the founder and president. In diagram 2, everyone is on the same level except for someone named "chet." I don't know who Chet is, but I'm glad I'm not in his position. All the other diagrams show that everyone is more or less at the same level with no traditional hierarchical structure at all.

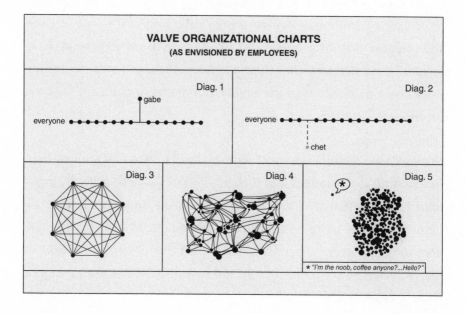

VALVE ORGANIZATIONAL CHARTS
(AS ENVISIONED BY EMPLOYEES)

Here are some examples of what this actually means for how the company works:

- Any group of employees can write and ship a software product without approval from a manager. If the employees think it's ready to ship, it ships.
- Any group of employees can start a search for a new hire and begin interviewing candidates. After interviews and wide discussion, if there is a candidate whom people want to hire and to whom no one objects, then the candidate is hired.

- When candidates are hired, their salaries are usually only a small part of their compensation. They can also receive bonuses of between 5 and 10 times their salaries, determined by the opinions of their peers.

Of course, not everyone likes this structure. One former employee, for instance, says it is a "lot like high school," where the popular kids have a lot of informal power.[7] In a sense, she was saying that Valve felt more like a community, where people have informal power derived from their reputations, rather than like a hierarchy, where people have formal power derived from their positions. Perhaps that's something we will see more often in the highly automated organizations of the future.

In short, new technologies will probably lead to two major changes in hierarchical decision making. First, more tasks will be done by automated systems that are tools or assistants for the humans. Second, the humans will do more nonroutine tasks, organized in more flexible, decentralized ways. When executed well, these changes will lead to hierarchies that are more flexible and more intelligent than many of those we have today.

CHAPTER 7

Smarter Democracies

The next species of supermind is a *democracy*. The most visible examples of democracies today are in governments. In democratic countries around the world, from Norway to South Korea, citizens vote to elect legislators who in turn vote to enact laws. The laws created by these democracies are then interpreted and enforced by hierarchies in the other branches of those governments.

Many people are surprised to realize that democracies are important in business, too. For instance, in any publicly held company, shareholders vote to elect the members of the board of directors who in turn vote on major decisions that are implemented by the companies' hierarchies. Democracies are also important in nonprofit organizations, from your local Rotary club to the American Federation of Teachers, where members vote to elect their leaders and make other important decisions.

In its pure form, we define a democracy as *a supermind where decisions for the group are made by a vote of its members*. Democracies, of course, come with lots of variations, like who is eligible to vote; whether decisions are made by majority vote, plurality vote, or in some other way; and whether group members express their preferences by voting directly or through their elected representatives. But the key aspect of a democracy is that the ultimate decision-making power comes from all the members of the group, not just its leaders. And that allows far more possibilities than in a hierarchy for how large groups of people can cooperate in achieving widely shared goals.

In democratic countries today, even though we don't always like the outcomes of democratic voting, we often have a kind of vague, implicit assumption that voting somehow magically results in good outcomes. But this assumption is not true, even in theory!

In 1785, a French political scientist, the Marquis de Condorcet, mathematically showed one of the limits of making decisions by voting: If the average voter is more likely than not to vote for a good outcome (assuming we know what that is), then the more voters there are, the more likely it is that the election will result in a good outcome. But if the average voter is more likely than not to vote for a *bad* outcome, then the more voters there are, the more likely it is that the outcome of the election will be *bad*.[1]

In other words, elections lead to good outcomes only if the average voters have both the knowledge and the motivation to vote wisely. While this is sometimes true of voters, there is certainly no guarantee that it is always true. And even if all voters vote for what they think they want, it's quite possible that many of them do not know what actions (or which candidates) are most likely to achieve their desired outcomes.

In spite of their limitations, however, democracies are still one of the best ways we know to aggregate the opinions and desires of many individuals. Unlike members of hierarchies, voters in democracies are not bound by decisions in which they did not at least have a voice. So when everyone in a group needs to abide by a particular decision, democracies often provide a good way of making a decision that reflects a broad range of viewpoints and that even dissenting members of the group will usually view as legitimate.

But precisely because a democracy doesn't always reflect the views of any single individual, it is less likely to exhibit the kind of coherent intelligence we often hope for from individual humans. For instance, democracies usually can't commit themselves to future actions in the same way hierarchies can. They can change their minds suddenly without any explanation. And they can certainly make decisions that seem silly or inconsistent.

HOW WILL INFORMATION TECHNOLOGY MAKE DEMOCRACIES SMARTER?

New technologies can help democracies become smarter in a number of ways. First, by lowering the costs of communication, advances in IT have the potential to help voters be better informed and therefore better able to vote intelligently. In fact, in my book *The Future of Work*, I argued that a key factor enabling the spread of democratic forms of government around the world, starting in the late 1700s, was the spread in the previous two centuries of what you might think of as one of the earliest kinds of information technology: the printing press. Without voters who are well-enough informed to vote sensibly, democracies don't make much sense, and the printing press (and newspapers) made the spread of information possible on a much larger scale than ever before.

Of course, merely having the *potential* for voters to be well informed does not guarantee that they actually will be. For instance, today's social media can give hoaxes and false news stories a level of influence they would never have had before social media existed. And so it's certainly possible to use these techniques to make democracies dumber, not smarter, by disrupting the flow of accurate information to voters.

In a sense, as the world has entered the age of social media, we are all like people from small towns visiting a big city for the first time. At first it's hard to know whom to trust among all these new people. But over time, people who live in big cities usually learn pretty well how to tell who is trustworthy and who isn't. I think—and hope—that as social media continues to pervade and influence our society, we will develop both technical and cultural methods for doing the same thing online.

New technologies also make it much faster and easier to count votes in a democracy. This in turn should lead to democracies being used to make many more decisions, not only in governments but also in companies and other organizations. For instance, the Whole Foods grocery chain already lets employees vote on whether to hire new members of their teams, and the Mondragon federation of worker cooperatives, in Spain, lets workers vote on major corporate decisions, including electing the equivalent of the board of directors.[2]

VOTING AS A WAY OF REPRESENTING THE DESIRES OF VOTERS

There are two traditional ways of using democracies to make decisions that take into account the interests of all the voters. First, in a *direct democracy*, each person votes directly on all decisions. This form of democracy was used in ancient Athens, and it is used today in the cantons of Switzerland, in business partnerships, and in many civic organizations and informal groups. This has the obvious advantage that all voters can represent their own interests very directly. But it has a disadvantage: voting on all decisions that arise in a large group can be so time-consuming as to be completely impractical for most voters.

A much more common kind of democracy, *representative democracy*, solves the problem of not having enough time to vote on everything by letting voters pick representatives who then make decisions on their behalf. Representative democracy is used in many governments today, including the US Congress and the British Parliament. While this requires far less time from the voters, it does not represent their interests nearly as precisely as direct democracy does.

Liquid Democracy, Pirate Parties, and Voting Agents

Fortunately, new information technologies now make it possible to create forms of democracy that combine the best of both direct and representative democracies, forms that would never be feasible on a large scale without new technologies. These new forms have names like delegative democracy, proxy democracy, and smartocracy. The name I like best is liquid democracy. All these methods involve ways of letting people use online systems to delegate the right to vote on their behalf in much more fine-grained ways than traditional representative democracies permit.[3]

For instance, these schemes usually allow you to vote directly whenever you want to but to give others the right to vote for you when you don't want to do so yourself. You can give one person the right to vote for you on foreign policy decisions, for example, and give someone else your voting rights on financial decisions. And the people to whom you delegate your vote can, in turn, delegate it further. For instance, the person who has your voting rights for financial matters might delegate them further to one person for tax questions and to someone else for budgetary matters. In this way, you can have your interests represented by people with very specialized knowledge and enough time to consider decisions thoughtfully. If you don't like the ways these people are voting on your behalf, you can always transfer your voting rights to someone else or vote directly yourself.

This method doesn't require any more of your time as a voter than you want to spend, but it gives you a very powerful way of expressing your interests in as much detail as you see fit. This method can potentially be used in governments, businesses, or any other kinds of organizations. In fact, proxy voting by shareholders in large corporations is a simple (offline) version of this approach that has been used for decades.

Liquid democracy has also been used by several nascent political parties in Europe and the United States, where candidates agree to vote in their respective parliaments according to the web votes of their constituents.[4] For instance, in 2012, in the early days of Germany's Pirate Party, a linguistics professor named Martin Haase was one of the most powerful members of the party—not because he had campaigned for office or given hard-hitting speeches but because more people had delegated their voting rights to him than to any other party member. Often the votes he controlled were enough to sway a decision.

Since then, other loosely affiliated Pirate parties have won regional races in a number of European countries, several seats in the European Parliament, and 10 seats in the parliament of Iceland. In fact, for a period of several months in 2015, public opinion polls showed the Icelandic Pirate Party to be the most popular party in the country.

One interesting feature of these systems that makes them easier than you might think to adopt in any representative democracy is that they don't require a constitutional change. All they need is for voters to elect a majority of representatives who will vote however the voters in the liquid democracy decide.

Outside the world of politics, Google has pilot-tested a liquid-democracy approach to making business decisions, like which logos to use for internal Google projects and which foods to serve in the "micro-kitchens" scattered throughout Google's offices.[5] While none of these uses of liquid democracy has yet achieved widespread influence, I suspect that we will look back on them as having been harbingers of an approach that will become much more common in many kinds of organizations in the future.

Here's one more twist that makes this even more intriguing in the long run: What if instead of delegating your voting authority to another person you could delegate it to a computerized agent? Some of these agents would just advertise their policy positions and let you (or others to whom you had already delegated your vote) decide whether you wanted your vote to be cast based on those positions. Other agents might try to guess how you would want them to vote based on all kinds of detailed knowledge about you. And, of course, some developers of voting agents might try to game this system by fooling you into thinking that their agents would reflect your interests when they really wouldn't. But it seems unlikely that a system like this would be a lot *worse* than the representative democracies we have today, and it's quite easy to imagine that it could be a lot better.

VOTING AS A WAY OF FINDING WHAT'S TRUE

In addition to aggregating people's values and preferences, democracies can also be very useful as a way of aggregating people's opinions about what is true. For instance, when lots of nonexperts vote on possible answers to a question, they often arrive at an answer that is just as good as one that an expert would give. In the Galaxy Zoo project, for instance, hundreds of thousands of online volunteers are helping astronomers by classifying the shapes and other characteristics of a million galaxies in distant parts of the universe that astronomers have previously observed through telescopes.[6] Even though a single volunteer might mistakenly classify an astronomical object, when many volunteers look at that same object and vote on how to classify it, the results of the group's votes are extremely accurate, allowing the classification to happen much faster than if it were being done by a handful of experts.

In the Eyewire project, led by my former MIT colleague Sebastian Seung (now at Princeton), online volunteers use a similar voting approach to help neuroscientists map the neural connections in detailed images of the brain taken with an electron microscope.[7] Interestingly, the human volunteers work together with AI algorithms, indicating connections the algorithms have missed and letting the algorithms complete the marking of new connections the humans notice. This approach makes it possible to map far more parts of the brain far more rapidly than would be possible if all the mapping had to be done by professional scientists and their paid assistants.

The Good Judgment Project

Counting votes is a fairly simple way of combining people's opinions, but some of the most interesting examples of what you might call democratic truth finding involve more than just voting; they rely on more sophisticated ways of combining opinions. For instance, the Good Judgment Project,[8] led by Philip Tetlock at the University of Pennsylvania, was part of a competition organized by the US intelligence community's Intelligence Advanced Research Projects Activity (IARPA). Teams led by different universities competed to develop innovative methods for predicting the answers to a wide range of questions about geopolitical events, such as:[9]

- Will Serbia be officially granted European Union candidacy by December 31, 2011?
- Will the six-party talks on the Korean peninsula resume before January 1, 2014?
- Will the London Gold Market Fixing price of gold (USD per ounce) exceed $1,850 on September 30, 2011?

In each case, the groups didn't make simple yes-or-no predictions. Instead they tried to estimate the probability of the events occurring. New questions usually had end dates several months in the future, and groups were able to update their predictions every day until the end date.

The Good Judgment team was the hands-down winner of the IARPA competition, and their success presents us with a number of lessons. First, the Good Judgment team didn't assemble a panel of the world's best-known experts on geopolitical questions. Instead they encouraged anyone who was interested to join the crowd of thousands of online volunteers the project assembled.

Next, they found that some of the members of this crowd were reliably and significantly better than others at making accurate predictions. The researchers could determine, to some degree, who the best predictors would be by examining characteristics such as how intelligent they were, how open-minded they were, and how frequently they updated their predictions. And after there was enough data on how good the volunteers' predictions actually were, the best predictor of any one volunteer's future accuracy turned out to be that volunteer's accuracy in the past.

The Good Judgment team also found that a small amount of training in forecasting techniques improved people's predictive accuracy, as did sharing information, effort, and prediction rationales among small teams of 12 to 15 people. The best-performing teams, by far, were the ones composed of what the researchers called superforecasters, people who were among the top 2 percent of all forecasters in terms of accuracy.

Finally, they found that certain sophisticated ways of statistically combining individual predictions led to more accurate group predictions than those resulting from simply averaging individual predictions. For instance, they found that group predictions were more accurate when they put higher weight on more recent predictions, on predictions from people who had been more accurate in the past, and on people who updated their predictions more frequently. They also found that people tended to be too conservative in their predictions, so the statistical accuracy of the predictions was improved by mathematically adjusting the team predictions to be more extreme (that is, further from a 50 percent probability and closer to either 0 percent or 100 percent).[10]

It's tough to quantify exactly how successful the project's predictions were, since there aren't any obvious, publicly available sources of standardized predictions to which we can compare their results. But we do have one very intriguing suggestion. In November 2013, the *Washington Post* editor David Ignatius reported that "a participant in the [IARPA] project" (who presumably had access to classified sources inside the US government) told Ignatius that the superforecasters from the Good Judgment Project "performed about 30 percent better than the average for intelligence community analysts who could read intercepts and other secret data."[11] In other words, when you train, select, and combine the best forecasters from a more or less random online crowd of part-time workers, you get results that are substantially better than those from the multibillion-dollar apparatus of the US intelligence community!

Here's the key lesson for us: For the kinds of questions the Good Judgment Project studied, extremely good results came from a clever set of statistical adjustments that significantly improved the performance of a simple democracy (which we can define as the simple average of individuals' predictions). Would exactly these same adjustments work for all kinds of questions about which groups could "vote" on answers? Probably not. But the clear statistical results in this project point the way toward a very intriguing possible future for truth-finding democracies. Perhaps instead of traditional democracies, we should have more sophisticated democracies where carefully designed algorithms combine the opinions of group members to produce much more accurate results.

In fact, this is surprisingly similar to the basic architecture that IBM's Watson system uses. As we saw in chapter 4, Watson includes many different computational agents, each with a different kind of expertise, producing evidence for or against different possible answers. Over time, machine-learning algorithms built into the system refine the weights they give to these "opinions" from the different agents. The result is a very robust system for taking into account many different kinds of knowledge while learning along the way how best to combine all these different points of view.

The Good Judgment Project involves a very similar architecture, except that all the agents are people who are connected by computers. A huge opportunity, I think, is to create "democracies" that include both people and computers. Some of the voters would be people. Some would be machines. Each would have their own different kinds of knowledge and expertise, and each would have a track record of accuracy for solving various kinds of problems in the past. In addition, a separate set of computer agents would be continuously learning how best to combine all these votes into results that are more accurate than either people or computers could produce alone.

VOTING SEPARATELY FOR FACTS AND VALUES

There's an intriguing implication of what we've just seen. In many places where democracies exist today—such as in governments—we usually let people vote on issues that involve both questions of fact (what's true?) and questions of values (what do we want?). But if two different kinds of democracies are needed for these two kinds of questions, perhaps we should more clearly separate democratic decision making into two separate processes.

The first process would be designed to predict the outcomes of actions we might take, such as increasing taxes or changing labor laws. This fact-based process would assess the likely outcomes of proposed actions in terms of measures such as household income, employment rates, and crime rates. In today's world, predictions like these are often made by experts with relevant credentials. But perhaps this process should instead involve combinations of people and computers that have previously demonstrated their ability to make accurate predictions about similar questions in forums like the Good Judgment Project.

The second process would be something like the legislative process we use today—or perhaps a liquid-democracy form of that. Voters would start with the fact-based predictions from the first process and then choose the actions that are most likely to achieve their goals.

Condorcet's theorem told us that democracies only work well when the average voter has the knowledge to vote for a good answer. By dividing the work of democracy in this way, we let the people who are good at making accurate predictions vote on the results various actions would likely produce, and then we let those who know what we want vote for the results we want most.

In summary, democracies in government, business, and elsewhere can get smarter by using new technologies to do three things. First, they can allow voters to express their preferences and values in a much more fine-grained way by delegating to other people or machines the task of voting on their behalf for many more detailed issues than would otherwise be possible. Second, they can facilitate much more accurate ways of determining what is (or will be) true using sophisticated combinations of the judgments of many more people and machines. Finally, they may be able to make even more intelligent decisions by separating the first and second functions more clearly.

CHAPTER 8

Smarter Markets

The next species of supermind is a *market*. This form of collective decision making is ubiquitous in our world, with markets for everything from turkey sandwiches and televisions to pharmacists and factory workers.

We can define a market as *a supermind where decisions are made by individuals mutually agreeing to trade resources with one another.* Usually, but not always, one participant in the trade (the seller) provides a good or service, and the other (the buyer) provides money. The group decision in a market, therefore, is a combination of all the individual decisions that are made by mutual agreements among trading partners.

In a market, individual members of the group have a lot of control over how to allocate their resources. We don't all have to agree which cars are best, for instance. I can drive a Toyota; you can drive a Honda; and the total allocation of societal resources to each brand is just the sum of all our individual decisions. Unlike voters, who all have to live with the same president, and unlike members of a hierarchy, who have to follow orders from their superiors, participants in a market are not bound by any decisions they didn't agree to.

Of course, markets differ in terms of who can participate, how quickly and efficiently trades can occur, whether they are "rigged" by outside forces, and many other factors. But the essence of a market is that mutual agreements among many pairs of trading partners lead to overall group decisions about how to allocate all the group's resources, whether those resources are cars, cotton, iPhones, recorded music, or people's time.

Some of our animal relatives have very primitive forms of markets. For instance, chimpanzees sometimes trade meat for grooming and even for sex.[1] But since the earliest forms of barter among our hunting-and-gathering ancestors, human markets have developed to such a remarkable degree that they are now one of the most important kinds of superminds on our planet. Markets—often aided by instantaneous electronic communication—allocate societal resources among more and more kinds of goods and services all the time.

A market is the first type of supermind we've seen so far where no individual sees the whole problem for which the group is trying to make a decision. For example, there is no CEO of the global cotton market who is thinking about how to allocate all the cotton in the world to shirts, sheets, and bandages. There aren't even any individuals who vote on how to make this overall allocation. Instead the group decision *emerges* from the interactions of thousands of buyers and sellers all over the world.

Economists have shown that—at least under certain conditions—this group decision-making method leads to an optimal allocation of a group's resources, in the sense that no other allocation could make some individuals better off without making others worse off.[2] And even when these conditions are not met, markets are often a very efficient way of allocating scarce resources to the people who want them most and providing incentives for everyone to produce the things that are most valuable to others.

Markets also have their drawbacks. While they are remarkably good at efficiently allocating resources to fulfill human desires, they are completely blind to things that are not included in the prices that buyers have to pay. For instance, when businesses that pollute the environment pay no price for this, markets will efficiently allocate other resources as if the cost of this pollution is 0, even if the actual costs to society are far greater.

One way of dealing with these limitations of markets is to have another kind of supermind (such as a government) overseeing a market. A government might impose a tax on pollution, for instance, thus harnessing the vast power of the markets to allocate resources in ways that minimize pollution while still efficiently providing the other goods and services that consumers want.

HOW WILL INFORMATION TECHNOLOGY MAKE MARKETS SMARTER?

We already know that the cheap communication enabled by information technology can dramatically expand the global reach of markets. We see the results of this every day in the global markets for everything from BMWs to iPhones. Many years ago, my son, who was then about 13 years old, found the key component for his Halloween costume on eBay. It was a headband for the Japanese anime character Naruto, and the seller was, as far as I could tell, one guy operating out of his bedroom in Hong Kong. But this one guy made my son, in Massachusetts, a happy customer. Whether the guy knew it or not, his business was part of a global economy that takes advantage of information technology to intelligently decide how to use resources from all over the world to satisfy the desires of millions of people—including 13-year-old Massachusetts boys.

In addition to providing cheaper communication, new technologies also provide automated tools for buyers and sellers. For instance, many financial investors use software programs to buy and sell stocks on their behalf. These automated bots are usually less intelligent than the human stock traders they replace, but because they are so fast and available, they help make markets more efficient and thus—in an important sense—more intelligent. The same is true for online retailers like Amazon that use software on their websites to sell you things. The software might not have the general intelligence of a human store clerk, but it has the compelling advantage of being fast, convenient, and always available. I think these conventional electronic markets only scratch the surface of what's possible in the future.

Predictions as a Kind of Decision

To make any decision, you usually need to make *predictions* about the likely results of different actions you might take. Often, just deciding what prediction you're going to make is itself an important decision. And it turns out that markets can be surprisingly useful in making predictions.

It's obvious that both people and computers can make predictions. But what's not so obvious is that computers are often much better at doing this than people, even in situations where you might not expect them to be.

For instance, in his book *Thinking, Fast and Slow*, Daniel Kahneman reviews decades of work in psychology that compares intuitive predictions made by people to algorithmic predictions made by machines.[3] In a typical study, for example, trained counselors predicted the grades college freshmen would receive at the end of the school year. They based their predictions on 45-minute interviews with each student as well as each student's high school grades, aptitude-test scores, and four-page personal statement. The researchers also predicted grades for the same students using a statistical algorithm that considered only high school grades and one aptitude test. In spite of the fact that the human counselors had much more information—and, of course, much more general intelligence—than the algorithm, the researchers found that the algorithm made more accurate predictions than 11 of the 14 counselors.

This is not an isolated case. For over 50 years, researchers have conducted similar studies, predicting outcomes such as the longevity of cancer patients, the success of new businesses, the future career satisfaction of workers, the likelihood of violent crimes, and the future prices of Bordeaux wine. About 60 percent of the studies found that the algorithms were significantly better than the people at making these predictions, and the rest found no significant difference between the two. As Kahneman points out, even if the algorithms are no more accurate than people, they are generally so much cheaper and easier to use that they are still a better way of making the predictions.

Of course, there are certainly situations where algorithms' lack of general intelligence is a stumbling block. For instance, I'm sure that all major airlines must have algorithms that do a good job of predicting the volume of passenger travel on their various routes based on factors like holidays, the time of day, and the day of the week. In fact, I suspect that the predictions from these algorithms are usually better than those from very knowledgeable airline employees most of the time.

But when something important happens that the algorithms don't know about, they can't immediately adjust their predictions based on this new information. For instance, if these algorithms were trying to predict air travel on September 12, 2001, the day after the World Trade Center attacks on September 11, they would have done a terrible job. But any human who was remotely conscious of world events would have known that there would be essentially *no* passenger air travel on that day. In other words, virtually any human could have done a better job of predicting this than the standard airline algorithms.

Using Markets to Make Predictions

So how should we make predictions? Could we perhaps combine people and computers in some way to take advantage of the unique capabilities of both? That's what my former student Yiftach Nagar and I set out to investigate.[4] We wanted to try to help groups make better predictions about the future actions of opposing groups such as terrorists, military enemies, or business competitors. But for our experiments, we chose a simpler problem: trying to predict the plays in an American football game.

Now, the obvious possibility would be to use the machines as assistants to the people. For instance, the machines might help people analyze the game situations more systematically. Or they might give people detailed statistics about the past performance of all the players on the field.

But we decided to experiment with a more novel possibility. Could the machines act as peers to the humans in a special kind of market?

Here's how it worked: We showed groups of people videos of a football game, and just before each play began, we stopped the videos and asked people to predict whether the play would be a run or a pass. Rather than asking our subjects to just make a simple prediction, we asked them to express their predictions by participating in a *prediction market*. Somewhat like futures markets, prediction markets let you buy and sell "shares" of predictions about possible future events. For instance, if you think the next play will very likely be a pass, you should buy shares of this prediction. If your predictions are right, then you (typically) get one dollar for each share you own, and if your predictions are wrong you get nothing.[5]

But the market lets you express your opinions even more precisely than that. If you think, for instance, that the probability of a pass is 60 percent, then you should be willing to buy a pass prediction for anything up to 60 cents, and you should be willing to sell one for anything over 60 cents. That means the resulting price in the overall market is essentially an estimate of the probability of a pass play based on the collective opinion of all the people participating in the market.[6]

Alongside our market of human observers, we also programmed software bots to make similar predictions and trade among themselves. The bots made their predictions using rudimentary machine-learning algorithms and limited information about the game situation (such as which down it was and how many yards to the next first down).

Finally, in some cases, we had the people and the bots participate in the same markets together. In those cases, when the human participants bought and sold predictions, they didn't know whether they were trading with a person or with a bot.

As we hoped, we found that the markets in which both people and software bots traded together worked better than those with only people or only bots trading. The combined markets turned out to be significantly more accurate overall, and less susceptible to various kinds of errors. For instance, even though the bots were more accurate, on average, than the people, there were several plays where the bots made severe errors but the people mostly predicted correctly. On some of these plays, for example, the football-savvy humans recognized that the players were in a "shotgun" formation, indicating a higher probability of a pass. The bots, however, had no information about the team formations, so they were more likely than their human counterparts to incorrectly predict runs on these plays.

In the combined markets, the people and the computers were all acting as peers, trading with one another, but they each had different kinds of capabilities. The computers were less likely to be distracted by the specific features of a given situation, more able to systematically apply statistical methods to minimize their errors, and less likely to be overconfident in their own judgments.

The people, on the other hand, had access to more information than the bots did (such as the physical locations of the players on the field and the comments of the game's broadcasters), and they were better able to respond sensibly to different situations. This combination of diverse approaches resulted in overall predictions that were better than either the people or computers made alone.

It's easy to imagine that cyber-human prediction markets like this could be used in many ways. Google and Microsoft, for example, have already let their employees use prediction markets to estimate completion dates for internal projects. The University of Iowa has been using prediction markets to predict the winners of US presidential races for decades. The Hollywood Stock Exchange website uses prediction markets to predict movie box-office receipts. In all these cases, the predictions from the prediction markets are usually as good as or better than any alternative prediction methods. Our results suggest that predictions for these and many other kinds of things could be even better if computer bots were involved, too.

Taking Cyber-Human Prediction Markets Even Further

One of the intriguing possibilities about using a market for prediction is that it provides incentives for people to get involved if, and only if, they can be useful. For instance, in routine situations (like predicting airline travel on a normal day), computers can often do a good job, and humans have little incentive to participate. Since their predictions would be no better than the predictions the computers are already making, the humans would be unlikely to make much money from trading, so why would they bother?

On the other hand, in unusual situations (like predicting air travel on September 12, 2001), where the humans can see that the computers' predictions are very wrong, the humans have a clear incentive to intervene. They have the potential to make significant profit from trading against bots who, literally, don't know what's going on.

In either case, humans who *think* they are better at predicting than they actually are will usually lose money, so they are likely to become discouraged and give up. Or if they enjoy participating as a kind of entertainment (like gambling), then the money they lose will provide even more incentive for participation by the people and bots who are actually good at predicting.

And here's one of the most intriguing possibilities: What if each participant has his or her own "stable" of bots? Then participants will compete to create smarter and smarter bots. If your bots are better than mine at making accurate predictions, then you will make more money than I will. So each of us has an incentive to create bots that are as accurate as possible. But we also want our bots to know their own limits and participate only when they have a reasonable chance of being successful. The upshot here is twofold: providing an incentive for bot designers to make increasingly smarter bots will lead to advances in AI, and the prediction markets in which those bots participate will become more accurate.

It's important to note, by the way, that this approach can be useful with the artificial intelligence that we have today. In fact, it can even work with simple prediction algorithms, like statistical regression, that have existed for decades.

Cyber-Human Markets for Everything

Most of what we've just been saying applies to far more than just prediction markets; it applies to many other kinds of markets, too. Today's financial markets are leading the way, with investment managers increasingly relying on quantitative, often AI-based, trading algorithms. And the firms with the better algorithms can be far more profitable than their competitors.

But it's not hard to imagine a future world where this approach becomes common in many other industries. Imagine, for instance, a fully automated online shoe retailer: let's call it Shoeless. Shoeless has automated buying bots continually scanning the prices at various wholesale shoe suppliers, looking for the best deals. The shoes these bots buy are automatically sent to an Amazon warehouse, then Amazon handles fulfillment and customer service.

At the same time, Shoeless has its own website, where its automated sales bots are always experimenting with a variety of ads and constantly adjusting prices based on the type of customer who's viewing the ad, current wholesale costs, and current inventory levels. The owner of Shoeless might occasionally hire human contractors to update the website and the automated buying and selling algorithms, but the number of human employees of the company could be 0. Could such an automated retailer outperform a traditional retailer, where people do more of the work? Today, maybe not. Sometime in the not-too-distant future? Quite possibly.

But the real point is that, in a certain sense, we can let the market decide what kind of retailers are most effective. The companies that work well—whether they are fully automated, semiautomated, or not automated at all—will make money. Those that don't work well will go broke. And over time, the invisible hand of the market will continually redirect resources to the places that are—at that moment—most effectively providing what customers want.

Of course, it's not quite this simple. There are many situations where markets don't perform in practice the way they should in theory. But markets do have a very important ability to continually adapt to changing situations, including changes in what can and cannot be automated at any given time. So in a sense, markets have a kind of general intelligence that includes and goes beyond the general intelligence of the individuals within them.

Chapter 9

Smarter Communities

The next species of supermind to consider is a *community*. Communities are everywhere. For example: the residents of my neighborhood in Boston, my daughter's friends on Facebook, high-energy-physics researchers all over the world, the doctors who practice medicine in my hometown in New Mexico, and the people who write and edit articles on Wikipedia.

We can define a community as *a supermind where decisions are made by informal consensus or according to shared norms, both of which are enforced through reputations and access to resources.*[1] In other words, upstanding members of the community, who uphold the community's shared norms, get the respect and admiration of their peers; they have more influence in making consensus decisions, and it is usually easier for them to access group resources like help and companionship from other group members. Members who violate the community norms lose respect, influence, and access to resources. In extreme cases, violators may be publicly shamed, ostracized from the community, or punished in other ways.[2]

All communities use informal consensus, shared norms, and reputations in making decisions, but they also differ in many ways, including how rigid their boundaries are, how formalized their decision-making processes are, and how they enforce their norms.

Communities are pervasive in nature as well as in human societies. Beehives, ant colonies, wolf packs, and baboon troops are all examples of communities, and so were the bands of our hunting-and-gathering human ancestors. We can think of a community as the basic type of supermind from which all the others we've seen so far grew. And if you find a decision-making supermind that isn't clearly one of the other types, it's probably safe to consider it a community.

HOW WILL INFORMATION TECHNOLOGY MAKE COMMUNITIES SMARTER?

The information-processing capabilities of new technologies can dramatically affect how communities reach consensus and establish reputations. But evaluating how these changes lead a community's decision making to be more intelligent requires an understanding of what the community is trying to achieve in the first place. Since communities can take lots of different forms, let's look at examples from communities that are trying to accomplish work-related goals and communities that are seeking to help their members be happier.

HOW CAN INFORMATION TECHNOLOGY HELP COMMUNITIES ACHIEVE WORK-RELATED GOALS?

Many communities have obvious goals that can be used to evaluate their effectiveness. For example, the Wikipedia community is creating an online encyclopedia. The neuroscience community is trying to scientifically understand the vast mystery of how brains work. The community of Xerox copier repair technicians is trying to keep Xerox photocopiers functioning properly.

Consensus Decision Making in Wikipedia

In many cases, new information technologies can help these communities make better decisions to achieve their goals. The Wikipedia community, for instance, couldn't even exist without the Internet and wiki software, which allow a very unusual kind of consensus decision making. Unlike a traditional encyclopedia, which has an established set of authors and a hierarchical editorial process, Wikipedia allows anyone to change an article at any time. And if someone else thinks the article should be changed again, he or she can keep changing it. But when there is an informal consensus that the article is okay, then no one changes it further—at least for now.

If two people disagree about whether a particular change is a good idea, the Wikipedia culture strongly encourages them to hash out the issues in online discussions where other people can participate, too. And in the unusual cases where this mostly amicable process doesn't lead to a decision everyone accepts, some rarely used higher-level dispute resolution processes are also available.

Wikipedia's software also maintains records of what each contributor has done, an important part of building and recognizing reputations in this community. And, in some cases, Wikipedia bots make some of the simple editorial decisions automatically.

Even though hardly anyone (including Jimmy Wales, Wikipedia founder) expected this online consensus process to really work, the combination of Wikipedia's software and culture has somehow allowed it to work remarkably well.[3]

Could this process work in a face-to-face environment with large numbers of editors? I suspect not. Imagine, for instance, a football stadium with 70,000 people in it. (That's about the number of active Wikipedia contributors at the time I write this.) And imagine that these people are trying to create an encyclopedia using only paper and pencil, face-to-face conversations, and the public address system.

They could probably accomplish something, but I suspect that they would almost certainly end up using some kind of crude hierarchical process. There would be occasional instructions issued to everyone on the loudspeaker, and there would be lots of smaller groups scattered throughout the stadium where editors at different levels would solicit and approve articles on various topics.

But I think the same group of 70,000 people could be far more effective using the Wikipedia software. The online nature of the interactions allows people to rapidly shift their attention from one topic to another, and it allows people from a huge group to form an ever-shifting constellation of many parallel small groups, each of which works temporarily on a specific article or other topic. And that, in turn, makes the radically decentralized consensus process work in a way it almost certainly couldn't in a large face-to-face group.

Communities of Practice

Community of practice is a term for a community of people who do the same kind of work and learn how to do it better from interacting with one another.[4] A classic example of this was described by anthropologist Julian Orr, a former colleague of mine when I worked at Xerox's Palo Alto Research Center (PARC). Julian studied how Xerox copier repair technicians did their jobs.[5]

A key insight of his research was that, even though the technicians were usually alone while they repaired a copier, the time they spent socializing with one another at breakfast, at lunch, and on other breaks was a critical resource for their work. There they exchanged all kinds of information about how to fix the real problems that actually arose in their jobs, not just the standard error codes and repair techniques documented in the official manuals. For instance, factors like temperature and humidity could affect the machines in ways that went far beyond the cases described in the official manuals, and by exchanging stories about their actual experiences, the technicians became much more effective at repairing the machines.

The community Orr studied was a face-to-face one, but—partly as a result of his work—Xerox later created an online tool called Eureka that technicians could use to share tips with one another all over the company. In a process similar to scientific peer review, the technicians themselves—not higher-level managers—decided which tips were useful and which weren't. And, also like scientists, the reputations the technicians established by contributing tips were powerful motivators. At one meeting, for instance, a technician received a spontaneous standing ovation from his coworkers because they respected the tips he'd shared on Eureka. Xerox estimated that, by making the repair-technician community more effective, the system saved the company $100 million.[6]

In the long run, it seems clear that information technology has huge potential to help work-related online communities make more intelligent decisions. At a minimum, it can make the communication needed to reach a consensus and establish reputations much faster, cheaper, and easier. And, in cases like the Wikipedia bots, automated systems can sometimes make decisions themselves that contribute to the consensus decision making and reputation formation of the community.

Will these changes always lead to more intelligent communities? Of course not. But if used wisely, these new technologies have vast potential to help create new kinds of decision-making communities that can do many things more intelligently.

WILL ONLINE COMMUNITIES MAKE THEIR MEMBERS HAPPIER?

For communities that are not work-oriented, it's less obvious how to determine their goals and measure their intelligence. But it's clear that new technologies can provide many kinds of benefits for these communities, too.

Some communities, like Facebook, are designed to fulfill the social and emotional needs of their members. For example, there are many people today (including my daughter) for whom Facebook, Instagram, Twitter, and similar systems are the primary ways they interact with their friends.

Other communities (like Yelp and TripAdvisor) are focused on helping their members decide where to eat or stay, based on reviews from thousands of other customers. Amazon and Netflix do more than just show reviews from other community members. They also use sophisticated algorithms to recommend products you might like based on the preferences of other people whose tastes are generally similar to yours.

But today's media are also full of stories about how these communities can actually reduce the happiness of their members. For instance, my MIT colleague Sherry Turkle argues that the relationships we have with our friends online are often much less fulfilling than traditional face-to-face conversations.[7] Seeing all the carefully curated "good times" your friends are having on Facebook may make you less satisfied with your own life. And sometimes, the online world can be a facilitator of seriously harmful bullying and shaming.

In general, it seems that online communication can have both positive and negative effects on community members' happiness. So far, at least, the net effect is unclear.

HOW DOES TECHNOLOGY AFFECT THE BOUNDARIES OF A COMMUNITY?

For a group to function as a community, it needs to have a critical mass of shared norms and values. But sometimes the values of subgroups in a community diverge so dramatically that the whole community is in danger of fragmenting. The United States experienced an extreme version of this during the Civil War, over 150 years ago. I saw a milder version in the 1960s, when young people, antiwar activists, and so-called hippies rejected the values of the establishment to the point that, for a while, the country really did feel like it was fragmenting into separate communities. The election of Donald Trump as US president highlighted a similar kind of fragmentation, in this case between those who voted for Trump and those who didn't.

Information technology can play an important role in both bringing communities together and splitting them apart. On the one hand, IT has the potential to increase shared information and norms across larger groups. For instance, in the 1960s, most Americans got their news from one of three national television networks and a small number of other publications. If Walter Cronkite said it, many Americans believed it was true. That almost certainly helped spread more shared norms across a country that previously had strong regional differences.

But in the 2016 election, many Americans got their news from Facebook and other online media that created highly tailored news feeds for each individual.[8] If you had liberal friends and interests, you were rarely exposed to conservative news outlets, and vice versa. In a community where each subgroup saw a different set of facts about the world and had a different value system for interpreting those facts, the shared norms needed for the overall community to function effectively were greatly weakened. In a sense, the United States seemed to be fragmenting into two separate communities.

By the time you read these words, it's likely that the US political situation will have changed substantially from the ambiguity that prevails as I write this, in mid-2017. But whatever happens, it's likely that IT will continue to play a major role in fragmenting some communities and uniting others.

TECHNOLOGY FOR ACHIEVING MORE INTELLIGENT CONSENSUS

As we've just seen, the early evidence is mixed about whether IT will help a community reach a better-informed and more logical consensus.

But I think there is reason for optimism about technology's ability to do this in the long run.

One intriguing approach to facilitating consensus is called online argumentation (or online deliberation). If a group has little agreement about what is true and what values are important (as is the case in some political discussions), this method probably won't help much. But for a community that already agrees on many things, this approach can help make new decisions in a clear, systematic way.

Online discussions today often include lots of repetitions, digressions, and people talking past each other or just ignoring each other. Based on philosophers' notions of how to summarize the essential logical structure of arguments, online argumentation helps reduce the random and disorganized nature of many of today's online discussions.[9]

The basic idea is that, instead of just adding to a free-flowing online discussion, group members can contribute their points of view in an online map that explicitly represents the logical structure of the argument: What is the decision to be made (the *issue*)? What are the possible decision options from which to choose (the *positions*)? And what are the *arguments* for and against each option?

One of the leading researchers in this field is Mark Klein, a principal research scientist in our MIT Center for Collective Intelligence. Mark has developed an online tool called the Deliberatorium to support the approach. For example, Mark demonstrated the power of online argumentation by using it to summarize an online discussion (from the travel website Planeta.com) about the merits of buying carbon-emission offsets to compensate for the pollution resulting from your airplane travel.[10] The original online discussion included 13 pages of text and was filled with digressions and repetitions. But when Mark translated the discussion into an argument map in his system, he found that all the discussion content could be summarized in the following eight lines.

IS CARBON-EMISSION OFFSETTING A GOOD IDEA?

 Yes

- 👍 Carbon offsets do reduce greenhouse-gas emissions
- 👍 It is getting easier to find good carbon offsets
- 👍 Many major meetings are using them

👂 **No**

- 👍 Can have unexpected consequences
- 👍 It fosters complacency
- 👍 It's too easy to cheat

The diagram shows one *issue* (whether carbon offsets are good) and two different *positions* about this issue ("yes" and "no"). Even though it's not shown here, another position might be "We don't know yet." Each of the positions shown has several *arguments* supporting it. (The thumbs-up icons indicate arguments *for* the position; thumbs-down would indicate arguments *against*.)

In this case, Mark did the mapping himself, but the approach really gets interesting when many different people can each contribute different pieces to the discussion. In order to express your opinion in this framework, rather than just entering a new comment at the end of the current list of comments, you need to first decide what kind of entry yours is (issue, position, or argument), then decide where it fits in the argument map. If necessary, you may need to break down what you want to say into several separate items to make it fit the structure.

For instance, suppose you just read a report saying that, on average, only about 30 percent of the cost of carbon offsets is actually spent on reducing carbon emissions, and the rest goes to investors, auditors, and others. To add this point to the discussion shown above, you might create a new argument below the statement "Carbon offsets do reduce greenhouse-gas emissions." Your new item would be an argument against that point (indicated by a thumbs-down icon), and it might say something like "Reductions are only 30 percent of costs" (see bold line below). In the more detailed window that comes up if someone clicks on your new item, you might include a link to the report you read.

IS CARBON-EMISSION OFFSETTING A GOOD IDEA?

 Yes

 Carbon offsets do reduce greenhouse-gas emissions
     Reductions are only 30 percent of costs
 It is getting easier to find good carbon offsets
 Many major meetings are using them

 No

 Can have unexpected consequences
 It fosters complacency
 It's too easy to cheat

To be sure your new item is appropriately classified and formatted, a human moderator would usually need to approve the item before it becomes visible to other users. Once it's posted, users can rate any item, so the items people find most important can be displayed more prominently.

Mark and his collaborators have used this approach to help a number of groups debate issues of importance to them. In one case, for example, students at the University of Naples debated how Italy could better use biofuels, and over the course of three weeks, they created what experts said was a remarkably comprehensive and well-organized review of the key issues and options.

In another case, Intel conducted a deliberation on how it could use "open computing" (in which users are given greater access to computing tools and data). The discussion resulted in a well-organized overview of key issues from 73 contributors, many of whom were outside the company. And in a third case, over 600 members of the Democratic Party in Italy debated controversial questions about possible changes to Italy's election laws.[11]

In addition to Mark and his colleagues, a number of others have used similar tools to help answer a wide variety of business, technical, and public-policy questions.[12] And it's easy to imagine using this approach inside companies to engage a wide range of people in systematically analyzing the merits of alternative corporate strategies, new product possibilities, different job candidates, and competing health insurance packages.

Public Disputations

David Brin, the visionary science fiction author, has even advocated using public "disputations" similar to those in the Deliberatorium to debate major public-policy matters and other questions.[13] He suggests that, like football games and presidential debates, these online disputations could become a form of public entertainment. The whole process might last weeks or months online and feature periodic live events as well as referees, judges, and detailed rules to ensure that contentious issues are analyzed logically rather than swept under the rug by evasion or emotional slogans.

Could something like this actually work on a large scale? Could we, for instance, use a process like this to help evaluate proposals for the government's role in health care in the United States? There might be widely viewed live debates involving prominent politicians and well-known experts. There might be well-funded groups conducting background research to support various points of view. And, most important, the result would be a concise online map of the key issues, positions, and arguments.

Not everyone would agree on which arguments were most compelling, but if the process were done well, most people would agree that the different points of view were fairly and accurately represented. Would this guarantee that good decisions would be made? Of course not. But it could certainly help citizens and legislators make better final decisions.

I've been optimistic about these and other possibilities for online argumentation ever since I first heard about the topic, in 1986.[14] And I'm surprised that the approach hasn't already been more widely used in business, politics, and elsewhere. But I suspect that this may be one of those transformative ideas—like the idea of democracy itself and the idea of the World Wide Web—that are tried in various forms on small scales for many years before conditions are finally right for them to take off on a large scale.

But if that does happen, I think this approach could help online communities make far more intelligent decisions than any communities—face-to-face or online—do today. Even if a community doesn't ever come to a consensus, this way of laying out the structure of arguments has the potential to help other decision makers—including hierarchical managers and democratic voters—make far better decisions than they do today.

COULD INFORMATION TECHNOLOGY ENABLE CYBER-SOCIALISM?

When Karl Marx and Friedrich Engels developed the theory of communism, in the 1800s, they wrote about "primitive communism," the egalitarian sharing of food and other property practiced by ancient hunting-and-gathering societies. They also predicted that society would return to a more developed form of "pure communism" in the future.[15]

While there is certainly no scholarly consensus that this Marxist theory of history is valid, there is substantial evidence that primitive hunting-and-gathering societies did embody many aspects of the socialist principle: from each according to his ability, to each according to his need.[16] For instance, the English anthropologist E. E. Evans-Pritchard, who studied the hunting-and-gathering tribes of the Nuer people in the Nile valley, said, "In general it may be said that no one in a Nuer village starves unless all are starving."[17]

Even though there have been many experiments with communist and socialist economies in the last century or so, none of these societies has been able to replicate on a large scale the level of socialist sharing that occurred in the small communities of hunting-and-gathering bands. But is it possible that IT might enable this community-style decision making to operate effectively in much larger groups? And might this make something like primitive communism feasible on a much larger scale? Of course, we don't know for sure, but I think there is reason to believe it might be possible.

A Scenario for Cyber-Socialism

Let's think about how such a society might work. Since the term *socialism* has somewhat more flexible connotations today than *communism*, we'll use the term *cyber-socialism* for this new form of IT-enabled socialistic decision making.

By the way, let me be clear that I am not *advocating* this way of organizing a society. I'm not yet sure whether it would be possible to work out the details of this scenario in a way that would make it both feasible and desirable. But I think it is very intriguing to contemplate radical new possibilities like this one, and I think it is very likely that some version of this will be tried in the future.

The key idea is that IT makes it possible to create publicly visible reputations for everyone in a group, derived from detailed tracking of their actions. Imagine, for instance, that you could walk into a grocery store and leave with any combination of bread, eggs, ice cream, and beer you want. Though you don't actually pay for anything, the value of what you take is tracked. Alongside your consumption, all your contributions to others are tracked, too. Every time you write software, cook meals, or cut someone's hair, the value of what you contribute is recorded.

Now imagine that some combination of your peers, various kinds of experts, and bots make estimates of how much you are *capable* of contributing to society and how much you *need* of the goods and services available. For instance, perhaps your coworkers evaluate how much they think you are capable of contributing at your job and report on how much you actually do contribute. Your doctors evaluate how much medical care you need and whether you have a disability or illness that prevents you from working.

Finally, imagine that very sophisticated algorithms analyze all this data to calculate a multidimensional reputation for you based on what you have contributed and used relative to your abilities and needs. For instance, if you contribute as much as you are capable of and use only what you need, then you would have a good reputation and be entitled to participate in all the benefits of society. If you are disabled, for example, you may have significant medical expenses and be unable to work, but since you're still contributing as much as you are capable of, you can still be a respected member of society.

Some people will be able to contribute much more than they need, and they will have an even better reputation because of their net contribution to society. Perhaps these high contributors would be widely recognized and respected in the way we often respect wealthy or famous people in our society today. If you are one of these people, you would be a socially desirable mate, and you might get to go to the front of the lines in stores, theaters, and airports. Inequalities in material consumption would presumably be smaller in this society than they are in ours, but you might also have access to a few material benefits (like nicer cars or special housing) that wouldn't be available to others.

On the other hand, if you contribute less than you are able to or use more than you need, then you would not be doing what is expected of you, so you would have a reputation as a slacker or a moocher. And if you also use more than you contribute, then your reputation would be even worse. Your parents probably wouldn't be proud of what you had achieved, few people would want to be your friends, and you would be low on the priority list when it comes to receiving government services. If you continued to violate the community norms about how much you should contribute and use, you might be subject to various kinds of penalties, and in extreme cases, you might even be asked to leave the society altogether.

In other words, a cyber-socialist economy would decide how to allocate human labor, food, and other resources in a very different way from the system that prevails in capitalist economies. Instead of mutual agreements between buyers and sellers in a market, decisions about resources would be based on societal norms that are embodied in the way you're rated by other people and in the algorithms for computing reputations. These societal norms would be enforced by the consequences of having good or bad reputations. Also, unlike a purely market-based economy, a cyber-socialist economy would explicitly take into account people's needs and abilities, not just what they consume and produce.

Could This Actually Work?

One obvious question is whether it would even be possible to create reasonable estimates of what you contribute versus what you are capable of contributing and what you use versus what you need. It's not obvious that this would be possible, but there are a number of reasons for thinking it might well be. For instance, in recent years, there have been intriguing speculations about ways of using modern computational power and access to data to calculate useful economic quantities that would not have been feasible to calculate otherwise.[18] And as we saw in the Valve example in chapter 6, it's also possible for people to estimate the contributions of their coworkers.

Another question is whether people would be motivated enough by potential benefit or harm to their reputations to really exert their best efforts. Why wouldn't a talented person, for example, try to hide his or her abilities and contribute just enough to satisfy society's minimal expectations? I'm sure that's what some people would do (as some do today). But I think there is reason to believe that many people would be motivated by a desire to have a good reputation.

Think, for instance, how hard some people try to increase their followers on Twitter or Instagram. Think how important it is to some people to have lots of "likes" on their Facebook posts. And think how much many of us care—in our ordinary, offline lives—what our friends and neighbors think of us. Could these motivations be as powerful in a cyber-socialist system as the financial motivations of a capitalist economy? I don't think the answer is obvious, but I think it's quite possible that they could be.

Still another question is whether the loss of privacy needed to operate a system like this would be worth it. In fact, this illustrates how the goals of a supermind (in this case, a community) can be very different from those of the individuals in that supermind. The community's goal here is to have a fair way of dividing up the work and resources among the members of society. But this system for accomplishing that goal requires the individuals to give up quite a bit more privacy than many people would want to surrender. Is the trade-off worth it? I think that depends on the people and the situation, so I don't think there's a simple answer. But I think that questions like this—about trade-offs between the goals of a supermind and its members—are worthy of much discussion.

Would a system like this take substantial resources to operate? Yes. And would it be subject to many kinds of abuse? Yes. But our current systems also have problems like these, and it's not obvious that the difficulties of a cyber-socialist system would be worse than what we have today. And if it worked well, this kind of economy—in contrast to a capitalist economy—could allocate society's resources in a way that many people would consider fairer. It would also likely reduce the extremes of material wealth between the rich and the poor. So it seems to me worthwhile to think further about how a scenario like this might actually be implemented in a way that could be feasible and desirable.

An Early Example: China's Social Credit System

Intriguingly, China is already experimenting with something it calls a social credit system, which has some of the characteristics of the scenario we've just seen.[19] The Communist Party has said that it wants to roll out a nationwide version of the system by 2020, so this may be a harbinger of much bigger things to come.

For starters, the system keeps track of financial behavior, such as whether people keep up with their insurance premiums, tax payments, and credit card bills. The system is also expected to include information about various kinds of social behavior, such as cheating on subway fares, jaywalking, causing disturbances on airline flights, and violating family-planning limits.

For instance, in China, if your parents are over 60, the law requires you to visit them regularly and ensure that they have enough food; children who fail to fulfill these filial duties might be reported in the system. In the long run, the system may also include data about various kinds of online behavior, such as how many hours you play video games per day, how courteously you interact with other users in online forums, and how reliable the information you post is.

All this data will then be used to compute various "social credit" ratings that will lead to many kinds of benefits and penalties. People with high scores, for instance, may have access to luxury hotels, certain government jobs, favorable loan rates, and "green lanes" that entitle them to receive faster government services or faster security screening at airports. People with low scores might have limited access to good jobs, favorable mortgage rates, and good schools. They might even be unable to stay in certain desirable hotels or eat in certain restaurants.

The government planning documents for this system say its goal is to "allow the trustworthy to roam everywhere under heaven while making it hard for the discredited to take a single step."

Is this a good idea? Certainly the system has the potential to be an insidious "big brother" that attempts to invade and control more and more of Chinese citizens' lives. But some observers say that a comprehensive data-based system like this one might be better than the subjective judgments that Communist Party officials have traditionally made based on the *dang'an* dossiers they maintained on urban workers.

In any case, how well the system works depends on many details, like how easy it is for citizens to see and correct their own records, how transparent the algorithms for calculating reputations are, and whether the resulting reputations are publicly visible or seen only by government officials. And different communities will need to decide for themselves whether the potential benefits of such a system outweigh its costs.

For the purposes of this discussion, I think the key point is that new information technologies are changing the political calculus of how to organize large groups. Could these new technologies allow, on a vastly larger scale, the kind of decision making based on norms and reputations that was common in ancient hunting-and-gathering communities? Could they, for instance, allow a new form of large-scale cyber-socialism to compete effectively with market-based economies? We don't know for sure, but experiments like China's social credit system will certainly provide fascinating indications about what might be possible.

So are new information technologies guaranteed to make communities more intelligent? Of course not. But I think they offer some very intriguing possibilities for the creation of much more intelligent communities than any we've ever seen.

CHAPTER 10

Smarter Ecosystems

All the species of superminds we've discussed so far require some overall framework for cooperation: hierarchical authority, democratic choices, market agreements, or community norms. When there is no such framework for a group, it belongs in our last species of supermind, an *ecosystem*.

The most obvious example of an ecosystem is the collection of all the living things on our planet. These living things interact with each other in various ways, but there is no single person or group that tries to coordinate them all. In other words, our global ecosystem is itself a kind of supermind.

We can view lots of other groups as ecosystems, too. For instance, all the superminds in the United States—all the markets, hierarchies, democracies, and communities—can be viewed as a kind of ecosystem. Similarly, we can talk about a city, a state, a government, or a company as being an ecosystem made of other superminds. In each case, many different individual superminds interact with each other to make various kinds of overall group decisions.

We will define an ecosystem as *a supermind where individuals interact without any overall framework for cooperation. In the short term, decisions are made by the law of the jungle: the individuals with the most power get what they want. In the long term, decisions are made by survival of the fittest: the individuals that survive, grow, and reproduce most successfully control the most resources.[1]*

It's important to realize that ecosystems are a different type of supermind from the others we've seen. In a sense, they are the environment in which all the others interact. But ecosystems also make decisions. Through short-term competition for power and long-term evolution, they "decide" which of the other superminds (or other individuals in the ecosystem) will get to make specific decisions in each situation.

As an example, let's think about the ecosystem of superminds in the United States, and let's begin with a simple civics lesson about citizens electing government officials as part of a democracy. The citizens try to vote for candidates who will represent their interests when making and carrying out laws, but elected officials often pursue their own individual interests, too. However, if an elected official's actions stray too far from the citizens' interests, the voters can vote that official out of office in the next election. Thus, in this part of the supermind jungle, there is a kind of balance of power between the (mostly) hierarchical governments and the democracies that choose them.

The story continues with other parts of society: Government hierarchies interact with markets by creating laws about product safety, contract disputes, insider trading, and many other things that affect markets and hierarchical businesses. Most of the time, businesses and other market participants obey these laws because governments can punish them when they don't.

But the balance of power here is not as one-sided in favor of the government as it might at first appear. In the jungle of politics, businesses and markets have powers of their own. It's completely legal, for instance, for businesses to donate money to political campaigns, and it's clear that these donations sometimes affect how elected officials act. Furthermore, the political ecosystem doesn't stop with what is legal. As anyone who has ever watched television crime dramas knows, it's certainly not unheard of for criminals to bribe government officials to affect how the laws are enforced.

Of course, the story doesn't stop there, either. Communities—including neighborhoods, friendship networks, religious groups, and many others—shape the values their members express in democracies and markets. Your taste in clothes, restaurants, and cars as well as your political views on abortion, climate change, and taxation are shaped by the communities to which you belong, and in turn you make your voice heard in markets and democracies.

But influence works both ways here, too. Markets and governments influence communities as well. Advertising, for instance, tries to change the buying preferences of individuals and communities. Commercial entertainment can also profoundly shape community values. For example, some people attribute the remarkably rapid change in the attitudes of American communities toward gay marriage to television shows like *Modern Family*, which portrays gay marriage in a favorable light.

All these examples so far illustrate the short-term operation of power and influence in the supermind ecosystem of the United States. In the longer term, a different kind of power operates as well: the power to survive, grow, and reproduce as conditions change. For instance, there are many more software companies and many fewer steam-powered factories in the United States today than 100 years ago because the technological possibilities available to businesses have changed over that time.

More subtly, the relative power of different kinds of superminds may change over time as ecosystems evolve. For instance, political scientist Robert Putnam, in his book *Bowling Alone*, published in 2000, lamented the decline in local community organizations like bowling leagues, parent-teacher associations (PTAs), and the Red Cross. He attributed this in part to people spending more time watching television. In other words, markets are controlling more human time (through advertising-supported television viewing), and local communities are controlling less. Stated even more simply, markets appear to have been evolving more successfully than local communities in the US ecosystem in recent years.

Ecosystems are the foundational species of supermind that existed before all the others we've discussed. The others only evolved because they were able to survive and reproduce successfully. And ecosystems are always waiting in the background to decide which of the superminds and individuals within them will get to make a given decision.

In essence, ecosystems serve the desires of the most powerful, the longest lasting, and the most numerous members of the group. But they are completely agnostic about what leads their members to succeed in these ways. They simply reward what works, regardless of whose desires are served.

HOW WILL ECOSYSTEMS CHANGE WITH INFORMATION TECHNOLOGY?

How will new information technologies change the ways ecosystems make decisions? Let's begin with two simple observations. First, if technologies make superminds smarter, and if smarter superminds are more powerful—though neither of those things is a given—then the new technologies will essentially increase the level of competitiveness for all the superminds in an ecosystem. For instance, when consumers get used to how easy it is to buy books on Amazon, they may expect the same level of convenience when buying back surgery from their doctors. If the consumers don't get what they want from their current doctors' offices, they're likely to go to other superminds in the market for medical services.

Second, simply by making communication faster and easier, new technologies will often increase the speed of evolution in ecosystems composed of superminds. Superminds reproduce and evolve by spreading their ideas, and, because of advances in IT, this can now happen far faster than it used to. For instance, if Amazon figures out a new user interface that makes its website particularly easy to use, other groups all over the world can instantly see these good ideas and often quickly copy them in their own user interfaces.

Will more intelligent individual superminds and a faster spread of new ideas make the overall supermind ecosystem more intelligent? That depends on what goals we think the overall ecosystem should be achieving. And to figure that out, we need to take a step back and think about how the goals of a supermind relate to the goals of its members.

SUPERMINDS HAVE WILLS OF THEIR OWN

It seems obvious to say that the goals of superminds are different from those of their members. But it's useful to be reminded of how important these differences can be. Markets allocate resources in a way that all the buyers and sellers agree to, but as we saw earlier, no individual in the market has that goal, and markets can be ruthless in their treatment of individuals who don't have many resources to trade. Communities try to serve the interests of their members, but they sometimes systematically—even violently—oppress some of their members, such as those in racial and other minorities. Sometimes a supermind's goals can even be different from those of its most powerful members. Uber, for instance, forced Travis Kalanick to resign in 2017, even though he was not only the CEO of the company; he also held a majority of the company's voting shares.[2]

In some cases (like the firing of a CEO), we may be able to identify specific individuals who play a key role in a supermind's decision. But often, the decisions just *emerge* from the actions of many people in the group. Who is responsible for a community's racism, for instance? Usually it's not any single individual or even any small group. Who is responsible for the outcome of an election? Again, it often depends on many factors and many individuals. In other words, even though superminds are composed of individuals, the superminds themselves have wills of their own that are different from those of some or even all of the individuals within them.

MOST SUPERMINDS HAVE A GOAL OF INCREASING THEIR OWN SURVIVAL OR REPRODUCTION

One of the foundational lessons from Charles Darwin's theory of biological evolution is that the characteristics that help organisms survive and reproduce become more common over time.[3] As a number of social scientists have observed, this lesson applies not just to biological organisms but also to superminds.[4] Of course, as we've seen, superminds don't transmit their characteristics using biological genes and sexual reproduction. Instead their characteristics are based on *ideas* (sometimes called memes[5]) that can be transmitted by many forms of communication and then imitated and combined in a vast number of different ways.[6]

But since there is constant evolutionary pressure for superminds to survive and reproduce, we are much more likely to see superminds that do whatever helps them survive or reproduce, whether they have any conscious intention of doing so or not. In fact, even if a supermind *wants* to do something that is good for its own members but decreases the survival or reproduction rate of the supermind itself, that kind of supermind would almost certainly be doomed. Over time, it and other superminds like it would become very rare or just die out.

For instance, companies—like many in the dot-com era—that give their employees lavish pay and benefits but don't produce commercially viable products don't last long. But companies—like Costco and Trader Joe's—that provide unusually good jobs for their employees can be very successful if they do that in a way that also allows them to lower costs, increase customer satisfaction, and be more profitable.[7]

Sometimes the characteristics that help a supermind survive are even opposed to the group's original goals. For instance, sociologist Robert Michels described what he called the iron law of oligarchy, a common pattern of organizational evolution that he observed first-hand in the German Socialist Party.[8] When organizations committed to the ideals of democratic decision making grow, he argued, at some point it becomes impossible for everyone to participate in decision making. This means that a small subset of the group's members needs to take responsibility for analyzing and recommending decisions and carrying out other administrative functions for the group. These elite members then acquire a vested interest in maintaining their positions and in preserving the organization itself, even when that requires doing things that contradict the organization's original goals.

In other words, many superminds have an implicit goal of fostering their own survival or reproduction whether they know it or not and whether this is in the interests of their members or not.

WHO'S IN CONTROL HERE?

We've just seen how the goals of superminds and their members can be very different. And that should worry us. It should worry us a lot. Because we individual humans share our planet with vast numbers of very powerful superminds: multinational corporations, national governments, global markets, and many more.[9]

If these superminds are looking out for their own interests, not ours, what hope do we humans have? That is one of the most important questions underlying everything in this book, and we'll see a number of instances of it.

But here's a surprisingly optimistic observation: *Superminds whose primary members are humans often exhibit a general long-run tendency to do what's good for the people in them.* Why?

There are two parts to the argument for why this is true. First, as we've seen, the participants that have the most influence in an ecosystem are those that successfully survived or reproduced in the past. But what makes one supermind with human members more likely to survive or reproduce than another? Quite often, it is being able to attract more human members.

Throughout human history, this has probably been most obvious in wars and other violent conflicts. Of course, weapons, battlefield strategy, and many other factors can affect who wins a war, but having significantly more soldiers on one side than the other is often a decisive advantage.

The same principle applies in many other parts of human life, too. Larger companies, larger markets, larger communities, and larger countries are all very often more powerful and more likely to survive than smaller ones.

Being able to attract more members also helps superminds reproduce. Superminds reproduce when other superminds imitate them. So the superminds that attract more people to imitate them also cause their characteristics to be more common in the future.

The second part of the argument is that individual humans are more likely to be attracted to superminds that give them more of what they want. Sometimes people do this by joining an existing supermind and making it larger. At other times, they do this by starting a new supermind that has the characteristics they find attractive. Either way, the kinds of superminds that are attractive to people are likely to have more influence in the ecosystem than those that aren't.

Of course, in the short term, people may not have much choice about the superminds they join. For instance, if another country's armies occupy your country, you may be forced to become part of a nation you didn't choose. And it's possible for people to suffer a very long time in superminds to which they don't want to belong.

But in the long run (which may be many generations), people often have quite a bit of choice about the superminds in which they participate. If you hate the repressive government where you live, you may be able to leave the country or help overthrow the government. And if you can't do it yourself, maybe your children or your great-great-grandchildren will do it eventually.

If you don't like your job, you may be able to find a better job where you can be part of a different supermind and get more of what is important to you. Or if you can't, maybe your descendants will be able to get better jobs than yours. And even in the short term, if you'd rather watch a movie than socialize with your neighbors, you can choose to participate in the market for movies instead of in your neighborhood community.

So in summary:

- if people choose to participate in the superminds that give them more of what they want, and
- if the superminds that attract more people survive and reproduce more effectively,
- then in general, the ecosystem will choose the superminds that give more people more of what they want.

Of course, there will be many exceptions to this general tendency, and even in cases where this happens, it may take a long time. But in general, and in the long run, this seems to be a common pattern in human history.

Over time, for instance, tyrannical kingdoms seem to have become rarer and freedom-enhancing democracies more common. Material standards of living have increased dramatically, in part because industrial hierarchies and global markets have been more effective than small communities at giving more people more of what they want.

Even when these changes didn't actually make us happier, we often got what we *thought* we wanted at the time. For instance, a number of scholars believe that the transition from hunting and gathering to agriculture was a kind of trap.[10] Cultivating food rather than foraging for it allowed people to have a more plentiful and reliable supply of food, so it seemed luxurious and appealing.

But it also required a different—less pleasant—kind of work, and it allowed population densities to grow slightly faster than food production.[11] The net result was that farmers probably worked more hours per day than their hunter-gatherer ancestors, were less well nourished, suffered from more serious diseases, and died younger.[12] But at least the ecosystem gave people what seemed to them at first to be a more luxurious life.

So even though it doesn't always happen, ecosystems often favor the superminds that give more people more of what (they think) they want. In other words, ecosystems—more or less—try to do the things that provide the greatest good for the greatest number of people.

But here's something very surprising: this is exactly what utilitarian philosophers have said for centuries is the right thing to do—whatever provides the greatest good for the greatest number.[13] In other words, what ecosystems *actually* do is what many philosophers say we *should* do.

We can call this the *principle of evolutionary utilitarianism*:[14]

When ecosystems are composed of superminds whose members are people, the ecosystems, in the long run, generally try to provide the greatest good for the greatest number of people.

We'll see more about this in the following chapter, but for now, we can use the principle of evolutionary utilitarianism to answer the question with which we began this discussion: if we view the goal of an ecosystem as providing the greatest good for the greatest number of the people in it, then having smarter superminds and a faster spread of ideas should increase the ability of an ecosystem to achieve that goal. And so from that point of view, IT should indeed help ecosystems become smarter.

CHAPTER 11

Which Superminds Are Best for Which Decisions?

I f you were planning to buy a car, you would probably do some shopping around to compare different kinds of cars. If you were systematic about it, you might even create a table where you compared the cars you were interested in on the dimensions you cared about, like cost, fuel economy, and reliability. Or, more likely, you would try to find a source where such a comparison had already been compiled, like *Consumer Reports*.

In this chapter, we're going to create a similar kind of "buyer's guide," not for cars but for superminds. There are two reasons to do this. First, as we just saw in the previous chapter, figuring out which superminds are best suited to a given situation is a good way of predicting which ones the ecosystem will favor.

Second, because as individuals we are usually far less powerful than the companies, communities, governments, and other kinds of superminds all around us, these comparisons can help us figure out how best to use whatever influence we have to accomplish our goals.

If you want to help your company develop new products more rapidly, for instance, should you rely on the people inside your own company's hierarchy or use markets to find the best people and ideas outside your company? If you want to help combat climate change, would you be better off buying an energy-efficient car or protesting in the streets to change community opinions? If you want to reduce discrimination against women and minorities, should you try to pass laws against discrimination or start a company that competes more effectively because it does a better job of hiring and promoting the best people regardless of their race and gender?

Of course, the buyer's guide for superminds we're going to develop here won't answer all these questions by itself, because so many other factors are involved. But the comparisons we'll develop can help you think much more systematically about which kinds of superminds are likely to be most effective in different situations.

HOW CAN WE COMPARE SUPERMINDS?

The different types of superminds we will compare are our old friends: *hierarchies, democracies, markets, communities,* and *ecosystems.* To figure out which of these species of supermind is best suited for making a particular decision, perhaps the most important question we need to answer: Which one creates the most *net benefits?* We define net benefit as *the total benefit the supermind creates* minus *the cost of creating that benefit.* Net benefit is a quantity you want to maximize, whether the supermind you are analyzing is working for just your own company or for the whole world.

If you are interested in predicting which type of supermind the ecosystem will pick, or if you want to make the world better (in the sense of providing the greatest good for the greatest number), then you also need to compare the different types of superminds on the basis of *how effectively they distribute the net benefits they create.* A supermind that creates a great deal of net benefit for one person but not for anyone else may be nice for that person, but it is likely to have trouble attracting enough other people to even make it practically viable, not to mention socially desirable.

In other words, we want superminds where

- group decision making creates a lot of benefit,
- the cost of group decision making is low, and
- the net benefits of group decision making are effectively distributed.

To compare supermind types on these three dimensions, we'll define the different types precisely enough to make some of the comparisons based only on the definitions. We'll also draw upon previous research about these supermind types from many different fields, including economics, political science, philosophy, and sociology. In doing this, you'll get a whirlwind tour of key research results about group decision making from all these fields, and you'll see how they all fit together.

Economists, for instance, have written about the relative advantages of hierarchies and markets.[1] But even within the field of economics, different researchers have focused on comparing markets and hierarchies in different situations with few attempts to reconcile their differing results.[2] Political theorists and philosophers have written about the relative advantages of democracies and hierarchies.[3] And anthropologists, sociologists, and many other social scientists have studied how various kinds of groups create and distribute benefits to their members.[4] But as far as I can tell, this is the first time all these different types of superminds have been systematically compared in a way that combines results from all these fields.[5]

To illustrate the comparisons, we'll use examples of the ways food might have been produced and distributed in primitive human groups like the hunting-and-gathering societies in which all our human ancestors lived until about 12,000 years ago.[6] Then we'll see how the same comparisons also help explain today's supermind ecosystem and how this ecosystem is likely to change with increasing use of IT.

COMPARING COSTS OF GROUP DECISION MAKING

To compare the costs of group decision making in the different types of superminds, let's think about how decisions are actually made in each case.

- In a pure *hierarchy*, each decision is delegated to a single person who is responsible for that decision and who decides what the group will do, usually taking into account information, advice, or assistance from others. If a group of primitive humans were organized in this way, the leader of the group, or others that person had delegated, would tell everyone in the group what to do. For example, on a given day, they might tell some people to hunt deer and others to gather berries. The leader and the assistants would also decide what each person gets to eat.

- In a pure *democracy*, voters receive information about the available options, then each decides which option he or she thinks the group should choose. In a primitive human group organized this way, everyone would need to vote on every decision about who hunts and gathers which kinds of food and who gets what to eat.

- In a pure *market*, the group's decision is just the combination of many separate agreements among pairs of buyers and sellers who want to trade resources with one another. Before agreeing to a trade, the buyers and sellers usually communicate with competing buyers and sellers, too. In a primitive human group organized this way, different people might decide for themselves what kind of food, if any, they want to try to hunt and gather on a given day.

Then they could trade whatever they have with others to create a more balanced diet for themselves. But if they have nothing to trade, they get nothing to eat.

- In a pure *community*, the individuals make decisions based on the community's norms. These norms are an informal group consensus about what is right in different situations, and a large majority of the group members must agree on those norms for the community to function effectively. The norms in a community of primitive humans would guide what kind of work different people should do and how the food should be shared. For instance, maybe women would hunt and men would gather berries (or vice versa). These norms would evolve over time through discussions and experience, and the group would share and enforce them with rewards and punishments (such as extra food for those who are in good favor with the group and, in extreme cases, ostracism for those who aren't).

- In a pure *ecosystem*, the individual with the most power makes the group decisions. In a primitive human world organized this way, each person would be responsible for getting his or her own food, but powerful people could force others to gather food for them or take food from others whenever they want to. Determining who is most powerful would sometimes require fights or other competition, but direct competition could often be avoided if people could tell from looking who is likely to be the most powerful (for example, those who look big and strong).

Comparing Ecosystems and Democracies

Two of these forms of decision making are easy to compare. Ecosystems have a low cost of group decision making because there is very little group decision making at all. Each person has to find food to the best of his or her ability, and individuals may rarely even see one another. But when decisions need to be made, they are simple tests of strength: if Joe is stronger than Sue, he can take the berries she just picked. But if Ellen is stronger than Joe, she can take the berries herself. As shown in the table below, we rate the cost of this form of group decision making as low.

Type of Supermind	Cost of Group Decision Making
Hierarchy	Medium
Democracy	High
Market	Medium+/-
Community	Medium
Ecosystem	Low

Democracies have a very high cost of group decision making because most people in the group need to vote on most decisions. Everyone has to vote on whether Joe hunts or gathers today and, if so, where. They also have to vote on the same choices for Sue, Ellen, and all the other people in the group. And they have to vote on how much food each member of the group gets to eat. This means there has to be lots of communication so people will know enough to vote sensibly, and lots of time has to be spent making individual decisions, voting, and counting votes. All this information processing takes a great deal of effort, so we rate the cost of this form of group decision making as high.

Comparing Hierarchies, Markets, and Communities

The other three types of superminds (hierarchies, markets, and communities) all require the involvement of more people and the exchange of more information than ecosystems do, but they require less of these things than democracies do. Therefore we rate the cost of decision making for all these other types as medium.

We rate markets as "medium plus or minus" to call attention to the fact that, depending on the situation, markets may have either a higher or lower decision-making cost than hierarchies and communities do. To see why this is true, let's think first about the situations where markets have a lower decision-making cost than hierarchies.

When Do Markets Have a Lower Decision-Making Cost Than Hierarchies?

Such situations typically occur when the scale and scope of group decision making is large. For instance, to take a modern example, my decision about whether to eat rice, bread, or spaghetti for dinner tonight is affected by the availability in my kitchen of all these different kinds of carbohydrates. That in turn is affected by what I choose to buy at the supermarket. And, of course, my choices at the supermarket are affected by thousands of decisions made all over the world about whether, how, and when to produce and distribute these different kinds of food. Could a single giant "global food-production hierarchy" have made all these decisions? Perhaps. But that would likely have been much more expensive than the decision-making in the global food market.

One of the best articulations of why this is so comes from the Nobel Prize–winning economist Friedrich Hayek (writing about tin rather than food):

Assume that somewhere in the world a new opportunity for the use of some raw material, say tin, has arisen, or that one of the sources of supply of tin has been eliminated. It does not matter for our purpose—and it is very significant that it does not matter—which of these two causes has made tin more scarce. All that the users of tin need to know is that some of the tin they used to consume is now more profitably employed elsewhere, and that in consequence they must economize tin...

The marvel is that in a case like that of a scarcity of one raw material, without an order being issued, without more than perhaps a handful of people knowing the cause, tens of thousands of people whose identity could not be ascertained by months of investigation are made to use the material or its products more sparingly...[7]

In other words, a market can make very complex group decisions by letting thousands of individuals make their own small decisions, each taking into account his or her own private knowledge. All these smaller decisions are coordinated by a relatively small number of ever-changing *prices* for the items about which the decisions are being made. Often this means that markets can make an overall decision that is much better than what a vast hierarchy could have made and at a much lower cost.

When Do Markets Have a Higher Decision-Making Cost Than Hierarchies?

Even though markets are often cheaper to operate than hierarchies when many people and decisions are involved, they can be more expensive, too, especially in ever-changing situations that involve only a small number of potential trading partners. A number of Nobel Prize–winning economists, including Ronald Coase, Oliver Williamson, Oliver Hart, and Bengt Holmström, have analyzed the situations in which this is true.[8]

A key issue is that the *transaction costs* of making decisions in markets can sometimes be greater than those of hierarchies. For instance, say Ron promises to give Elizabeth a slice of deer meat in exchange for a bunch of grapes, but then he takes the grapes and never gives her the meat. That is a problem. A manager in a hierarchy can deal with problems like this by quickly punishing Ron, but markets require some mechanism outside the market itself. In the primitive world, this might be a community; in the modern world, it might be contracts and the legal system.

In the modern world, another important kind of transaction cost arises when one party has the potential to "hold up" the other party in the future. For example, imagine that I make a significant investment in retooling my tire factory to make a special tire in a size that only fits the cars you make. For the first year, you buy all my tires, and everything is fine. But then, in the second year, you find someone else who can make the same size tires for half of what you've been paying me, and you suddenly tell me that you will no longer buy my tires at the old price. If I had known this was going to happen, I would never have retooled my factory in the first place, but now I am stuck. The risk of things like this happening again makes me less willing to make similar investments in the future, even when they would be good for the overall economy.

On the other hand, if both my tire factory and your car factory were owned by the same company and managed as part of the same hierarchy, then neither of us would have to worry about writing complicated contracts to cover all possible contingencies or taking risks that the other would hold us up in the future.

In other words, having a single hierarchical management structure that can appropriately adapt to changing situations can often lead to lower long-term costs of group decision making. This is the best explanation we have for why hierarchically managed companies exist in our economy instead of every worker being an independent contractor who negotiates with others every day to do the work that needs to be done.

Comparing Markets to Communities

Like hierarchies, markets can have either higher or lower decision-making costs than communities. The same price mechanism that often makes markets cheaper than hierarchies also makes them cheaper than communities when coordinating large numbers of people and decisions.

On the other hand, communities, like hierarchies, are often better than markets at dealing with transaction costs arising from things like contract negotiations and hold-up problems. In a community, for example, people already have lots of reasons to go along with decisions that are dictated by community norms; if they violate these norms, they know that the community has many ways to punish them. But in a market, resolving issues that trading parties disagree about requires some extra effort that goes beyond the market itself.

COMPARING BENEFITS OF GROUP DECISION MAKING

The next factor to consider when comparing types of superminds is how much benefit they create by making group decisions. By definition, members of an ecosystem don't decide things together, so there isn't any benefit of group decision making in that type of supermind. For example, the people fighting about food in an ecosystem are not really any better off than if they were alone. Therefore, we rate ecosystems as having low benefits of group decision making in the table below.

Type of Supermind	Benefits of Group Decision Making
Hierarchy	High
Democracy	High
Market	Medium-
Community	Medium
Ecosystem	Low

We rate markets as "medium minus" because the participants in markets reap only one specific kind of benefit from collective action: buyers and sellers only trade with each other if they both think what they are getting is worth more to them than what they are giving up.

For example, Ron and Elizabeth wouldn't trade deer meat for grapes unless they both thought they would be better off after the trade than before it. Economists call this positive-sum trading because the sum of benefits for the two parties is greater after the trade than before. In a market, all the buyers and sellers benefit from this simple form of pairwise collective action.

All the other types of superminds can create agreements in much larger groups than just buyer-seller pairs. That means they can make decisions that are good for the group as a whole, even though some of the individuals in the group would never have agreed to them. This in turn gives these superminds the potential to create many other benefits that would be impossible in a pure market, so they are all rated higher than markets. These additional benefits fall into two main categories: the *basic benefits of cooperation* and the *benefits of bigness*.

Basic Benefits of Cooperation

As Thomas Hobbes famously remarked in his 1651 book, *Leviathan*, in a world without any form of human cooperation (in other words, an ecosystem), "there is...continual fear and danger of violent death, and the life of man [is] solitary, poor, nasty, brutish, and short."[9] Many philosophers and others (including John Locke, Jean-Jacques Rousseau, and, more recently, John Rawls) have also discussed the various kinds of benefits possible from human cooperation.

One of the most obvious benefits of cooperation is just avoiding the losses that can result from unrestricted conflict. If anyone who is stronger than you are can kill you or take anything of yours he or she wants, then you live in constant fear for your safety. You may have to spend much of your time trying to protect yourself, and you have less reason to invest your effort in creating things that others might steal. Being part of a group that restricts other individuals from harming you can be a very significant benefit. For instance, even though the winner usually gains something in a fight, both parties may have been better off if the fight had never happened in the first place.

Cooperation can avoid other kinds of problems, too. In a scenario that economists call the tragedy of the commons, for example, villagers in a small town let their sheep graze in the town commons without any restrictions. As a result, the sheep eat all the grass. No more grass can grow, so no one has grass anymore. But if the villagers had cooperated to limit the amount of grazing each one's animals could do, they could still have had grass.[10] This problematic pattern also occurs in many other group situations, resulting in such problems as environmental pollution and climate change.

Another potential benefit of cooperation results from what evolutionary biologists call reciprocal altruism.[11] In a community with reciprocal altruism, for example, Mary might give Sue an apple she picked without expecting any direct payment for it, and Sue might return the favor later. But if Sue always takes things from others and never gives things to anyone else, she is likely to acquire a bad reputation (as a "cheater" or a "taker") and be punished in some way. In a community with reciprocal altruism, everyone, on average, can be better off than they would be otherwise.

Benefits of Bigness

The basic benefits of cooperation that we've just seen can occur even in small groups, but many other potential benefits of cooperation increase as the size of the group increases. The most obvious of these are the ones that come purely from the greater power that larger groups have. For instance, as we've seen, larger armies can usually defeat smaller ones, and large companies usually have more power than small ones to influence suppliers, customers, and regulators.

The other benefits of bigness include various forms of economies of scale, scope, and specialization. In a primitive human group, for instance, everyone in the group will likely get better food if some people specialize in hunting while others specialize in cooking and preserving the food.

In modern times, as we've seen in Adam Smith's famous pin factory, letting different people specialize in different kinds of work can often lead to very significant improvements in productivity. A large integrated-circuit factory can often produce chips at a much lower cost per chip than a small one. And buying insurance to cover the risk that your house will burn down works better when there is a large group of insurance buyers rather than a small one.

Communities, hierarchies, and democracies can all, in principle, obtain these different benefits of collective action because they all have ways of getting everyone to go along with the group's decisions. But communities, in general, have looser methods for making and enforcing their decisions than hierarchies and democracies, so they are less likely to be able to fully capture these benefits. Therefore we rate hierarchies and democracies as high on this dimension and communities as medium.

COMPARING DISTRIBUTION OF BENEFITS

In order to compare how effectively different types of superminds distribute the benefits of group decision making to their members, we need a way to judge whether one distribution is better than another. But this is a very complex problem that has occupied economists and others—from the Marquis de Condorcet in the 18th century to Kenneth Arrow and many others in the 20th century.[12]

Many economists have analyzed this problem by saying that we can't sensibly compare one person's preferences to another's because there's no way of really knowing how strongly I feel about something compared to how strongly you feel about it. For instance, imagine that there is only one piece of deer meat left and that we're trying to decide whether Mary or John should get it. Also imagine that Mary hasn't eaten anything for a week and that John has just had a meal but is still hungry. If you hold the viewpoint that individual preferences can't be compared, you couldn't say which way of distributing the food was better, because both John and Mary want the meat. Economists say that a distribution in which no one can be made better off without making someone else worse off is Pareto optimal, after the late 19th and early 20th century Italian economist Vilfredo Pareto. So if John and Mary are both hungry, giving the meat to either one of them is Pareto optimal.

But in the real world, we often assume that preferences are, at least to some extent, comparable across individuals. For instance, we would almost certainly agree that it would be better for Mary to get the deer meat instead of John. In modern times, we believe that—at least up to a point—taking $100 from Bill Gates and using it to pay Medicare expenses for someone who has no money at all is better for society as a whole, even if that means Bill ends up with a little less money.

So to compare different superminds, we'll use the utilitarian philosophy with which we concluded the last chapter: we'll assume that it is desirable to distribute benefits in ways that provide the "greatest good for the greatest number." We'll also assume that superminds in which more people are involved in making group decisions are more likely to distribute benefits in ways that do this. This assumption isn't always true, but it certainly seems plausible in general.

Now, with these assumptions, we can compare the different types of superminds. First, we see that in both ecosystems and hierarchies, a single individual makes choices for the group. Of course, that individual might take the preferences of others in the group into account, but we can assume that, in general, he or she will do so less effectively than when more individuals in the group are directly involved in making the decision. So we rate both ecosystems and hierarchies as low on this dimension.

Type of Supermind	Distribution of Benefits
Hierarchy	Low
Democracy	Medium
Market	High
Community	Medium
Ecosystem	Low

Since both communities and democracies *do* involve more people in decision making, we rate both of them as medium on this dimension.

We rate markets as high for a special reason. As we saw in the previous section, markets can only make decisions that everyone involved agrees to. Even though that means markets can't create all the benefits that other groups can, it also means that the benefits markets *do* create always get distributed in ways that everyone, at least in some sense, is happy with.

SUMMARY

Here is a table that summarizes all the comparisons we've made so far:

Type of Supermind	Costs of Group Decision Making	Benefits of Group Decision Making	Distribution of Benefits
Hierarchy	Medium	High	Low
Democracy	High	High	Medium
Market	Medium+/-	Medium-	High
Community	Medium	Medium	Medium
Ecosystem	Low	Low	Low

The theory summarized by this table is the "buyers' guide" for superminds that we set out to create at the beginning of the chapter. It tells you the advantages and disadvantages of each type of supermind on each of these three key dimensions. One way of using the theory is to help explain (or predict) how human societies are (or will be) organized in different situations. And that's what we'll do in the remainder of this chapter.

EXPLAINING THE SUPERMIND ECOSYSTEM IN HUNTING-AND-GATHERING SOCIETIES

According to our best anthropological evidence, most early humans lived in small communities (called bands) of about 15 to 50 people.[13] Why would they do this instead of just living as individuals in a pure ecosystem? The preceding table helps us see why: the benefits of collective action in communities must have outweighed their costs. The table shows that communities have a higher cost of collective action than ecosystems do, but they also have greater benefits and better distribution of benefits.

In other words, if you were an early human, it was worth it to you to pay the costs of participating in and abiding by the decisions of your community, because in return you got important benefits like better and more reliable food.

Now, why didn't early humans use the other types of superminds more? Their communities did actually have some rudimentary elements of hierarchy (certain people had more influence than others), democracy (the group was more likely to do things that most group members wanted), and markets (there was some trading, especially between different bands).[14] But the disadvantages of these other types of superminds (like being expensive to operate) must have outweighed their advantages for most decisions.[15]

EXPLAINING TODAY'S SUPERMIND ECOSYSTEM

Today's world is far removed from the world of small hunting-and-gathering communities. Instead of hunting wild animals and picking berries, we usually buy our food at stores and restaurants. In other words, we have outsourced most of the stages of food preparation to a much larger supermind: the global market economy.

Why do we do that? The short answer is: markets can most effectively take advantage of the significantly increased economies of scale and specialization that are now available.

Why Are Greater Economies of Scale Available Now?

Two critical things have changed since hunting-and-gathering times to make much greater economies of scale possible. First, new technologies—starting with agriculture itself—have greatly increased the potential economies of scale for food production (and most other things). It is a lot easier to grow a whole farm full of wheat, for instance, and divide the results among many families than it is for each family to have its own wheat field.

Second, new information and transportation technologies have increased our ability to take advantage of these potential economies of scale because they have greatly increased the size of human groups that can effectively work together. If you can talk to almost anyone on the planet virtually instantly on your cell phone and ship most physical products almost anywhere on the planet in a matter of days, then much larger groups can work together in all sorts of new ways.

Together these two changes have combined the whole world's food production into a single supermind, and it's now an everyday occurrence to eat food from the other side of the planet. For instance, about 70 percent of the apple juice and 50 percent of the cod eaten in the United States today comes from China, and about 46 percent of the soybeans eaten in China come from the United States.[16]

Of course, other factors matter in food production besides just economies of scale. Sometimes we want local food (even from our own gardens) because it's fresher and more environmentally friendly to transport, among other things. But there are still good reasons to have much of your food produced on a much larger scale than your family or neighborhood could manage.

Why Are Markets a Good Way of Organizing Very Large Groups with Lots of Decisions to Make?

If you're going to get your food from a much larger group than your own family or neighborhood, the main question we want our theory to help answer is: How should that group of food producers be organized? The table on page 157 reminds us of four possible types of superminds we could use to answer that question: hierarchies, democracies, markets, and communities. The minus sign in the medium+/- rating for markets represents the idea that in very large groups with lots of decisions to make, markets often have a lower cost of decision making than the other three supermind types.

For instance, even though *communities* worked well for managing food production in small hunting-and-gathering bands, the costs of using informal consensus and reputations to do this in communities of millions of people would be completely prohibitive with conventional technology.

Or imagine having a vast global *hierarchy* that's responsible for feeding everyone in the world. This hierarchy (let's call it the United Nations Department of Food Services, or UNDFS) would own all the farms, all the food-processing plants, and all the grocery stores in the world. You might be able to tell UNDFS your food preferences, but you would ultimately only get the food it decided to give you. This would essentially be an extreme form of global socialism, but even today's socialist economies don't go nearly this far; they use markets for many parts of their food-production systems.

If we used a direct *democracy* to manage all the details of global food production, everyone would need to vote on every tiny decision in the entire worldwide food system. Should we plant wheat or corn in this field? Which kind of fertilizer should we use? How many loaves of bread does Bill Gates get? How many does his gardener get? Even thinking about this possibility makes it clear that the costs of such a system would make it completely infeasible.

Why Are There Hierarchical Firms in a Market Economy?

If markets are such a good idea, why don't we use them for everything? Why isn't every worker in the economy a separate one-person company? One reason, as we saw above, is that making decisions in markets is sometimes more expensive than in hierarchies (the plus sign in the medium+/- rating).

Another reason is that hierarchies can often create more benefits from group decision making than markets could alone (high versus medium-). For instance, imagine that Apple wants to design a new version of the iPhone, but instead of using long-term employees to create the design, they just asked all the companies that make iPhone components to design the new phone without anyone from Apple coordinating the details. Samsung might design the batteries, LG the display, Intel the semiconductors, Corning the glass screen. And instead of developing the software in-house, as it does today, Apple would ask another contractor to do that, too—say, a start-up full of recent MIT graduates.

All these suppliers would need to agree on many things, despite the fact that no one would really be in charge. For instance, if Corning wanted to use a thicker glass and Samsung wanted a larger battery, but those two changes together would make the phone too thick overall, then they would have to somehow agree on what to do without anyone else telling them how to make the trade-off. I suppose it's possible to imagine that this could somehow work, but it's easy to see how having a hierarchical company like Apple manage the whole design process would result in much better designs much more quickly.

Why Are There Government Hierarchies in a Market Economy?

As we saw above, markets can run into trouble when there are some people who don't agree to a decision that would be good for the group as a whole. For instance, government hierarchies (with their legal systems and police powers) can resolve problems when people don't fulfill their contracts. They can also help prevent sellers from lying about their products (truth in advertising), and they can insist on health and safety standards.

Governments can also do other things that communities want but markets can't do well themselves. For instance, they can provide services for which there is a kind of natural monopoly (such as highways and national security). They can redistribute income from rich people to poor ones, and they can provide funding for research that benefits everyone but that no single company would pay for alone.

Why Are There Democracies in a Market Economy?

Purely hierarchical governments, with leaders like kings and emperors, have been overseeing markets for thousands of years, and they still do so in some countries today. But many countries have established democracies that oversee their hierarchical governments. The table on page 157 helps us understand why.

In the column showing the costs of group decision making, we see that democracy is more costly than any other form of supermind. It would be far too expensive to use democracies to make all the detailed decisions of a market economy or even of the hierarchical government that oversees it. But democracy is rated higher than hierarchy at distributing benefits. Of course, a particular king or other hierarchical government may always do what is best for most of the people in a country. But the table assumes that, in general, democracies usually do a better job of that than a single leader or government hierarchy would without democratic supervision.

What Role Do Communities Have in a Market Economy?

Communities are always in the background of any kind of economy. As we saw above, they certainly shape the opinions of voters in a democracy. In a sense, the mission of a democratically elected government is to carry out a community's wishes. Communities also do many things themselves. For instance, communities can provide entertainment (when friends visit with each other instead of watching television), prepare food (when people cook for friends or family members without being paid), and help the underprivileged (when donations to charities, rather than government programs, provide food or other support).

But in the democratically governed market economies that are typical of developed countries today, communities have effectively delegated much of their decision making to the other types of superminds. To summarize, community members have implicitly said something like this:

When we lived in small hunting-and-gathering bands, we made all our group decisions about food and other things by a kind of informal consensus of the whole community. But our communities are now way too big for that to work anymore; we just don't agree enough, and coming to a consensus would take forever. We don't want kings or other rulers to tell us what to do, either, because that doesn't give us enough of what we want. So we'll use democratic voting to help us decide what to do as a whole group.

But we don't have enough time to vote on all the detailed decisions about the specific jobs that people in our group will do and how much they will get of the food, clothing, and other resources our group has. So we'll let markets take care of most of those decisions for us.

However, markets need some way of resolving disputes between buyers and sellers, and they can't do everything we want (like sometimes taking money from those who have a lot and giving it to those who have very little). Unfortunately, supervising markets in all these ways still requires far more detailed decisions than we have time to vote on individually, so we can't use democracies for that, either.

Instead we'll let hierarchical governments supervise markets on behalf of the whole community. But we'll supervise the governments in two ways. First, we'll elect the leaders of the governmental hierarchies. And second, we'll elect our representatives to vote on high-level policies (called laws) that codify what we want done.

In that way, we as a community will be able to use the other types of superminds to get—more or less—what we want without having to worry about all the details ourselves.

Below is a diagram that summarizes how all the species of superminds interact in making decisions in a typical modern democracy. The arrows indicate which superminds oversee (or control) others.

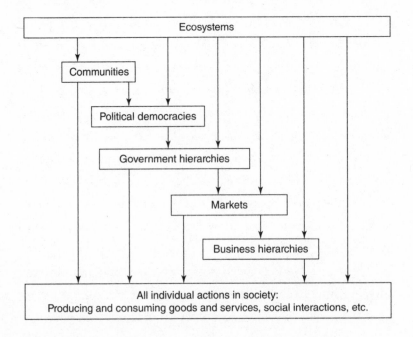

HOW WILL INFORMATION TECHNOLOGY AFFECT THE BALANCE OF POWER AMONG TYPES OF SUPERMINDS?

In addition to helping *explain* the kinds of superminds that have evolved in primitive and modern ecosystems, our theory can also help *predict* how IT is likely to change the balance of power among the different types of superminds in the future. To do that, we'll consider two ways IT could affect superminds. First, IT is likely to *increase the size of groups*. And second, for any given group size and supermind type, IT is likely to *decrease the costs of group decision making*.

Increasing the Size of Groups

As we've already seen, modern communication technologies—like the Internet—have dramatically increased the size of groups that can make decisions together. That means that many more people—and resources—can be brought to bear on whatever problems these large groups want to solve. But it also usually means that the costs of making group decisions increase, since involving more decision makers usually requires more effort. However, there is one notable exception: markets.

The minus sign in the medium+/- rating for markets indicates that markets often have lower costs of decision making in large groups than any other supermind type (except ecosystems). Therefore, as information technologies continue to increase the size of groups that can make decisions together, it's very likely that markets will take over even more of these decisions.

For instance, much of the social interaction that used to occur in face-to-face communities is now occurring in the online communities hosted by Facebook. But since a company is providing the infrastructure for these communities, market motivations affect the community in ways they never would in a purely face-to-face community. When Facebook employees design the software that decides what items to include in your news feed, for example, they are not just thinking about what news items will help build a stronger and more satisfying community for its members. They are also thinking about what news items will lead to more long-term advertising revenue for Facebook.[17]

Decreasing Costs of Group Decision Making

While IT doesn't eliminate all the costs of communication and information processing needed for group decision making, it certainly reduces them. This means that supermind species that were previously too expensive may become affordable in many situations. And if these supermind species provide enough other benefits, then they will outcompete other species and become more common.

In other words, as IT reduces many of the costs of group decision making, the supermind types that will benefit the most are the ones that previously suffered the most from high decision-making costs. If we look at the table on page 157 again, we see that democracies have the highest cost of group decision making (high), and markets (the plus sign in the medium+/- rating) are next highest.

So while IT will potentially benefit all types of superminds, the ones that are likely to benefit the most are democracies and markets. For instance, we should expect that IT-enabled innovations like liquid democracy will enable more democratic voting in governments and in businesses and that markets will continue to take over functions in our society that were previously done by other types of superminds.

SUMMARY

The theory we've developed in this chapter brings together knowledge about group decision making from many different disciplines to help us

- understand which types of superminds are likely to be most common in different situations and
- decide which kinds of superminds are most likely to help us achieve our goals.

This systematic approach to comparing superminds is one of the most important benefits of looking at the world from the perspective of superminds.

Part IV

How Can Superminds Create More Intelligently?

CHAPTER 12

Bigger Is (Often) Smarter

In November 2009, my colleagues and I launched a new online platform called Climate CoLab.[1] The goal of this platform is to crowd-source the process of finding solutions for one of the most important problems facing humanity today: global climate change. On the day we launched, only a few dozen people were registered members, mostly people we already knew. By the end of December 2009, we had 193 members who had created 20 proposals for different approaches to the climate-change problem. Over the years, the Climate CoLab community has continued to grow, sometimes doubling or tripling in a year. By early 2018, the community had over 100,000 people, including some of the world's leading experts on climate change as well as businesspeople, students, policy makers, and many others from all over the world. Together, these people have developed and evaluated over 2,000 proposals for how to solve many aspects of the climate change problem.

Climate CoLab is not just about *deciding* what proposed actions are best. It's primarily about *creating* good ideas for what to do in the first place. And it illustrates two of the most important ways new technologies can help superminds be smarter, regardless of their goals:

- *Involving more individuals.* When comparing the brains of animals from different species, having more neurons is strongly associated with more intelligence.[2] And computers with more processing elements (like transistors) can store and process more information. So it certainly seems plausible that increasing the number of elementary processing units in a system can help make the system smarter. One way IT can help make superminds smarter, therefore, is by increasing the number of people and machines they include.
- *Organizing the work in new ways.* No matter how many neurons there are in a brain or how many transistors there are in a computer, if these parts aren't connected properly, the system will have no intelligence at all. So another critical way IT can help make superminds smarter is by letting us explore a vastly larger set of possibilities for connecting and organizing large groups of people and computers.

In this chapter, we'll talk about the benefits of having more individuals; in the next, we'll talk about new ways of organizing work.

EXAMPLE: CLIMATE COLAB

Anyone who wants to participate in the Climate CoLab community is welcome to. Based on surveys we've done, we know that our community is well educated (more than half have some postgraduate education), older than you might expect (the median age is between 30 and 39), about two-thirds male (63 percent), and very international (about half are from outside the United States).[3]

The main way activity is organized in the Climate CoLab community is through a series of annual online contests on topics ranging from how to generate cleaner electricity to how to change public attitudes about climate. In each contest, after members submit proposals, judges select the most promising entries as finalists. From the finalists, the judges then select the Judges' Choice Award winners, and the community votes for the Popular Choice Award winners.

At the Climate CoLab conferences, the winners of the Judges' Choice and Popular Choice Awards have the opportunity to present their ideas to groups that can potentially help implement them. The winners are also eligible for one overall grand prize ($10,000 at the time of this writing), awarded by the judges. All proposal authors are eligible to share another award purse (also currently $10,000) for their contributions to integrated proposals, as described below.

But in our surveys, contributors generally tell us that their main reason for participating is not the chance to win money but the chance to help solve a world problem while learning and interacting with others who have similar interests.

Winning Ideas from Climate CoLab

Of the many proposals that have emerged from the Climate CoLab contests, one of my favorites is for a system called SunSaluter, which won the grand prize in 2015. SunSaluter is a low-cost solar panel that rotates during the day to follow the sun across the sky, generating 30 percent more electricity than a fixed solar panel. The panel's rotation is powered by dripping water and gravity, and as the water drips, it is filtered to produce four liters of clean drinking water per day. So this single device can produce both electricity and clean water — two basic needs for the hundreds of millions of people in the world who don't have them.

One of the most interesting things about this proposal is that it didn't come from a professor at MIT or Stanford, an engineer at a major energy company, or anyone else you might expect. It was submitted by a young Canadian woman from Calgary named Eden Full, who invented SunSaluter at the age of 16 and later dropped out of Princeton to pursue the development of SunSaluter full-time. She now leads a nonprofit organization that helps entrepreneurs in countries like India and Malawi establish businesses using this technology.[4] As we'll see, the fact that Eden wasn't part of the academic or industrial establishment is not unusual in crowdsourced contests.

Other winning Climate CoLab proposals have included, to name just a few,[5]

- a way of combining Google Maps with infrared photographs taken from airplanes to show people how much wasted heat is escaping from their homes;
- a plan called China Dream, from a nonprofit organization in China, for developing and promoting an aspirational lifestyle for Chinese consumers that is more environmentally sustainable than the "American dream";
- a way for individual countries to charge emission levies on ocean shipments coming to and leaving from their ports, without violating international law, providing significant economic incentives for shippers to avoid their ports, or requiring any global international agreements.

Of course, Climate CoLab wasn't solely responsible for the development of all these ideas. Some of them were based on work their developers had been doing for years. But Climate CoLab's crowd-sourcing approach provides a way of framing important problems, finding people who have good ideas about these problems wherever they are, encouraging them to develop the ideas into a form that can be shared, systematically comparing these ideas, and then helping to bring attention and other resources to the most promising ones.

This crowdsourcing approach to problem solving is very different from the conventional problem-solving approach where you hire the best people you can find, pay them to work on your problem, and then hope they are successful. Neither is guaranteed to work, but crowdsourcing can often solve problems the conventional approach can't. And crowdsourcing is only one of a number of possibilities we'll see for how new technologies can make groups smarter by involving more individuals.

THE BRUTE-FORCE EFFECT

As we've already seen, there are many tasks in the physical world for which larger groups (like armies or companies) are better than smaller ones. We can call this the *brute-force effect*.

The same principle holds true for many tasks in the information world, too. In projects like Wikipedia and Climate CoLab, for instance, the sheer volume of work to be done requires large numbers of people to do it. And by reducing the costs of finding and communicating with potential members of a group, new technologies can make it easier to assemble such large groups. Think about how hard it would be to find the 70,000 or so people who volunteer to work on Wikipedia each month if the only tools you had were newspaper advertisements and word of mouth. And even if you did manage to find 70,000 people from all over the world who wanted to help, very few would actually be able to do so if they had to travel to a single physical location to do the work.

Even within an individual company of a fixed size, the number of people involved in solving any specific problem is usually very small. While it's not always desirable to do so, new information technologies make it far easier to involve many more people from throughout the company in solving specific problems, and doing so may generate much better solutions.

Searching for Red Balloons

One variety of the brute-force effect is useful during large-scale searches. One of the best examples of this is the US Defense Advanced

Research Projects Agency (DARPA) Red Balloon Challenge.[6] The purpose of the challenge was to explore how a group could quickly search a vast area for a few specific items of interest. Problems like this occur in a wide range of situations, from search-and-rescue operations to hunting down escaped criminals to reacting to health threats after disasters.[7] As an exercise to practice search methods that are applicable to all these situations, the DARPA challenge involved finding red balloons.

On December 5, 2009, at 10:00 a.m., DARPA positioned 10 large red weather balloons at 10 undisclosed but publicly visible locations scattered across the United States. The challenge, which DARPA had announced several weeks earlier, was to find all 10 balloons as rapidly as possible. The first group to do so would receive a prize of $40,000.

This might sound like an impossible—or at least extremely difficult and time-consuming—task. How could any single group of people ever find all these balloons in any reasonable amount of time? Well, one group did—it found all 10 balloons in only eight hours and 53 minutes—but it wasn't an ordinary group. The core of the group was a team from MIT, including my colleague Sandy Pentland and others in his lab. But the core MIT research team didn't do the actual searching. The group also included 4,400 people from around the world who registered on the MIT team's website and more than 100,000 others who visited the website during the challenge.[8]

How did the MIT team recruit this vast group? The answer illustrates the importance of incentives. They divided the $40,000 reward money into $4,000 per balloon, and they said that the first person to report the correct location of a given balloon would get half that amount—$2,000.

But if that money were the only incentive, anyone who wanted to look for balloons would be motivated not to tell anyone else about the challenge, because each new person recruited would have been more competition for the reward money.

So the MIT team also gave a share of the reward money to the people who helped *find the people* who found balloons. For instance, imagine that Alice joins the group, then recruits Bob, who recruits Carol, who recruits Dave. If Dave actually finds a balloon, he would get $2,000, but Carol would get half of that amount ($1,000), Bob would get half of Carol's reward ($500), and Alice would get half of that ($250). The MIT team would pay a total of $3,750 for that balloon, and they would donate the remaining $250 to charity.

By cleverly motivating everyone to not only look for balloons but also recruit others to the cause, this approach rapidly recruited a vast army of searchers. Together this group's brute-force searching solved the problem far faster than almost anyone expected. I can't imagine that this method would have been possible without the fast, cheap communication enabled by modern information technologies.

THE WISDOM-OF-CROWDS EFFECT

In his book *The Wisdom of Crowds*, James Surowiecki popularized another reason why large groups can be smarter than small ones.[9] He tells the story of the English statistician Sir Francis Galton, who, at a county fair in England in 1906, analyzed the results of a contest to guess the weight of an ox. It turned out that the average of all the guesses (1,197 pounds) was a remarkably accurate estimate of the actual weight (1,198 pounds). Surowiecki describes similar results for many other things, from estimating the number of jelly beans in a jar to guessing the location of a lost submarine.

The basic principle behind why this works is that when many people with no particular bias guess the answer, they should be equally likely to make errors on the high side and on the low side of the correct answer. When you average their answers, the errors should cancel each other out, leaving an accurate estimate. Usually, the larger the crowd, the more accurate the estimate.[10]

Limitations of the Wisdom of Crowds

Even though many people know about the wisdom-of-crowds effect, it turns out that this effect is more complicated than many readers of Surowiecki's book realize. First, the average is probably not the right statistic to use. I've been doing a version of this experiment in my MIT classes for years, asking students to guess how many jelly beans are in a jar. Contrary to what you would expect from reading Surowiecki's book, the average of their answers is often quite far from the correct answer—20–40 percent of the class members often make guesses that are more accurate than the average.

Part of the problem is that it's not unusual for a few students to make guesses that are way too high, and even one wildly high guess in a class can significantly distort the class average. Instead of the average, I've found that the results are usually much more accurate when I use the *median* of the students' guesses. The median is the number that's exactly in the middle of all the guesses, meaning that half the guesses are higher and half are lower. Unlike the average, the median isn't affected much at all by a few extreme guesses on either end. Even though Surowiecki implied otherwise, Galton himself used the median, not the average, and a number of other researchers have similarly found that the median is a better way of combining a group's guesses than the average.[11]

As Surowiecki notes, another very important condition for the success of the wisdom-of-crowds effect is that the guesses need to be independent of each other. If people are influenced by one another's guesses, this introduces biases that make the whole process less effective. For instance, in one compelling experiment, when group members saw information about one another's guesses, their guesses moved closer together, and they became more confident that their guesses were right... but their guesses actually became less accurate.[12] In other words, when members of the group shared information, they became less diverse and less effective at predicting the correct answer.

So even though cheap communication enables larger groups to exist, we still have to be careful about decision-making methods, since some ways of using that communication capability may actually make the group less smart.

SPECIALIZED KNOWLEDGE

Another important reason why large groups are often smarter than small ones is that they can include more people with different kinds of specialized knowledge. This is usually critical for solving complex problems. No single individual today, for instance, knows how to make something as simple as a modern pencil,[13] much less a jet airplane or an iPhone or an athletic shoe. All these human activities require many different specialized kinds of knowledge.

Complex societal problems—like what to do about global climate change—make even these manufacturing problems seem easy. Responding to climate change, for instance, requires many different kinds of detailed knowledge about what kinds of actions make sense in different places around the world. To respond to this need in Climate CoLab, we've specifically encouraged people with a wide range of specialized knowledge and interests to participate.

In the first few years of our work with Climate CoLab, we held only one or two contests per year on very general topics like "What international climate agreements should the world community make?" We got some interesting proposals in response to these questions, but most of them tended to focus on some narrow part of the overall global problem.

Then, in 2013, we began to systematically divide the problem of what to do about climate change into a family of a dozen or more related contests, each focused on a different aspect of the problem. For instance, we held separate contests for proposals on how to reduce emissions in transportation, buildings, and electricity generation, on how to change public attitudes about climate, and on how to put a price on carbon emissions (which most experts believe is a critical leverage point in addressing climate change).

When we divided the problem in this way, we began to receive many more detailed and interesting proposals. For example, in 2013, we held a contest on how to replace diesel energy with renewable energy, especially in developing countries. The winning proposal came from a nonprofit organization in India. It described how small Indian farms could replace their expensive, emission-intensive diesel irrigation pumps with much cheaper and more environmentally friendly foot-powered treadle pumps.

When we looked at this proposal, it was obvious that its authors were deeply connected to the culture of small farming communities in India. They even included a video featuring an Indian farmer named Budhiram, whose life was changed by using such a pump. By opening up the problem-solving process to such a wide global community, we received a very interesting proposal, one that was well suited to a particular situation and one that I don't think would ever have occurred to most professors who focus on climate change at places like MIT and Harvard.

UNUSUAL KNOWLEDGE

Another reason why large groups are often smarter is that they are more likely to include people who have unusual (and unexpectedly useful) knowledge. One good example is InnoCentive (see page 22), the company that uses open online contests to help companies find solutions for difficult problems. One of InnoCentive's clients was the Alaska-based Oil Spill Recovery Institute (OSRI), which created contests asking for methods to deal with crude oil when it spills into frigid ocean waters (which is what happened in 1989 during the *Exxon Valdez* oil spill). One specific challenge was how to separate oil from water on oil-recovery barges after the oil and water had frozen into a viscous mass.[14]

If this problem had been easy to solve, someone in the oil industry would have solved it long ago. But no one did. So OSRI decided to find out whether anyone in InnoCentive's global community of scientists, technologists, and other problem solvers could help. The winning solution to this problem came from John Davis, a chemist in Bloomington, Illinois, whose relevant experience was having worked on a construction site in a summer job. He realized that the same kind of vibrating devices that keep concrete from hardening prematurely on construction sites could also be used, with minor modifications, to keep oil from congealing in cold water. For submitting this winning idea, Davis received the $20,000 award, and OSRI had a solution to its problem.

It turns out, by the way, that solutions coming from unexpected sources are not at all uncommon in crowdsourced contests. In a study of 166 InnoCentive challenges, researchers Lars Jeppesen and Karim Lakhani found that the further away the problem solver's technical field was from the field in which the problem originated, the more likely he or she was to solve it.[15]

At first glance, this seems almost impossible: Why would people who know less about a problem than experts do be more likely to solve it? But the result makes much more sense when you consider that problems that can be easily solved by people in the relevant field never get posted on InnoCentive. Only the problems that stump the experts in the field get posted in the first place. But since the people who do solve the problems often already know the answer to similar problems in other domains, they can solve the problems more easily.

We found similar results in Climate CoLab. You might think that the people who are most likely to become finalists in Climate CoLab contests would be those who have been to graduate school and have prior experience with climate-change issues. But instead we found that the people who were *not* the usual suspects were just as likely to become finalists. Of the people who submitted proposals, people who had no graduate school training and no previous climate-change experience were just as likely to become finalists as those with the opposite characteristics.[16]

There's a very general lesson here: hard problems require unusual approaches. And really hard problems require many different kinds of approaches to different parts of the problem. Scott Page, in his book *The Difference*, even argues that in many cases, diversity trumps ability.[17] In other words, having many different kinds of problem solvers is often better than having people who are really good at one particular kind of problem solving. The journalist Matt Ridley says the amazing results of combining different ideas in this way are like "ideas having sex." Whatever you want to call it, the combination of different kinds of unusual knowledge is often key to many kinds of collective intelligence.

The most exciting aspect of this way of thinking is that, by reducing the costs of communication and coordination, new technologies are making it possible for groups of people with very diverse kinds of knowledge and problem-solving approaches to work together at a scale and with a degree of collaboration that has never before been possible in all of human history. That means that there's real potential for these kinds of problem-solving groups to come together and solve some of the complicated problems that have vexed the world's experts for years—including climate change.

UNUSUAL ABILITIES

Many important problems in biology research involve figuring out the three-dimensional shapes into which the molecules in a protein chain will fold. To do this, you need to know some facts about protein chemistry—such as which molecules in the protein chain can bond with which others—but mostly you need to be able to visualize all kinds of three-dimensional movements of the protein chains and search through millions of possibilities for the configurations that would actually be physically feasible.

It turns out that, in certain cases, some people are better at doing this than today's computers.[18] These people possess a certain kind of intuitive spatial visualization skill, and when they learn the chemical rules that determine what kinds of folds are possible, they are able to explore the possibilities more effectively than the vast majority of other humans—or a computer.

Here's the problem: we don't know who these people are. Their unusual skill isn't used in many jobs, so even the people who have it may not know it. But ideally, if you know how to test for it, you can find the people who have the skill, then use that skill to solve problems.

That's just what David Baker, Zoran Popović, David Salesin, and their colleagues at the University of Washington did in a project called Foldit.[19] They created a set of online games that involved folding protein molecules. Thousands of people tried the games, and the games were so much fun that the people who were good at them kept coming back. One of the best, for instance, was a 13-year-old American boy named Aristides Poehlman, who lived with his parents in Virginia.[20] Like Aristides, many of the best players were spending hours each week playing the games and studying each other's solutions. Not surprisingly, as they practiced, they got better and better.

Over time, the research team began to put complex problems into the game—problems that real scientists wanted solved. Sometimes it turned out that the online crowd was able to figure out the correct answers better than scientists were. For instance, in one of its greatest successes, the Foldit community uncovered the structure of an enzyme related to AIDS that had eluded scientists for 15 years. It only took the Foldit community three weeks![21]

Of course, not all problems in the world can be so precisely formulated, with clearly specified options and objective criteria for evaluation.

But I think that far more problems than we suspect *can* be formulated in this way, enabling a new way of creating very smart groups: scan large swaths of people for the "geniuses" at solving a particular kind of problem, then let these geniuses share their best ideas with each other and expect amazing results. Perhaps this isn't so different from how scientific and technological communities have worked for centuries, but new information technologies allow us to turbocharge this process in a way that has never before been possible.

LIMITS OF SIZE

We've seen some examples of how large groups can be much smarter than small ones, so perhaps it is worth spending a little time thinking about the limits of this possibility. Even though there are often benefits of having more people involved in solving a problem, there are usually costs, too.[22] At a minimum, larger groups require more of people's time than smaller ones, and if you are paying for that time, that means they cost more money. But there's another, often more important, problem with large groups: they usually need to expend more effort coordinating their own activities, not just doing the actual work. Even when they make this extra effort, the difficulties of working together may outweigh the benefits of having more people.

Of course, the best approach depends on the kind of work the group is doing and a host of other factors. But a common rule of thumb for face-to-face groups is that the optimal size of a group is somewhere between 5 and 10 people. Fewer than that and you don't get enough total effort applied and enough benefit from diverse points of view. More than that and the extra difficulties of working in a large group just aren't worth it.

But what if technology could help reduce the difficulties of working together in large groups? Some years ago, I had an experience that drove home for me both the problems and the potential of this possibility.

Comparing Occupy Wall Street and Wikipedia

In the fall of 2011, the Occupy Wall Street movement attracted global attention with its protests against the role of business in creating social and economic inequality. The heart of this movement was in the Financial District of New York City, and it so happened that I was on sabbatical at New York University at the same time. On several Saturdays, I went downtown to watch what was happening in and around Zuccotti Park, where the Occupy protesters were gathered.

The most interesting thing I saw was a group of people working to develop a mission statement for the Occupy movement. About 50 people were sitting on benches and other makeshift seats in the otherwise deserted lobby of a big office building. Anyone could join the meeting, and during the time I was there, I noticed Michael Moore, the well-known documentary filmmaker, watching the proceedings, too. A key part of the Occupy movement was a desire for participatory democracy, and in this spirit, the group was using a special formal process for consensus decision making.

When I joined the group, the members were working on the opening of the mission statement. They had already agreed on the words "We believe in a free and just society." Soon after I arrived, someone suggested adding a word: "We believe in a *truly* free and just society."

A great deal of discussion ensued. A little bit of this discussion was about the substantive pros and cons of adding the word *truly* to the sentence. For instance, people questioned whether the word *truly* was just redundant and unnecessary or whether it was useful to emphasize the point.

But the vast majority of the discussion was about procedural issues. For instance, the consensus rules the group was using said that anyone could "block" a group decision if he or she felt strongly enough to leave the group if the decision were adopted. At one point, one woman said she would block the addition of the word *truly*, then the group members spent a very long time trying to figure out whether or how they could override her block. Eventually the woman who initially blocked the addition of this word changed her mind. Then the group spent another very long time debating whether she was allowed to retract her own block.

When I finally left the group about two hours later, the group members still hadn't decided whether to add the word *truly*, and I was very pessimistic that they would ever succeed in producing anything of interest using their extremely cumbersome consensus process. Now, years later, after searching the web and news reports from the time, I think my pessimism was warranted. The Occupy movement did produce a few consensus documents, but as far as I can tell, it never succeeded in producing a mission statement.[23]

I don't think this necessarily reflects poorly on the Occupy protesters themselves. Instead I think it is a demonstration of the incredible difficulty of consensus decision making in any large face-to-face group. I saw very similar difficulties when I watched a group of antinuclear protesters plan a demonstration at a California nuclear plant almost 40 years ago and again when I observed a negotiating session among professional diplomats at the Paris climate talks in December 2015. In all these cases, a vast amount of time was spent on procedural issues rather than substance, and the limitation that only one person could talk at a time was incredibly frustrating in a large group where everyone's opinions were supposed to be heard.

So what's the solution? Should we just give up on making consensus decisions in large groups? I don't think so. I think Wikipedia illustrates the surprising possibilities for how technology can help. Tens of thousands of people work more or less simultaneously on different parts of Wikipedia using a genuine consensus process. Everyone who cares about any specific issue has a chance to have his or her opinions heard, and in the vast majority of cases, the final decisions are agreed upon by everyone involved.

Could the Occupy protesters have produced a high-quality mission statement relatively quickly if they had done it online using tools like the Wikipedia software and processes? We can't know for sure, but I think the answer is probably yes.

This doesn't mean that technology can magically solve all the problems of large groups working together. But we've already seen a number of examples of how technology may be able to greatly reduce the costs and increase the effectiveness of large groups working together. We don't yet know how far this can go. But perhaps, instead of decreasing in effectiveness when more than about 10 individuals are involved, groups may continue to increase in effectiveness as they grow to 100 or 100,000 or even 100,000,000 individuals.

CHAPTER 13

How Can We Work Together in New Ways?

In Adam Smith's famous pin factory, dividing the work of a single pin maker into many smaller tasks done by different specialized workers led to vast increases in productivity. But even Smith, when he wrote about this in 1776, probably didn't realize how important this division of labor would be in driving economic progress for centuries to come. Much of the prosperity we enjoy today—you might even say much of the collective intelligence of today's organizations—results from this specialization of work.

The early factories that Adam Smith described—in fact, the advances of the Industrial Revolution in general—depended on more than just new technologies. They also depended—crucially—on new ways of organizing the work. The individual workers weren't any smarter, there weren't any more of them, and they may even have had fewer skills than the craftspeople they replaced. But when their work was organized differently, their specialized collective intelligence at producing pins—and many other kinds of products—was greatly increased.

All new ways of organizing work include one or more of the following three elements:

- dividing the work in new ways,
- assigning tasks in new ways, and
- coordinating interdependencies among tasks in new ways.

In this chapter, we'll see examples of how new technologies help do all three of these things in ways that have the potential to make groups much, much smarter. None of these changes alone *guarantees* that groups will be dramatically smarter, but the huge economic benefits of mass production prove that merely changing how a group is organized can sometimes dramatically change how intelligent it is.

DIVIDING WORK IN NEW WAYS: HYPERSPECIALIZATION

The division of labor that Adam Smith chronicled was for physical tasks. I think new information technologies are going to enable another huge wave of division of labor, not for physical work this time but for information work. In an article we published in the *Harvard Business Review*, my colleagues Rob Laubacher, Tammy Johns, and I call this *hyperspecialization*.[1]

Topcoder

A company called Topcoder (now part of IT services company Wipro) illustrates what's possible. When Topcoder develops software for a customer, it breaks the work up into much smaller pieces than would be common in a typical software company. Then, for each of these pieces, it holds an online contest where members of Topcoder's worldwide community of over one million freelance software developers compete to do the task.

For instance, the contest organizers might provide a high-level description of the project's goals and challenge developers to create a specifications document that best translates those goals into detailed system requirements. (Topcoder hosts a web forum that allows developers to query the client for more details, and all those questions and answers become visible to all competitors.) The winning specifications document might become the basis for the next contest, in which other developers compete to design the system's architecture, specifying the various pieces of software to be developed and the connections between them. Further contests would be launched to develop each of the pieces separately, then others would integrate the pieces into a single working whole.

Because the company aggregates demand for specific tasks, it enables a developer who is particularly good at, say, designing user interfaces to spend the bulk of his or her time doing just that. Indeed, Topcoder developers are becoming increasingly specialized. Some focus on programming very specific kinds of software, such as small graphics modules. Some have discovered a particular talent for putting together software components that others have written. Some specialize in fixing bugs in other people's code.

In the great tradition of division of labor, this hyperspecialization pays off. Topcoder can often provide its clients with development work comparable in quality to what they would get through more traditional means, but at as little as 25 percent of the cost.

Microtasks on Amazon Mechanical Turk

Amazon's Mechanical Turk service is an even more extreme example of hyperspecialization. It's a kind of online labor market, but instead of finding people to do programming tasks that might take hours or days, Mechanical Turk finds people to do *microtasks*, which might take only a few minutes and earn them only a few pennies.

The name Mechanical Turk comes from a famous chess-playing machine that defeated chess players in courts all over Europe during the 18th century (see the image below).[2] The machine was eventually revealed to be a hoax, however. Its cabinet was cleverly constructed so that a small human chess master could hide, undetected, inside. It was the human, not a machine, who actually decided which moves to make. In other words, the Turk was a human pretending to be a machine, doing tasks that machines couldn't yet do. In the same way, Amazon's Mechanical Turk service uses people to do tasks that machines can't do yet—what the company calls "artificial artificial intelligence."

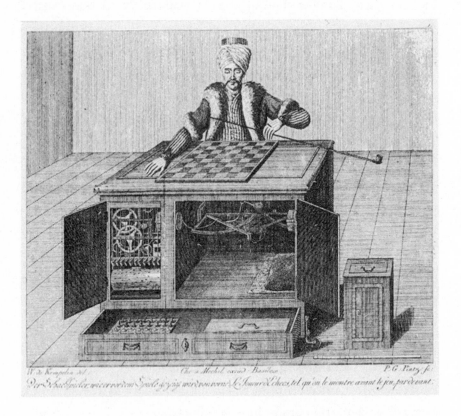

Amazon originally created the service to help it proofread the product listings on its own website. A typical task might have involved checking for misspellings in a single paragraph or determining whether two different pages were for the same product. But the service is now used for all kinds of other tasks: transcribing a few minutes of a podcast, taking a survey, extracting the names of items purchased from a shopping receipt. In some cases, the people who request these tasks also specify particular qualifications that workers must have before doing the tasks (such as getting correct answers on a series of qualifying tasks), so some of the workers (called Turkers) become hyperspecialists in particular kinds of microtasks. Companies like Facebook also routinely use Turkers and similar workers to fill in the gaps when their AI algorithms don't always know enough to sensibly select trending topics and do other kinds of content moderation.[3]

Of course, Topcoder and Mechanical Turk are only early examples of what's possible. What if it were super fast and easy to find someone who could fix the graphics in your PowerPoint slide? What if a law firm could instantly find someone online who is one of the world's experts on the rules of evidence in Texas murder trials and get the answer to a specific question about this topic in minutes?

To do this, of course, there will also need to be workers who specialize in being generalists—whose hyperspecialty is coordinating the work of other hyperspecialists. These workers will perform some of the functions that managers do in today's hierarchies, but their roles may be much more circumscribed.

There are certainly places where hyperspecialization isn't appropriate. In designing a radically new product, for example, the members of a design team may need to develop a shared understanding among themselves about what the product will do before they can think about delegating parts of the design to hyperspecialists.

Hyperspecialization is also a case where the goals of superminds may differ in important ways from the goals of the workers within them. Many people worry, for instance, about the risks of creating "digital sweatshops," where workers do mind-numbingly repetitive piecework at pay rates below the minimum wage in many countries. And hyperspecialized workers can sometimes contribute, unknowingly, to overall goals they would never support. For instance, they might be asked to synthesize chemicals that will be used in bombs or to identify the faces of protesters in photographs of public demonstrations in repressive countries.[4]

But people sometimes have concerns about hyperspecialization that are not justified. For instance, people often worry that hyperspecialists will become very bored doing the same kind of highly specialized work all day long and that the work will lose meaning when it is divided into ever-smaller parts. But this doesn't need to happen. Many medical specialists, for instance, focus on fairly narrow aspects of keeping their patients healthy but continue to find their work rewarding. And unlike assembly-line workers in a factory, who do the same specialized tasks all day, digital hyperspecialists can construct their own personalized task portfolios. An engineer, for example, might spend part of a day working on a difficult challenge for Inno-Centive, then relax by doing some less demanding work on Mechanical Turk.

Perhaps most important, online workers usually have much more choice about where they work than do workers who must come to a physical job location. So over time, we should expect to see quite a bit of competition to attract the most—and the best—workers. For instance, companies and other online communities will compete to create the best platforms and norms for using them, and governments will compete to create the best frameworks for regulating them.[5]

In any case, whether it's on Mechanical Turk, Topcoder, or similar sites that don't even exist yet, I think there will likely be much more hyperspecialized online work in the future. Because new information technologies make it possible to communicate across the planet instantly and nearly for free, hyperspecialized workers will be able to take advantage of global economies of scale for the specialized tasks they do. And by doing these tasks better and more cheaply than would ever have been possible before, they'll help make groups smarter than they've ever been before.

ASSIGNING TASKS TO PEOPLE IN NEW WAYS: SELF-SELECTION

In a traditional hierarchy, managers delegate tasks to other members of the group. But one of the intriguing things about many of the examples we've been discussing is how many of them involve workers selecting for themselves the tasks they want to do.

In addition to finding people who are *good* at these tasks, this is also a way of finding people who are really *motivated* to do the tasks. Topcoder's founder, Jack Hughes, for instance, believes that the discretion the company's software developers have in choosing what to work on is a leading reason for his community's high productivity.

InnoCentive's success illustrates how, if you broadcast your needs widely enough, the people with the highly specialized knowledge or abilities you need can find you instead of you having to find them. And cheap communication technologies make this possible on a scale our ancestors could never have imagined.

Semiautomated Matching of Tasks to People

New technologies can also play an active role in matching workers with people who have work to be done. Job-search sites like Monster.com and CareerBuilder.com provide simple examples of this. These sites bring together lots of jobs and lots of job seekers and provide automated search tools to help people on both sides of the matching process find each other.

But it's possible to go much further than today's job-search sites do. For instance, imagine a site that operates more like Match.com than Monster.com.[6] In addition to asking for objective information like your work history, it would also ask about your passions, what you do for fun, and the kinds of people you like to work with. If you're an employer, it wouldn't just ask about the specific job skills you want. It would also ask about your company culture and the kinds of people who do best there. Using all this information (most of which wouldn't be visible to others on the site), the system's algorithms could do a much better job of matching workers and jobs than people do for themselves with today's tools.

And it's important to note that, unlike today's job boards, this new kind of site could use its matching process for more than just full-time jobs. Employers could use it to match people to tasks of any scope, all the way down to tiny online microtasks like those on Mechanical Turk. For example, researchers are already experimenting with how to use various mathematical techniques to automatically send microtasks to the people who can do those particular kinds of tasks best, based on their past performance.[7]

Here's an analogy for what might happen: In 1995, one of the first things Pierre Omidyar, the founder of eBay, tried to sell on his new online market was a broken laser pointer.[8] The listing stated clearly that the pointer had cost $30 new but that it no longer worked, even with new batteries. He didn't really expect anyone to buy it. But someone did. For $14! This was one of the first signs Omidyar had that he was really on to something. And it illustrates one of the key contributions that eBay has made to the global economy.

If you have a broken laser pointer in your attic, it might have value to someone somewhere. But if the cost of finding that person is more than the laser pointer would be worth to him or her, then the broken laser pointer has no economic value. It's worthless to you, and you might as well throw it away. But if a new technology (like the eBay platform) can reduce the search cost to almost zero, then suddenly the broken laser pointer has economic value.

Now, imagine this same kind of thing happening not with the junk in your attic but with your time. If you are unemployed and would rather be working, then your time is wasted, just like a broken laser pointer in your attic would be. Even if you have a job but are capable of contributing much more than your current job allows, then your time is also, to some degree, being wasted.

But imagine that every single person on the planet could be

matched—as efficiently as Google matches ads to people—to the most productive or most enjoyable ways that person could spend his or her time. Especially for the increasing number of jobs that can be done online, there would be huge flexibility in what you do on a given day.

Maybe on some days you would pick the things that pay you the most. Of all the things that need to be done, these would be the ones that are most important to the people who want them and that you could do better than anyone else in the world. On other days, just for fun, you might pick the things you like most, even if they don't pay much at all. On most days, you might pick a combination of things that you enjoy and that pay well. In other words, you could choose your own ever-shifting diet of tasks from this online menu of things to do.

Over time, the matching algorithms would get better and better at figuring out what you're good at and what you want to do. They would also give you clear incentives to get better at the things that most need to be done.

Of course, there are many factors that would determine whether this kind of world would work well: How should these matching algorithms really work? At any given moment, is there an overall shortage of workers or jobs? How would we, as workers, learn to pick a portfolio of tasks that didn't bore us or exhaust us while providing the income we needed? How could we improve our skills for the new things that need to be done? And how would our norms of what it means to be a good worker change?

Internet pioneer Vint Cerf and his coauthor, David Nordfors, think of a system like this as a way to "disrupt unemployment."[9] But even more than that, I think it's a way to create groups that are more intelligent than any we've ever known before on our planet by picking the people who are best for every task from the entire population of the whole world.

COORDINATING INTERDEPENDENCIES AMONG TASKS IN NEW WAYS

By definition, all superminds consist of different individuals doing different activities related to some overall goal. And whenever a goal is broken into parts, there has to be some way of managing the interdependencies among the activities that different group members do.

In 1999, my colleagues and I developed a framework for analyzing all these different types of interdependencies. We classified them in three main categories: *Flow* dependencies involve one individual creating something that will be used by another (such as an engineer creating a design that will be used by a factory worker). *Sharing* dependencies involve multiple individuals sharing the same resource (such as money or a person's time). *Fit* dependencies involve different individuals making pieces that must fit together (such as the body, wheels, and seats of a car).[10]

For example, money is a shared resource, and all companies must manage the interdependency among different parts of the company so that they can't spend more money than they have (whether the money comes from revenue, loans, or elsewhere). Many management processes (like budgeting) and technologies (like accounting software) are devoted to managing this constraint. But what other kinds of interdependencies might new technologies help us manage?

One example comes from a research system developed by Haoqi Zhang and his colleagues at Northwestern University. This system lets crowds of Mechanical Turk workers help travelers plan their vacation itineraries.[11] As a user of the system, you might describe your desired trip something like this: "I want to spend a day in San Francisco checking out cool things in the city. I would like to have two 'fresh local food restaurant' activities, spend at least two hours on 'cool artsy' activities, and do at least one 'people-watching' activity."

The system presents this information to the Turk workers along with an empty framework for the itinerary. The Turkers then go to work, each suggesting different ideas for the itinerary. Meanwhile, in the background, the system is constantly calculating travel times, counting activities of different types, and checking to see whether all the travelers' goals are satisfied and the interdependencies are managed. Whenever they aren't, the system suggests "to-do" items to fix them.

For instance, the system might say to the Turkers preparing your itinerary:

- "Add more things to the itinerary (there are still four hours left empty)"; or
- "There are too many restaurant activities in the itinerary (we need exactly two, and the current itinerary has four)"; or
- "There isn't enough time to do all the activities scheduled for the morning (including travel)."

When studying the overall results of this process, Zhang and his colleagues found that the potential travelers said the itineraries met most or all of their goals, and the to-do items generated by the system significantly increased the rate at which the Turkers dealt with the problems.

In other words, the system was automatically tracking and managing interdependencies that might otherwise have required time and effort from people to manage. And by freeing people to do things that only they can do, the system makes the whole supermind of people and computers smarter.

Of course, this system is designed for a relatively simple task, and the particular interdependencies it helped manage were easy to represent in a way a computer could "understand." But it's easy to imagine similar approaches being used for much larger and more serious tasks.

For instance, what if you could use an approach like this to let many engineers work together on designing a mobile phone that met overall constraints on size, weight, battery life, and manufacturing costs? If the system can automatically keep track of how each engineer's design decisions affect these interdependencies and show the results to everyone involved, it can help the engineers explore many different design possibilities much more rapidly than would otherwise be possible. Thus it can help make this group of engineers smarter than it would ever otherwise be.

EXAMPLE: "CONTEST WEBS" IN CLIMATE COLAB[12]

To understand how a number of the ideas we've seen in this chapter can fit together, let's look at how we use *contest webs* in Climate CoLab.

It would be possible to use traditional hierarchies—or even a single community like Wikipedia—to develop complex Climate CoLab proposals. But what if we want lots of people trying lots of competing approaches at the same time while still sharing as much of their work as possible?

That's hard to achieve in a hierarchy or a single community, but markets—or, more precisely, *market economies*—do it all the time with systems called supply chains or supply webs.[13] For instance, GM may buy car seats from Johnson Controls and audio systems from Mitsubishi. Mitsubishi may in turn buy integrated circuits from Intel and plastic from DuPont (see the following illustration). But other companies are also competing in the markets for each of these types of products.

In Climate CoLab, we were inspired by the supply webs for physical products to create contest webs for our knowledge products. These contest webs let us create a kind of supply chain for knowledge in which different groups of people choose for themselves whether they want to work on solving specialized subproblems related to climate change or integrating solutions for these subproblems into overall climate action plans at the national and global levels.

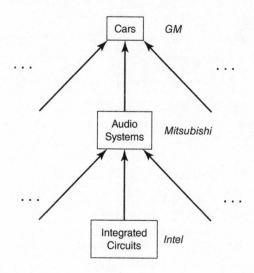

Just as physical components (like tires and seats) get combined into more complex products (like cars), information components (like proposals for changing transportation and electricity systems) get combined into more complex products (like national climate plans for China, India, and the United States), which can be combined yet again into even more complex products (like a global climate plan).

The contests where people compete to come up with basic ideas for improving things like transportation and electricity are called basic contests. Higher-level contests, where people compete to combine these basic proposals into national and global climate action plans, are called integrated contests.

For instance, one of our winning global proposals suggested that a digital currency called solar dollars (based on Bitcoin-like blockchain technology) could be used to encourage emission reductions in countries around the world. This global proposal contained subproposals for how the major countries and regions of the world could contribute to the overall plan (see the following illustration). The subproposal for Europe, for example, suggested that Greece could be used as a test laboratory for renewable energy approaches that could be used all over

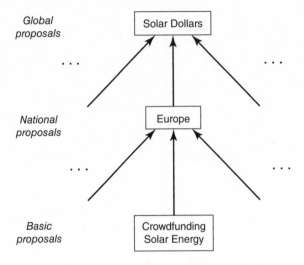

Europe. The Europe subproposal, in turn, included further subproposals for using techniques like crowdfunding to finance solar energy projects.

Advantages of Contest Webs

What are the advantages of our contest web? Unlike a hierarchy or community, this approach allows many members of a large group to simultaneously explore many alternative ways of solving an overall problem. Not only does this make the group as a whole more able to tolerate mistakes by single individuals, it also increases the chances that somewhere, in all the combinations being explored, innovative new ways of doing things will be discovered. In addition, it makes it easier for good ideas to be used in multiple places. For instance, if one person comes up with a good idea about how to crowdfund solar energy projects, then many other people can use this idea in their proposals for national and global plans.

In fact, as you can see in the following diagram,[14] there was quite a bit of this reuse in the 2015 Climate CoLab contests. The lines in the diagram indicate when a higher-level proposal used a lower-level one. The different shadings in the circles correspond to different author teams.

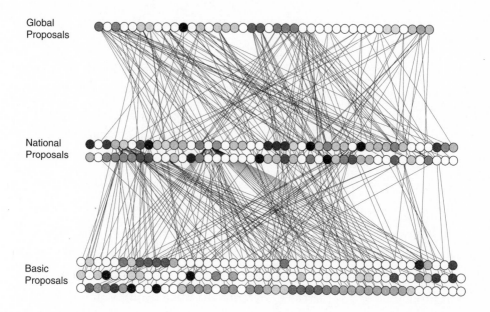

Global
Proposals

National
Proposals

Basic
Proposals

It's clear from the diagram that the global proposals (top row) included many different combinations of national and regional proposals (middle rows), which in turn included many different combinations of basic proposals (bottom rows). It's also clear that proposal authors reused work done by others as well as their own. In other words, many different people were simultaneously exploring many different combinations of the ideas represented in different proposals.

Incentives for Collaboration

Contest webs raise one more important question: Why would people create proposals that can be effectively combined with other proposals? Why would they, for example, try to make their national plan for India be compatible with national plans for other countries so they could fit together in a single global plan?

The similarity between contest webs and supply webs for physical products suggests an obvious answer to these questions: the creators of integrated proposals can "pay" the creators of the other entries they use, which motivates groups to create proposals that others want to use. To implement this idea in Climate CoLab, we created an artificial currency called CoLab points, which eventually get converted to dollars (in 2015, members received two dollars for every CoLab point), and we created an automatic pricing scheme to distribute these points.

Here's how it works: The judges in the global contest represent the "end customers" of the whole problem-solving system. They "buy" the global proposals they think are best for the prices, or points, they think they are worth. Then the points each global proposal receives are distributed automatically among the authors of the global proposal itself and the authors of all the national and other lower-level proposals it incorporates. The rules for distributing the points are designed to give the biggest rewards to people who created the parts of the overall proposal that require the most work and are most important to the overall problem.[15]

At each contest level, these rules motivate people not only to *compete* with the creators of other proposals in the contests they enter but also to *cooperate* with the creators of proposals in higher- and lower-level contests.

For instance, one winning global proposal focused on ways to mobilize citizens and organizations of many different sizes to combat climate change. This proposal brought together a team that eventually included more than 25 authors, many of whom had created lower-level proposals themselves and many of whom did not know each other before "meeting" on the Climate CoLab site. This team didn't just collaborate to create a global proposal: when we last talked to the members, they were also actively working together to raise money to implement the ideas in their proposals.

Using Contest Webs to Solve Other Problems

Of course, we don't yet know how widely applicable the system of contest webs can be. But the widespread usefulness of supply chains in the economy for physical products suggests that it has a lot of potential.

For instance, we have worked with other groups at MIT to apply the Climate CoLab approach to a range of global problems, including health care, education, and job creation. And in chapter 17, we'll learn how a company like Procter & Gamble could use the contest webs approach to do its strategic planning.

In other words, even with no more intelligence in our machines than we have today, we have the potential to create far smarter groups just by using computers' cheap communication and coordination capabilities to productively engage far more people and organize their work far more effectively than we usually do today. Of course, we don't know for sure how much this will increase the intelligence of human groups, but I suspect that most people far underestimate the amount.

Part V

How Else Can Superminds Think More Intelligently?

CHAPTER 14

Smarter Sensing

I n September 2015, Dr. Celina M. Turchi, an infectious-disease researcher in Brazil, got a phone call from a friend at the ministry of health who was stationed in central Brazil. The friend told her the ministry was hearing reports of a surprising number of babies being born in the city of Recife with small heads—a condition known as microcephaly. As she recalled, "The doctors were saying, 'Well, I saw four today,' and, 'Oh that's strange, because I saw two.'"[1] Seeing the babies, who seemed healthy except for their shrunken heads, devastated Turchi. "I went to three hospitals and a lab and as soon as I saw them, I couldn't stop thinking about them," she said.[2]

For months, no one really knew what was causing these symptoms. Some doctors speculated that it was an allergy, others that it was a disease called roseola, others that it might be due to a kind of facial rash. As part of many attempts to figure it out, doctors were testing blood samples for indications of diseases like parvovirus, dengue, chikungunya, and others.

Eventually they confirmed that the symptoms were linked to the Zika virus, a mosquito-borne virus that had been discovered in 1947 and named after the forest in Uganda where it was first found. For decades, no one paid it much attention because it was both rare and thought to cause only very mild symptoms.[3] Suddenly, though, it appeared to be linked to much more serious problems. In February 2016, after an emergency teleconference meeting with 18 experts and advisers from around the world, the World Health Organization declared the situation a public health emergency.[4]

As I write this, the end of the Zika story is not yet known. But we do know that the process by which the medical community identified this health threat is one that is critical to collective intelligence. In order to act intelligently, almost all superminds need to somehow *sense* what's going on in the world around them and then make decisions using this information. That's exactly what the medical community did in this case. No single individual figured this out alone; the conclusion depended on information gleaned from many people and places, which led to decisions made and actions taken in much larger groups.

In work I did with my colleagues Deborah Ancona, Wanda Orlikowski, and Peter Senge, we wrote about how *sensemaking*—the ability to make sense of what is happening in ambiguous situations— is one of the core capabilities of effective leaders.[5] In that work, we focused on sensemaking in individuals, but sensemaking is also a capability that groups can possess collectively.

Businesses, for instance, engage in sensemaking when they try to answer questions like: How do customers react when we tell them about our new products? How many new products did we sell last month? Are we having trouble hiring salespeople? What is the average interest rate we are paying on our bonds? What does the business press say are the hottest technology trends in our industry?

Sometimes groups do a very bad job of collective sensing. For instance, in 1975, when Eastman Kodak sold more than 85 percent of the film and cameras sold in the United States, one of its engineers, Steve Sasson, built what is widely credited as the first digital camera.[6] But for decades after this discovery, Kodak never figured out how to capitalize on the technology its own engineer invented. Now, of course, almost all cameras are digital, but in part because it never successfully reacted to this fundamental shift in its market, Kodak declared bankruptcy in 2012.

This wasn't a failure to sense the basic technological possibilities; Kodak had those facts before anyone else. But I suspect that the senior executives and the whole Kodak organization were so committed to film-based photography that they resisted seeing what was right in front of their eyes and thus couldn't make the changes necessary to respond to it appropriately.

Of course, many companies are *good* at collective sensing, too. For instance, in 1995, when the Internet was just entering the public consciousness, Bill Gates took one of his Think Week vacations, during which he read and thought about all kinds of books and papers that people from Microsoft and many other places had suggested he read.[7] When he came back from his vacation, he wrote what became his famous memo to Microsoft executives: "The Internet Tidal Wave." In this memo, he laid out the reasons why Microsoft needed to radically reorient itself to focus much more on the Internet.

Microsoft did exactly that, and it became one of the rare high-tech companies to be dominant in two technological eras: the PC era and the Internet era. In this case, the successful collective sensing was easier than usual because the CEO himself had the crucial insights (based on materials he'd been given by others) and immediately began taking action on them.

HOW CAN INFORMATION TECHNOLOGY HELP?

In order to do effective sensing, any supermind needs to gather and interpret information about the world. New information technologies let us do that on a far larger scale and with much greater depth of interpretation than was ever possible before.

For instance, the doctors and scientists studying Zika used technologies like e-mail and teleconferencing to share information around the world. And we've seen how the Internet helped find the unusual people who became "superforecasters" in the Good Judgment Project. These superforecasters were *sensing* what was going on in the world and summarizing what they sensed in accurate predictions about geopolitical events.

Big Data

By far the most visible way technology is improving collective sensing today is by using what is called big data and data analytics. The world is now awash in vastly larger amounts of data than we've ever had before. In medicine, we have DNA maps, drug costs, and medical test results. In business, we have GPS locations of millions of smartphone users along with their Twitter posts, Facebook likes, Google searches, and Amazon purchases. In government, we have videos of pedestrian movements, information on disability claims, and trading data that can indicate financial fraud. And all these new kinds of data can be analyzed in fascinating new ways.

I've never really liked the buzzwordy term *big data* because data alone is almost always worthless unless some supermind—such as a company, a government, or some other organization—analyzes it and acts on it. In fact, from a collective intelligence point of view, big data is just a name for dramatically richer ways of doing the *sensing* that has always been part of collective intelligence. But even though the white-hot interest in this term has waned, its importance has not gone away.

For example, take retail stores that use in-store video and touch-sensitive floors to sense every move customers make and then use that data to refine shelf layouts, product displays, and prices. Or even more intriguing are the stores that count the number of cars in competitors' parking lots—seen in aerial photographs—to get estimates of how well their competitors are performing.

In the medical domain, tracking detailed clinical histories of millions of patients can lead to insights that no single doctor or conventional medical researcher would ever discover. For instance, a study of data from the California-based Kaiser Permanente managed-care organization led to the discovery of the serious risks of heart attack caused by the drug Vioxx and resulted in the withdrawal of Vioxx from the market.[8]

Another important kind of data measures the behavior of physical objects. For example, many mechanical parts begin to behave in an unusual way long before they completely break down. They may become hotter, vibrate more intensely, or show greater mechanical stress. Once you recognize these patterns, you can take various kinds of preventive action *before* a part breaks. United Parcel Service, for instance, has used this approach to make preventive-maintenance decisions for its fleet of 60,000 vehicles, saving millions of dollars by doing so.[9] General Electric has built a whole new software business unit to profit from feedback about the equipment it sells. For instance, it expects to make very significant revenues from selling after-sales services, including maintenance plans based on predictive analytics using this new kind of data.[10]

All these examples illustrate the broader phenomenon called the Internet of things, in which physical objects—cars, houses, power plants, and many others—are connected to the Internet, gathering massive amounts of data and often acting on it automatically.

PRIVACY AND INFORMATION AS PROPERTY

The technologies that make it possible to analyze big data and do new kinds of collective sensing also raise important issues about who owns the data and who has the right to use it. For instance, does an online merchant from whom you buy Viagra have the right to sell information about what you bought? And does a data aggregator have the right to combine that information with detailed information about all the other websites you visited, all the Google searches you did, and so forth?

Many researchers, policy analysts, and others are talking about questions like these today, and I think this debate will only become more important in the future. Even though these issues are not the main focus of this book, let me briefly summarize my own intellectual journey on this topic over the last three decades. I first went through a stage in which I believed that almost everything would and should become public.[11] After growing up in a small town, I was already familiar with a world where the people you knew already knew lots of things about you, and I knew that wasn't all bad. In fact, it had many desirable consequences. For instance, if you knew that your reputation for being a polite and honest person would follow you for years in a small community, you were more likely to be polite and honest. My view about my own privacy was well summarized by a quotation from one of my former teaching assistants: "The boring have nothing to fear."

But in more recent years, I've come to believe that a very important subset of things should remain private, because if they don't, many kinds of desirable interactions will become difficult or impossible. Here is a quick summary of where I suspect we will end up, as a society, in a few decades:

- Most people will be much less concerned about their privacy than many privacy advocates today expect. For instance, most people will voluntarily share most information about what they buy, and they will receive some kind of monetary (or other) benefit by doing so.
- Most commercial transactions will include explicit terms about how the information can be shared, and these terms will be much better standardized and understood than the inscrutable "terms of use" on websites today, which most of us accept without reading.
- In general, data and knowledge of many kinds will have increasing economic value, just as land, capital, and machines acquired much

greater economic value as we moved from hunting and gathering to agricultural and industrial societies.

- Personal conversations (electronic or otherwise) will remain private. If your personal conversations were required to be public, there are many things you would never say. For instance, if I knew that all my friends and coworkers could find out everything I said to my wife about them, then I would be strongly motivated to keep many of my feelings about people to myself. And I think a world like that would be much less satisfying.
- Many business communications will remain private because it would be very difficult for most companies to conduct their business if they knew that their competitors could hear and see everything they did.

You could say that these are my best current guesses about how we will reconcile the trade-offs between what's good for superminds and what's good for the individuals in them.

CYBER-HUMAN SENSING

Regardless of what is kept private and what isn't, it seems almost inevitable that more and more things will be electronically sensed and recorded in the future. We already record vast amounts of information in e-mails, text messages, and photos. And increasingly ubiquitous sensors in the Internet of things will capture far more information than they do now. In many public spaces, every time a human moves a finger, walks a step, or says a word, it will be captured. And for more and more manufactured objects—like cars, watches, and cartons of milk—every time they move a millimeter, vibrate in unusual ways, or change temperature, it will be recorded.

People won't begin to be able to analyze this vast amount of data by themselves. But machines won't be able to do it alone, either, because they won't understand all the subtle nuances of things like body language, tone of voice, and the meaning of what *wasn't* said. In many cases, what we'll need is a combination of people and computers. One possible way to do this is with a system that mirrors the multilayered networks of neurons our brains use to interpret the sensory information they receive from the world.

Neural Nets

In your brain, neural signals from your eyes, ears, and other sensory organs are fed into successive layers of neurons connected in ways that interpret the signals at increasingly higher levels of abstraction. For instance, if you are looking at your mother, each photoreceptor neuron in your retina generates signals about the amount and color of light falling on it. When a number of nearby receptors see the same color, neurons in the next layer generate signals that indicate they're seeing a region of that color. Succeeding layers recognize even more complex patterns, such as edges, circles, squares, eyes, noses, and eventually your mother's face.

Many of today's machine-learning algorithms use artificial *neural nets* that work in a somewhat similar way. They're made up of multiple layers of simulated neurons, and each neuron connects via a system of links of varying weights to many other neurons.

In some cases, we will be able to combine human and computer sensing by letting the machines do the low-level sensing (such as recognizing suspected terrorists in a crowd), then letting people do the higher-level reasoning about what that basic data might mean. But there are some important limitations of this classic architecture as a way of merging human and computer sensing.

First, one of the limitations of the neural-net approach is that it usually requires vast amounts of data to properly adjust the weights on all the connections among all the simulated neurons. For example, recall the system that looked at 10 million digital images from You-

Tube in order to learn how to identify objects like human and cat faces (see page 72). But for many important problems, there just isn't enough data available to do this. If you want to predict terrorist attacks, for instance, there probably aren't enough recorded examples of past attacks for computers to learn with much confidence the different patterns such attacks might take.

Another limitation of the neural-net approach is that even if machines could learn some of these patterns, people wouldn't usually be able to understand how the machines reached their conclusions. For instance, if the machines tried to explain their reasoning, they would just be able to say something like, "I predicted this attack because the following 23 million connections in my database had the following 23 million values between 0 and 1."

Are there other ways of combining people and computers to make sense of complex situations but without these limitations? Yes, there are. To illustrate what's possible, let's look at how a deeply integrated cyber-human system could be used to sense the risks of terrorist attacks based on various kinds of data.

A CYBER-HUMAN SYSTEM FOR SENSING POTENTIAL TERRORIST ATTACKS

First, we need a way of keeping track of thousands of facts and relationships in a form that is useful to both people and computers. One particularly promising technical approach for doing this is called Bayesian networks. These networks express the key facts and relationships in a situation in terms of probabilities that both people and machines can understand.[12]

Priming the System

To get started, the system would need to be primed with lots of information about possible events and the probabilistic relationships among them. For instance, as we now know, the 9/11 attacks involved using airplanes as weapons. Various people in the US government had contemplated this possibility before the attacks, and it is quite possible that, if the US intelligence community had assembled scenarios for dozens of different types of terrorist attacks, this would have been one of them. If these experts had also tried to identify telltale warning signs for this type of attack, they would likely have thought of people with terrorist connections trying to buy advanced flight simulators or taking courses to learn to fly large jet aircraft.[13]

It's quite easy to believe that, if a system like this had existed in 2001, experts would have been able to enter into the system a description of the event patterns that might lead up to this kind of terrorist attack. For instance, they could have entered the probabilities that, if an attack using planes as weapons was being planned, various other kinds of events (like terrorists taking flying lessons) would occur. That's not to suggest they would have been clairvoyant about the method of the 9/11 attacks; they would also have entered similar events and probabilities for many other kinds of potential attacks, including detonating explosives in public places, releasing biological agents in public, and driving vehicles into crowds of pedestrians.

Detecting Actual Threats

Once a system like this is operating, it would be continuously taking in many different kinds of information and automatically computing the combined implications of all its observations. For instance, FBI agents in field offices around the country might fill in specially designed forms listing the names of individuals who were taking flying lessons. CIA analysts in Washington might fill in other forms listing individuals who had been in al-Qaeda training camps in Afghanistan. When a fact wasn't certain, the uncertainty could be represented by a probability (e.g., an 87 percent chance that this person was in an al-Qaeda training camp). Based on all the information it had, the system would be constantly updating the probabilities for many different kinds of attacks as well as for the potential participants in and locations of these attacks.

As it turns out, different people in the US government did have access to information that might have been used to avert the 9/11 attacks—if only they had put it together properly. For instance, in July 2001, an FBI agent in Phoenix sent a memo to FBI headquarters suggesting that there was a possible "coordinated effort by Usama Bin Ladin" to send students to US flight schools. The FBI agent based his theory on the "inordinate number of individuals of investigative interest" attending flight schools in Arizona.[14]

The next month, independently, the FBI in Minneapolis investigated Zacarias Moussaoui. Moussaoui was taking flight training for a Boeing 747, but he had none of the usual qualifications for such training. Questions he asked raised the suspicions of his flight instructor, who reported him to the FBI. Moussaoui was arrested for immigration violations, but even though other intelligence agencies had information linking him to al-Qaeda, this information was never connected to the reports about flight training, so no further investigation occurred.[15]

Part of the reason these two pieces of information were not connected has to do with restrictions on sharing information between agencies like the CIA and FBI. But even if the information had been shared much more widely in the intelligence community, there's still no guarantee that any of the busy human analysts would have put the pieces together and realized their significance.

However, if there had been a cyber-human system like the one we've just talked about, it seems quite possible that the system would have independently noticed the implication of these two facts about Moussaoui and brought it to the attention of a human. Of course, the system might also have noticed many thousands of other potential threats, and it would be useful to us only if it used probability estimates or some other way of prioritizing the threats so that the most important ones would be ranked first. But even this simple kind of

automatic pattern recognition across many diverse sources of information could potentially be of huge value.

It's also possible to do even more.

Entering Facts Automatically

Everything we've talked about so far assumes that professionals in the
intelligence community would have to enter all the information
needed in the system. But, of course, computer systems can also capture many kinds of useful information automatically. For example,
they can automatically track certain facts (like who takes flying lessons
and who communicates via e-mail with suspected terrorists) and enter
these facts into the system with no need for human involvement.

Artificial neural networks can also be continuously analyzing various kinds of data from social networks, security-camera video, and
other sources to identify potentially interesting facts for human analysts to review. Some of these facts probably shouldn't be entered into
the system until humans confirm them. But in other cases, the artificial neural networks will be so good that human confirmation won't be
needed; the facts can just be entered into the system automatically,
along with appropriate probability estimates.

Letting Humans and Machines Estimate the Same Probabilities

One of the advantages of using a technology like Bayesian networks is
that both humans and computers can understand and estimate the same
probabilities. For instance, if human intelligence analysts intercept
online communication that leads them to believe the probability of a terrorist bomb going off at the Super Bowl is much higher than they previously thought, they could manually adjust the human estimate of the
probability of this event. And the system could then adjust all the other
probabilities within it to be consistent with this new information.[16]

In fact, you could even imagine letting both people and computers participate in prediction markets, like those we saw in chapter 8, to estimate the probabilities of key events. Since people would be paid for making accurate predictions, this would provide a clear incentive for them to spend their time estimating the probabilities for which their knowledge is most important.

Could This Really Work?

There's no guarantee that a system like this would always recognize potential terrorist attacks, because in many cases the necessary information simply won't be available. Such a system could also raise privacy issues if it has access to too much information.

Perhaps even more important, there are all kinds of institutional and legal barriers that make it hard to do some of these things. For instance, there are rules that prevent certain kinds of information sharing between agencies and, sometimes, within agencies. And even if sophisticated cyber-human systems could produce extremely accurate probability estimates of potential threats, that doesn't guarantee that the human decision makers would trust them.

But I think the above scenario suggests a direction in which intelligence communities could move to create a supermind that uses the differing capabilities of people and computers to collectively do much more effective sensing of terrorist threats. Is the US intelligence community already doing things like this? I don't know, and its members probably wouldn't talk publicly about it if they were, but I wouldn't be surprised if they are still a long way from anything like the complete system we've just imagined.

I also think there is huge potential for using approaches like this for sensing not only in the detection of terrorism but also in many other areas. For instance, terrorism prevention has some parallels with other types of crime prevention, and, as we'll see in chapter 16, police detectives could use a similar approach to identify and investigate suspects. And in chapter 17, we'll see how a similar approach could be used to sense and combine many kinds of information to estimate the likely success of different possible strategic choices a company might make.

We've seen in this chapter how collectively intelligent groups need to sense what is going on in the world around them. We've also seen examples of how information technologies are enabling new ways of combining people and computers to do this sensemaking in business and in terrorism prevention.

In chapter 5, we talked about how, in a perfectly intelligent supermind, all decisions would take into account everything that is known to every member of the group. When you first read that, you may have thought it seemed like an impossibly utopian ideal. But in this chapter, we've now seen how deeply integrated cyber-human sensing systems might actually make something like that possible someday.

It wouldn't be because all the people talked to one another enough to know everything everyone else knew, or because some mystical connection allowed everyone perfect knowledge of one another's thoughts. Instead it would be because each person added his or her own information to a system that automatically calculated the combined implications of everyone's information. And because the system then let each person see the implications that were most relevant for his or her own decisions.

Today we wouldn't think of trying to run a serious company without a consolidated accounting system that keeps track of the combined results of all the company's financial transactions and packages this information for the people in the company who need to know about it. In the future, it may become just as unthinkable to run a serious organization that doesn't do something similar with many other—much more subjective—kinds of information. In fact, our great-grandchildren may find it hard to understand how the organizations we belong to in the early 21st century could have made so many of their decisions with their eyes—figuratively—closed.

CHAPTER 15

Smarter Remembering

A few days before writing this paragraph, I flew from Boston to Albuquerque, New Mexico, to visit my mother and sister. The flight, on American Airlines, was—fortunately—uneventful, but as I think about the trip now, I realize that it would have been completely impossible if the supermind called American Airlines hadn't had a vast store of collective memory.

Let's start with the fact that American Airlines has been flying passengers since 1930, and it doesn't need to figure out how to do it all over again every time a passenger arrives at one of its gates. Some of this memory is embedded in the physical objects the airline uses—planes, food carts, maintenance equipment. These objects reflect lessons learned by generations of humans, from the ancient inventors of the wheel to the Wright brothers at Kitty Hawk to the Boeing engineers in Seattle.

But if a new group of people had to figure out how to operate all this equipment every day, I wouldn't want to be on any of the flights that somehow managed to take off. Instead American has over 100,000 employees, each specializing in a particular job. The pilots remember how to fly airplanes; the maintenance crew remembers how to refuel a plane; the flight attendants remember where the pretzels are stored and how to evacuate the passengers in case of emergency.

A surprising amount of what American Airlines knows is embedded—not just in the brains of its individual employees but also in the organizational routines that combine their actions. The pilots know how and when the maintenance crew will refuel the plane. The flight attendants depend on the ground crew to restock the food and drinks before each flight. All this collective memory was in place long before I even knew I wanted to fly to New Mexico.

When I reserved my flights, I used my American Airlines frequent-flyer number, so the airline remembered me, too. And since I've flown lots of miles on American, they assigned me a good seat and let me board early in the process. When I handed my boarding pass to the gate agent, she put it on the scanner, and American's computer system remembered my reservation, confirmed my right to take the flight, and recorded that I was on board. When the plane landed in Albuquerque, I deplaned and enjoyed the warm New Mexico sunshine while American's computers remembered that I had earned another 1,536 miles in my frequent-flyer account.

Of course, there's nothing unusual about this. We take all these kinds of collective memory for granted. But almost nothing in our daily lives—or in the functioning of our whole society—could happen without them. No business could survive without remembering how to create something customers want to buy. No scientific community could make progress without individual scientists being able to "stand on the shoulders of giants" who preceded them. No markets could function without people knowing how to buy and sell things to one another.

But how do superminds remember all these things? Whenever you, as an individual, remember something, you must somehow *encode* it, *store* it, and later *retrieve* it. When superminds remember, they have to perform these three functions, too.

But to do this, the individuals in the supermind need to coordinate their work somehow. Often, for instance, different members of a group specialize in different topics. I know one married couple in which the husband always drives the car and the wife is always the navigator, telling him where to go. Teams, companies, and virtually all other groups have analogous ways of dividing the work, deciding who will remember what and evaluating one another's credibility on various topics.[1]

A key aspect of *collective memory*, as opposed to *individual memory*, is that collective memory usually requires *communication* between individuals. If you and I are part of the same group, and you need to "remember" something that only I know, then we have to communicate with each other in order for you to be able to do so.

HOW CAN INFORMATION TECHNOLOGY HELP GROUPS REMEMBER?

Perhaps the most important information technology for helping groups remember is so obvious that you probably don't even think of it as information technology: *writing.* Starting around 5,000 years ago, this first major information technology profoundly transformed the ways human groups remember. When something was written on papyrus or a piece of clay, it could be stored for a very long time, but the encoding and decoding processes (writing and reading) required years of specialized training to learn and a large amount of time and expense to carry out. Storing large amounts of written material was expensive, and it took centuries to develop efficient methods (like alphabetical filing) for organizing large amounts of information so retrieval could be done efficiently.

The second major information technology—the printing press—made it vastly cheaper and easier to make multiple copies of something that had been written, which made it possible for vastly larger groups to use writing as a tool for group memory.

Now, the third major wave of information technology—electronic communication and computation—is once again profoundly changing the costs and capabilities of encoding, storing, and retrieving information. Ever since early applications like computerized accounting in the 1950s, these new technologies have been transforming the ways groups remember everything from personal photos to interactions with customers to medical histories.

In many cases, these technologies make the process of encoding much simpler. For instance, when the initial activities to be remembered (such as online purchases) take place digitally, the encoding happens automatically, as a by-product of the action itself. New technologies can also automatically record audio, video, and many other kinds of sensory information as well as generate what is called metadata about factors like when and where these things were recorded and who was involved. Increasingly, they can do a pretty good job of automatically transcribing many kinds of speech into text, too, and, as we've seen, they are getting better at recognizing many of the patterns in sensory information, such as the pictures of people in video images.

Perhaps the most obvious advantage these new information technologies have over human memories and paper-based technologies is that they can provide almost perfect storage for an almost unlimited amount of information.

But the biggest remaining limitation of technology-based memory is retrieval. Technologies like Google's search engine often do an amazingly good job of retrieving the information you want, but for many kinds of questions, they are still far less useful than a knowledgeable human. In fact, one of the important lessons researchers learned about knowledge management in the 1990s was that often the most useful thing an online knowledge management system can do is help you find the *people* who have the information you need rather than the *documents* with that information.

INCREASING THE SIZE OF A GROUP'S WORKING MEMORY

If you ever took an introductory psychology course, you probably remember learning about the difference between *working memory* and *long-term memory*. Working memory is where you store the information you are working with at the moment—the telephone number you want to call, the different car models you're thinking about buying, the reasons for and against going to the movies tonight. Working memory is very temporary: you quickly forget whatever was in it unless you keep thinking about it. It's also limited in size: you can't keep more than about half a dozen "chunks" of information in working memory at a time. (Try remembering a 15-digit number without writing it down!)

Long-term memory, on the other hand, lasts indefinitely, even without your thinking about it, and it can include vastly larger amounts of information than working memory. This is where you store facts like the name of the first president of the United States, where you went to high school, and what your first pet looked like.

It's clear that information technology can increase the size and reliability of a supermind's long-term memory. But what about working memory? In a face-to-face setting like a business meeting, a whiteboard is a simple tool for increasing the size of a supermind's working memory. When you write items on a whiteboard, they remain visible and accessible to people in the room. That way, everyone can continue to compare and combine the different items on the board without having to remember them all.

Information technology can perform a similar function for much larger groups whose members aren't all in the same room. For instance, you could say that this is one of the most important functions of the online argumentation systems we saw in chapter 9. They increase the size of a supermind's working memory for complex arguments. Often, in a group discussion, people remember the arguments that were made most recently or the ones with which they already agreed. But with an online argumentation system, everyone in the group can easily see the whole set of arguments at any time with all the key positions and supporting arguments conveniently summarized. This can increase the group's ability to make sensible decisions based on the information summarized in the argument map.

Or think about online contests like those in Climate CoLab. They can play a similar role in identifying and comparing large numbers of decision options. Instead of key decision makers and the public focusing only on the solutions they heard most recently or on those that came from the most famous people, everyone can see a complete list of all the ideas that have been proposed by everyone who has contributed.

Of course, any list of ideas can get pretty long, and Climate CoLab uses various ways of sorting lists (such as expert judging and community voting) to bring attention to some of the most promising possibilities. Having the whole list of possibilities collected in a single place where all the items can be systematically compared increases the group's ability to make the best choices.

In fact, psychologists have found that one of the factors most strongly correlated with a person's general intelligence (as measured by IQ tests) is the number of things he or she can keep simultaneously in working memory.[2] Perhaps the same is true of groups, and by increasing the size of a group's working memory, we may be able to increase the group's intelligence.

REMEMBERING MILLIONS OF MEDICAL CASES

When physicians learn to practice medicine, they may see thousands of patients per year, and when they see a new patient, they often use their memories of similar cases to diagnose the new one. These detailed case memories—and the ability to see patterns and recognize similarities in new cases—are critical parts of how medical students become effective physicians.

Something similar happens in the medical community as a whole. When doctors see a new set of symptoms occurring together, like they did for Zika, they may name a new disease and (we hope) discover good treatments for it. But medicine isn't always an exact science, and like the Xerox copier technicians we saw earlier, doctors often share "war stories" about their interesting cases and ask one another for help in diagnosing the difficult ones.

What if we could supercharge this whole process with new kinds of IT? That's what a group called the Human Diagnosis Project (Human Dx) is trying to do.[3] Instead of using IT to *automate* the process of an individual doctor diagnosing a patient, the group is using it to *support* the process of a medical community in making a collaborative diagnosis.

Here's how it works: When doctors and other clinicians see patients they would like additional opinions on, they enter the symptoms, along with the results of any lab tests and potential diagnoses, into the Human Dx system. Then the system helps them easily share the case with colleagues around the world and get their advice about further tests, diagnoses, and treatments. For instance, if you're a nurse in a remote village in Africa, you might use a system like this to get opinions from specialists in Japan or Germany that would help you better treat your patients. And even if you're a leading expert at Massachusetts General Hospital, in Boston, you could still sometimes benefit from getting others' opinions.

A worldwide group of physicians and medical students has already used Human Dx to diagnose thousands of medical cases. Preliminary results from analyzing these cases suggest that the combined diagnoses of groups of clinicians are significantly more accurate than those of individual physicians.[4] That means this tool for collaborative diagnosis can already be useful in improving medical treatment today.

But here's the most intriguing possibility: as a system like this grows, it could eventually contain many millions of cases of human illness. According to the World Health Organization, there are only about 70,000 known human diseases, and a mere 10 of these accounted for 30 percent of all US hospital stays in 2010.[5] So the knowledge base would quickly contain many thousands of cases of common diseases and eventually most others. At that point, diagnosing a perplexing case—perhaps of an extremely rare disease—would often just be a matter of Human Dx *remembering* other patients with similar symptoms and what their eventual diagnoses were.

Of course, writing the software to determine what is similar won't always be easy. But one early study of cases already in the database suggested that a machine-learning algorithm could do diagnoses with about the same accuracy as medical students (66 percent) and only slightly less than that of physicians (72 percent).[6]

To use a system like this, humans will often need to recognize and categorize the symptoms and other information that goes into the system. And expert physicians may need to diagnose difficult cases that don't fit any of the known patterns.

But increasingly, medical personnel—and even patients—could almost immediately get likely diagnoses for their cases based on the collective memory of a medical-community supermind that has seen— and remembered—far more cases than any individual physician could ever see in a lifetime.

In this chapter, we've seen that memory is critical to the functioning of almost all superminds. We've also seen how new information technologies will help superminds get closer to the ideal of perfect memory and how this can often make superminds much, much smarter.

CHAPTER 16

Smarter Learning

In 1769, Nicolas-Joseph Cugnot of France built what many historians regard as the first automobile, a three-wheeled vehicle powered by a steam piston.[1] Over the following two and a half centuries, a combination of markets and hierarchical companies in the automobile industry repeatedly learned how to make cars better and better. This learning wasn't just a matter of sensing things and remembering them; it was mostly about learning by doing—improving through experience.

For instance, a German company led by Nikolaus Otto produced the first modern internal combustion engine in 1876. Then companies led by men with names like Daimler, Benz, Ford, and Chrysler continued to refine automobiles, adding and improving new technologies for functions like steering and braking.[2]

By the early 20th century, there were hundreds of small automobile companies, each of which produced only a few handmade cars.[3] In the same period, Ford Motor Company developed the assembly line and used it to produce the Model T in very large quantities.[4] Soon other car companies adopted these mass-production techniques and pioneered even more organizational innovations themselves. For instance, General Motors pioneered multidivisional hierarchies, and Toyota pioneered just-in-time inventory management.

The auto industry also adapted to many kinds of changes in its environment. When the world was at war, automakers produced vehicles for armies. When the world was at peace, they produced more cars for civilians. When gasoline prices rose in the late 1970s, the industry produced more fuel-efficient vehicles. Later, after gas prices fell in the 1980s, average fuel efficiency declined.[5]

Some of this learning occurred when individual hierarchically organized companies improved with experience. For instance, when Ford introduced the Model T, in 1908, it sold for $850, but by 1925, Ford reduced its costs enough to sell a Model T for less than $300.[6] Some of the learning occurred when different companies tried lots of different things and then other companies adopted the ideas that worked well (like assembly lines). Some learning was a simple result of the forces of supply and demand in markets: when customers didn't want to buy gas-guzzling cars, companies produced fewer of them. And some of the learning was a result of how markets encourage what economist Joseph Schumpeter called creative destruction: the companies that figured out how to profitably sell cars grew larger, and those that didn't went out of business.

All this learning was collective learning by superminds. Some occurred in hierarchies, some in markets, and some in scientific and other communities outside the auto industry itself. For this collective learning to occur, individuals certainly had to learn things. But individual learning alone would never have been enough for the whole auto industry to learn, change, and adapt as it did.

Of course, even though the auto industry is unusually visible and important, similar kinds of collective learning happen in virtually all industries and all parts of society.

EXPLOITATION AND EXPLORATION

In general, there are two important approaches to learning, both for individuals and for superminds: *exploitation* and *exploration*.[7] When you learn by exploitation, you keep doing the same kind of activity over and over, improving over time. For example, the psychologist Hermann Ebbinghaus used the concept of a *learning curve* to analyze how fast you improve by repeatedly practicing something. Business theorists have used the same concept to analyze how fast organizations improve as they get more experienced at certain activities.[8] Ford benefited from this learning-curve effect, for instance, when it was able to reduce the price of the Model T over time, because repeatedly building the same kind of cars helped the company learn how to streamline the process.

When you learn by exploration, on the other hand, you keep trying new things to see what works and what doesn't, then you do more of the things that work. Children often learn this way when they play, and so do pharmaceutical companies when they experiment with many possible new drugs in the hopes that a few will be blockbuster successes that pay for the ones that don't pan out. Markets are often especially good at exploration because they can easily try many approaches at the same time. For instance, when there are many high-tech start-ups in a single industry, even if only a few are successful, the overall market still learns what works and what doesn't.

Of course, most people and most superminds use both exploitation and exploration in some combination, but it's useful to think of them as two distinct types of learning.

HOW CAN INFORMATION TECHNOLOGY HELP?

One of the most obvious ways IT can help superminds learn is by helping groups remember and share the lessons that individuals have learned separately. We saw this earlier in the system that Xerox service technicians used to share tips about fixing copiers. We also see it when companies learn from trade magazines, conferences, and other media about best practices developed elsewhere in their industries.

Another obvious way IT can help superminds learn is by automating work that humans already know how to do. For instance, in the 1990s, many organizations did business process reengineering (BPR) projects where they analyzed their business processes and tried to improve them, often using computers to automate some of the work. In these early reengineering projects, introducing computers was often a big and expensive disruption. But today, to take advantage of the continuing opportunities for more computer support, we should design our processes from the beginning in a way that makes the boundary between what people do and what computers do as flexible as possible.[9]

CYBER-HUMAN LEARNING LOOPS

One way to do this is by creating *cyber-human learning loops*, in which people and computers work together and get better and better over time, often by letting the computers do more and more of the work (see the diagram below).[10]

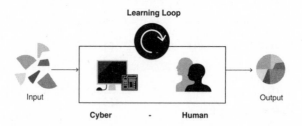

To make a cyber-human learning loop, we need to systematically track as much data as is practical about the inputs, actions taken, and outputs and then analyze this data to continually improve performance. For doctors, lawyers, and copier repair technicians, this data might include facts about the cases they handle and their outcomes. For salespeople, it might include characteristics of potential customers, actions the salespeople took, and the amount of any eventual sales. For accountants, it might be facts about their clients' financial situations and the information contained in their final tax returns. In other words, we want to use as much data as possible to accelerate the learning curve for a cyber-human supermind. To see how this approach could work, let's think about the job of a police detective.

Creating a Cyber-Human Learning Loop for Crime Solving

I confess that I have no real-life experience with the work of police detectives, but from watching plenty of television crime shows and reading many crime novels, I (ahem) consider myself something of an expert on the topic. To make the example very concrete, let's think about the work of one of my favorite fictional detectives: Harry Bosch, the star of many of Michael Connelly's novels.

Harry, as you might guess, is a very good detective: smart, creative, savvy, and completely dedicated to his job. He's also a bit of a rebel, lacking patience for bureaucratic rules and politically motivated superiors. You might call him an old-school detective, too, since he never seems eager to use new technology. But in the long run, I think he might eventually become a big fan of the ideas we're about to discuss.

How could a cyber-human learning loop help Harry and his colleagues solve crimes better and faster? First, I'm afraid Harry would have to stop relying on the loose-leaf binders he calls murder books, which contain all the paper documents collected in the course of an investigation. Instead, all the information about a case would need to be stored online and—as much as possible—formatted in a way that machines can understand. Much of what goes into the murder books would be recorded automatically from phone calls, e-mails, online interactions, and dictated daily summaries of case developments.

These case records would also include the final disposition of the cases: who was charged, what evidence was used at trial, and whether the defendant was eventually found guilty.

Remembering previous cases. If all you had was one of these online murder books, it probably wouldn't be much more useful than Harry's paper murder books. But let's assume that our cyber-human learning loop could draw upon much more than just one murder book and Harry's memories about his past cases. It could also draw upon all the records in all the case files in the whole Los Angeles Police Department, where Harry works. Maybe it could even have access to all the case files in the entire US law-enforcement community, or perhaps even in the world.

Now, of course, this raises all kinds of privacy questions, so let's assume that some of the information is excluded for privacy reasons. But there's still a *lot* of information potentially available that even Harry, with his decades of police experience, doesn't have on his own. For instance, some of these case files may help identify a serial killer who used a particular method in a crime far away and long ago.

Recognizing common patterns. But things really get interesting when the system doesn't just help remember things but also helps recognize patterns that no one, including Harry, has ever noticed before. For instance, even I know (from my extensive experience with fictional crimes) that when a husband is murdered and there are no other obvious suspects, his wife becomes a prime suspect. But how many other patterns are out there in the world that no one has learned to recognize yet? Over time, the machines in a cyber-human learning loop will identify more and more of these patterns and show them to the human detectives. In chapter 14, we saw how a cyber-human system could use patterns that humans had previously entered into it. But here we see how a system might *learn new patterns* by looking at lots of examples.

The cyber-human learning loop can also help identify—and improve—patterns in the *process* of solving cases. For instance, what if the probability of solving a crime increases when more people besides just the lead detectives express opinions about what to do next? Or what if it's the opposite? Maybe even subtler aspects of the crime-solving process are critical. It seems to me, for example, that Harry usually gets very little sleep while he is working on a big case. What if it turned out that, statistically speaking, the probability of solving a crime increases when the lead detectives get more sleep?

Automating common patterns. A key part of cyber-human learning loops is that computers gradually take over more and more of the work. For instance, I once had money stolen from my wallet in a locker at the MIT gym. The officer who took my police report said that the detectives might look at video from the security cameras in the gym. But I suspect that my case wasn't important enough to justify their taking the time to do that. Lo and behold, they never found the thief.

Computers could be useful in cases like this by learning to do more of the work over time. For instance, when human detectives look at videos to solve petty thefts like mine, they typically look for suspicious people in the area around the time of the crime. In my case, one of the gym attendants told me that there had been three similar thefts in the same month as mine, so a human detective would probably have combed through videos to see if there was a single person who was there at all three times.

This is something that computers can do pretty well, even with today's relatively limited facial-recognition technology. Instead of having to scan all the video themselves, the human detectives could just give the computer the three dates and ask it to scan for faces that were present at all three times. That might have helped the police catch the person who stole my money without diverting much of their time and effort from more important cases. And, over time, computers might even be able to do this automatically as soon as a petty-theft crime report is entered into the system.

In general, computers could gradually become increasingly helpful by doing things like suggesting potential experts, analyzing phone logs, or even suggesting hypotheses about who did it, why, and how. The key point here is that Harry's colleagues shouldn't try to computerize the whole crime-solving process once and for all. Instead they should create a flexible system that tracks lots of data about each case, helps people and computers learn from all this experience, and makes it easy for detectives to shift more and more of the work to computers over time.

Cyber-Human Learning Loops in Medicine, Law, Accounting, and More

Similar kinds of learning loops could be used to help many other kinds of superminds learn to do their work much more effectively, too. For instance, in the previous chapters we saw that doctors could build libraries of medical case histories by asking their colleagues for advice and letting a computer record the interactions. It's also clear that automated systems could then use these libraries to find treatment patterns that work for various combinations of symptoms in different kinds of patients. Lawyers could do something similar with legal cases, repair technicians with records of service calls, and accountants with tax returns.

Over time, computers would be able to do more of the work themselves. For instance, in tax accounting, there are already tools on the web that can automatically prepare simple personal tax returns. Cyber-human learning loops will let machines watch humans prepare more complex returns and gradually learn what actions the humans take in different situations. At first the machines may just suggest actions to humans. Eventually the machines can just automatically take the actions that humans always approve.

I think it will be a very long time before computers will have enough general intelligence to do everything that humans do, but in the meantime, superminds made up of people and computers will be able to continuously improve their performance by learning from their own experiences extremely effectively.

LEARNING FROM EXPERIMENTS

As we saw above, another powerful way to learn is exploration—systematically exploring different possibilities to see what works. For instance, the economist Ricardo Hausmann suggests a way of doing this for learning how to use tablet computers in classrooms.[11] What if we encouraged lots of teachers to try lots of different things with different kinds of students in different kinds of schools and then looked for patterns in what worked where? Maybe fifth-grade boys in affluent suburbs who like video games learn best when you let them play educational games that have fantasy themes from their favorite video games. And maybe eighth-grade girls in low-income neighborhoods who like soccer learn best when you constantly show them how their performance in online tests compares to that of their friends. Or maybe it's the opposite!

The point is that there are so many variables to consider and so many patterns to find that we should let as many people as possible use their creativity to come up with interesting things to try. Of course, in some cases we'll need to do carefully controlled experiments to see which results are just a matter of good luck and which are repeatable, but this approach encourages a supermind composed of teachers all over the world to rapidly explore lots of interesting possibilities.

Of course, it's not just people who can come up with hypotheses and test them. Computers can do that, too. For instance, the automated systems at sites like Facebook and Quora are always experimenting to see what kinds of news items you respond to and then sending you more like those.

Adam the Robot Scientist

One of my favorite examples of computers learning from experiments is Adam the robot scientist.[12] Developed by Ross King and his colleagues at Aberystwyth University and the University of Cambridge, Adam has the intelligence and the physical capabilities to carry out the whole scientific process: originating hypotheses, devising experiments, running those experiments, interpreting the results, and then formulating new hypotheses. Adam's specialty is understanding the genome of baker's yeast, a popular laboratory species.

The researchers provided Adam with a database that included what we already know about the genes and enzymes involved in yeast metabolism, and his job was to help figure out which genes are responsible for producing the "orphan enzymes" in baker's yeast—enzymes that hadn't yet been linked to any genes. To do this, Adam ran thousands of experiments using fully automated centrifuges, incubators, pipettes, and growth analyzers. At each step of the way, Adam explored new hypotheses based on the results of previous experiments. The only role for a human technician was to periodically add consumed solutions and remove waste.

Eventually Adam discovered three genes that, together, coded for one of the orphan enzymes, knowledge that had gone undiscovered by human researchers for decades. The scientists who developed Adam confirmed his results with separate manual experiments. They believe Adam is the first machine to "independently discover new scientific knowledge." Later, the same team developed another robot scientist, named Eve, that uses a similar approach to do automated drug testing.[13] For instance, Eve has already discovered that a drug previously developed for treating cancer may also be effective at preventing malaria.

Adam and Eve are interesting examples for many reasons. First, they show that machines can do parts of the scientific process that have previously only been done by humans. Second, they show how cyber-human learning loops can be used inside a scientific laboratory. The scientists who developed Adam and Eve haven't put themselves out of a job; they have just improved the efficiency with which they can do their work. The robot scientists can still do only the most routine kinds of scientific hypothesis generation and testing, but that frees up the human scientists to do more difficult and creative work.

These examples provide another answer to the question we've been asking throughout this book: How can people and computers work *together* to be more intelligent than either could be alone? In this case, it was useful for robot scientists to automate as many of the physical parts of experimentation as possible. And it was useful that they could autonomously generate and refine hypotheses, too.

But why not also let people see the results of all the thinking the machines have done and then suggest new hypotheses of their own? Why not let the machines help refine and test those human hypotheses—before they run any new experiments—by scanning the existing scientific literature more thoroughly than humans ever could? Why not let both humans and machines participate in debates (like those discussed in chapter 9) about which hypotheses are most promising to study next?

And, of course, similar kinds of semiautomated hypothesis generation and experimentation can be used in many fields besides science. What if we could use this approach to figure out what sales techniques work best online, what kinds of ads work best with potential voters, and how best to optimize factory operations?

We've now seen how IT can help superminds improve by learning more effectively from both their own experience and systematic experiments. Of course, this isn't guaranteed to make superminds smarter, but I think it certainly makes it more likely that they will be.

Part VI

How Can Superminds Help Solve Our Problems?

CHAPTER 17

Corporate Strategic Planning

Throughout this book, we've seen how superminds can help solve many kinds of problems. Now we're ready to combine the things we've learned in examples to show how superminds can help solve three important kinds of problems we face today. We'll see that effective problem solving often requires more than just picking one type of supermind that is well suited to the problem—it usually requires picking a combination of superminds that can work together as a larger supermind.

We'll start, in this chapter, by looking at how superminds can help companies do strategic planning.

WHAT IS CORPORATE STRATEGIC PLANNING?

Companies use the term *strategic planning* to mean many things. In some large companies, for instance, the "strategic planning process" is really just a euphemism for the annual budgeting process: all units of the company send their budgets up the hierarchy for approval, accompanied by descriptions of how they'll use the money. But in technology start-ups, the whole conceptualization of the business itself is a kind of strategic planning: What product or service will we provide?

How will we provide it? To whom will we sell it? Why will customers buy from us instead of our competitors?

The kind of strategic planning we'll focus on here is the process by which large companies make genuine strategic decisions about changes, whether those changes are in the combination of markets they address, the products and services they provide, or the competitive advantages they hope to achieve. To make our discussion concrete, we'll use Procter & Gamble (P&G), the legendary consumer products company, as an example and talk about how P&G could do strategic planning in new ways.

Bear in mind that the new possibilities for strategic planning that I'll suggest are just that: possibilities. I have no reason to believe that P&G is doing these things today. But I think that P&G—and many other companies—are likely to do things like this in the future.

HOW HAS P&G DONE STRATEGIC PLANNING IN THE PAST?

P&G's former CEO, A. G. Lafley, has written about the strategic-planning process P&G used under his leadership, and we'll base our discussion here primarily on his writings.[1] According to Lafley and his collaborators, P&G focuses its strategic decision making around a series of key questions about the company's overall *goals*, the *markets* it wants to address, the *value for customers* it provides, the *activities* that provide this value, and the ways it can gain strategic *advantages over its competitors*.

For example, in the late 1990s, P&G used this process to decide whether to try to become a major player in the global beauty-care sector. A key problem was that P&G didn't have a credible brand in skin care, the largest and most profitable part of that sector. Its only entry was the struggling Oil of Olay[2] brand, which had relatively small sales and an aging customer base. P&G identified several possible strategic options, including: abandoning Oil of Olay and acquiring an established brand from a competitor; keeping Oil of Olay as a low-priced, mass-market brand for older customers and improving its wrinkle-reduction performance; moving Oil of Olay into the higher-priced prestige distribution channel of upscale department stores; or reshaping the brand to be a "masstige" brand sold in special display cases of mass-market retailers at a price point somewhere between mass-market and prestige products.

To evaluate these options, Lafley and his colleagues specified "conditions for success" that would have to be true for each choice to be successful. For instance, they believed that for the innovative "masstige" option to work, the following had to be true: the potential customer segment would need to be big enough to be worth targeting, P&G would need to be able to produce the product at a cost that would allow a lower selling price than the full-on prestige products in the category, and mass-market retailers would need to be willing to create special display cases for this new product category. A key part of the process was doing research to gauge whether these conditions were true.

According to Lafley, the strategy-development process was organized as a series of meetings with a carefully selected team of people from different parts of the company. For instance, the strategy team didn't just include senior executives and their staff members; it also included promising junior executives and operations managers who would help implement whatever decisions were made. The result of all this work was P&G's decision to revive the Oil of Olay brand by moving it into the new "masstige" category.

Lafley and his collaborators also suggest that a similar process was used to develop strategies at other levels of P&G—not just in specific product categories (like skin care) but also in larger product sectors (like beauty products) as well as throughout the whole corporation.

INVOLVING MORE PEOPLE IN GENERATING POSSIBILITIES

This traditional P&G strategic-planning process involves a relatively small group of people and appears to rely heavily on the time-honored communication technology we call meetings. Today, the cost of many kinds of online communication is much less than it was in the 1990s, when P&G did this work. But imagine that the company were going through this process today. What would it look like if it were to use online tools to open up the process to many more people from inside and outside the organization?

One approach could resemble the online contest-web approach we saw in Climate CoLab. There could be separate challenges for strategies at different levels of the P&G organization, from the Oil of Olay brand to the global beauty-care sector to the entire corporation. And the strategies proposed for the higher levels would be different combinations of strategies at the next lower levels.

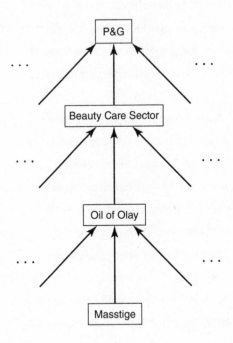

In each of these challenges, anyone in the company could propose a strategic option, and others could then comment on or help develop the ideas. Eventually there would be one "winner" in each challenge—the strategy that was eventually chosen—but during the planning process, it would be important to consider a number of different options.

In the Oil of Olay challenge, for example, people might propose strategies like the ones we saw above. In each case, they would need to describe key elements of the strategy, such as product characteristics, customers, and competitive advantage. With regard to the "masstige" strategy that P&G eventually chose, for instance, a proposal might say that P&G's labs would give the product broader antiaging effects than its competitors and that it would be advertised and packaged as a prestige brand even though the price would fall somewhere between mass-market and prestige levels.

But by opening the process to lots of people, surprising new options might arise. For instance, if this process were used today for P&G's cosmetics strategy, a group of young, tech-savvy employees—who would never have been included in the corporate strategic-planning process in the 1990s—might propose a whole new cosmetics concept involving skin and eye makeup specially formulated for each customer based on smartphone photos customers take of their own faces and questions they answer about their style preferences.

In the challenge at the next level up, for the *global beauty-care sector,* people could propose strategies that included options for Oil of Olay as well as for Cover Girl cosmetics, Pantene shampoos, and other current or potential P&G brands. In each case, the proposals would need to describe how the strategies for all the brands would fit together into a coherent sector-level plan. For instance, Pantene and Cover Girl might do joint advertising in certain channels, and Pantene and Head & Shoulders shampoos might try to avoid competing too directly with each other.

Of course, these are the kinds of questions P&G already thinks about in its strategic-planning process, but with more people involved, there would be many more chances for innovative new approaches to emerge and more chances for people with detailed knowledge of, say, specific manufacturing difficulties to bring their expertise to bear on larger corporate strategies.

At the *overall corporate strategy* level, proposals could include combinations of strategies for each sector: beauty, grooming, health care, and so forth. For instance, the overall corporate strategy Lafley described for P&G included elements like using large-scale R&D capabilities to build highly differentiated products with global distribution. So in a coherent corporate strategy, each of the sector and brand strategies should include differentiated global products.

Who Can Participate?

Unlike Climate CoLab, a company like P&G probably wouldn't want its entire strategic-planning process open to the general public. But with an online process, I think many companies would probably be happy to involve far more of their own employees than are involved in today's face-to-face processes. Ideally, companies might want this process to be open to any of their employees who wanted to participate and maybe to some people outside the company, too. As we learned in Climate CoLab, the best ideas sometimes come from surprising places.

SEMIAUTOMATED TOOLS TO HELP GENERATE MORE POSSIBILITIES

So far we've talked about relying solely on people to come up with strategic possibilities. But machines can be helpful here, too. In many aspects of strategy, there are generic possibilities that arise over and over again, and machines can automatically prompt people to consider these possibilities in relevant situations.

For instance, Michael Porter, who pioneered the modern academic field of corporate strategy, articulated three generic strategies that companies in almost any industry can use: *cost leadership* (being the low-cost producer), *differentiation* (being unique on dimensions, like quality, that customers value), and *focus* (tailoring products to a narrow segment of customers).[3] P&G generally uses the differentiation strategy, but in other situations it could be useful for strategic planners to be explicitly reminded to consider all these possibilities.

In a sense, machines could help strategy teams *remember* good ideas that others have had in similar situations. For instance, software tools embedded in an application for generating strategy proposals could automatically suggest possibilities for generic strategies like these:

- Integrate forward (that is, take on some of the tasks done by your customers) or backward (take on some of the tasks done by your suppliers).
- Outsource more of the things you do internally to freelancers or other more specialized companies.
- Move into related market segments (such as higher- or lower-priced products, nearby geographical regions, or other types of products purchased by your customers).

When you pick one of these options, the system could automatically give you a template for the kinds of details you should specify for each type of strategy.

A Strategy Recombinator

In addition to just suggesting individual possibilities to consider, software tools could also suggest combinations of possibilities. In 1999, Avi Bernstein, Mark Klein, and I used a semiautomated approach like this to develop ideas for new business processes. We called it the Process Recombinator,[4] and I think a similar approach could work for strategies, too.

For instance, if people created several possible answers to key strategic questions (such as those involving choices among products, customer segments, and competitive advantages), then it would be easy for a system to automatically generate many possible combinations of these options for people to quickly evaluate. One possible kind of competitive advantage, for example, might be letting customers use smartphones to customize their products. So the system could automatically suggest the possibility of doing this for all of P&G's products: cosmetics, shampoos, toothpastes, laundry detergents, potato chips, and others. Of course, many of these combinations would be silly or impractical and could be very quickly eliminated, but some might be surprisingly useful. And even silly options sometimes give people other good ideas.

For instance, in the early 2000s, P&G developed a process for printing entertaining pictures and words on Pringles potato chips. A strategy recombinator might have led to an idea that seems promising to me: using this technology to let customers buy Pringles that are preprinted with images the customers specify themselves.[5]

INVOLVING MORE PEOPLE IN EVALUATING POSSIBILITIES

One of the good things about involving more people and tools in generating possibilities is that it results in more ideas to consider, which often increases your chances of finding good ideas. But that also works the other way: if there are too many ideas, it can become hard to sort through them. What do you do when you have too many ideas? One solution is to involve more people in evaluating the ideas.

Involving Specialists and Outsiders

In a good contest web for corporate strategy, for instance, you probably want one group of people evaluating whether it is technically feasible to make a product, another group estimating how much it will cost to make the product, and still another group predicting whether people will buy it. In many cases, you won't care whether these people are inside your company or not. For instance, you might want an outside market researcher to estimate demand for skin-care products at different prices.

It's also often possible for people who aren't experts to do some of the work of evaluation. For instance, one aspect of evaluating a strategy is figuring out whether the different parts of the strategy are consistent. In P&G's case, its overall corporate strategy involves selling innovative, differentiated products at a global scale. So if someone created a strategic option that involved selling a low-cost, conventional laundry detergent only in Germany, that would *not* be consistent with P&G's overall strategy because it involves a conventional product, not an innovative one, and a local strategy, not a global one. That means this strategy should probably be screened out. And it wouldn't require an expert in marketing or strategy to tell this; even Amazon's Mechanical Turk workers could probably do it.

Using an Evaluation Funnel

To make the evaluation process efficient, you probably want to use something like the "funnel" approach that many companies use for new product development. At each stage, the best ideas are selected to move to the next stage, where they receive further development and evaluation. In the early stages, many half-baked ideas are considered and rapidly filtered out, but by the later stages, a much smaller number of promising ideas receive substantial attention.

For instance, when P&G evaluates a strategic option, it first evaluates the conditions for success that it thinks are *least* likely to be true. In the Oil of Olay case, the biggest uncertainty was whether customers would pay a higher price, so that's the one the company tested first. P&G found that customers would, in fact, pay a higher price, so that kept the strategic options that included high prices open. However, many options are eliminated after evaluating only one or two questions, thus saving large amounts of unnecessary evaluation effort.

Using Prediction Markets, Online Argumentation, and Voting

Even after doing research about some of the questions, there may not be a clear answer either way. In these cases, it may be worth using some of the techniques for online group decision making that we saw in chapters 8 and 9.

For instance, P&G's ability to produce a new version of Oil of Olay at a competitive price may depend on technical uncertainties about the manufacturing process that have not yet been resolved. One simple way of aggregating people's opinions about this question would be to take a poll among experts about the likely costs. A more interesting possibility would be to create a *conditional prediction market,* in which many people make predictions about what the eventual costs would be if the product is produced. Then, if the product *is* produced, people are paid for the accuracy of their predictions. If the product is *not* produced, everyone just gets his or her money (or points) back.

Either way, it might be useful to let people enter detailed arguments online for and against the different points of view, which could inform the people who are participating in the prediction market. Any of these approaches could provide a strong basis for making a final decision, drawing upon the best information available in a vast community of people with a wide range of expertise.

Recognizing Diamonds in the Rough

There's an important caveat here, though. Sometimes the best and most innovative ideas are so unusual that most people don't recognize them in their early stages. For instance, in the 1970s, when Steve Jobs and Bill Gates were first playing around with what we now call personal computers, most people in the world would not have had any idea that these strange, awkward devices would turn out to be among the most innovative and influential products of the next few decades.

It's certainly not easy to rapidly filter ideas without missing many of these "diamonds in the rough." Maybe we will just have to accept that it's very hard to detect the biggest breakthrough ideas in their early stages. But perhaps there's a way.

I suspect that some people are much better than others at recognizing these nascent breakthroughs. For instance, in my consulting work with Peter Schwartz and Stewart Brand, cofounders of the Global Business Network consulting firm, I have come to think of them as prototypical examples of people with this knack for recognizing good ideas long before most others do. And I think many of the best venture capitalists, like John Doerr (with whom I worked when we were in college together), have this ability, too. The question is whether it's possible to identify people who have this skill long before they reach the level of eminence of Peter, Stewart, and John.

Of course, we might be able to do this just by choosing people who have reputations for being very in touch with what's going to happen next. But it might be possible to do it more rigorously by setting up something like the process we saw in chapter 7 that Philip Tetlock used to identify "superforecasters." By systematically tracking over time how accurately (and how early) people predict technological advances and other kinds of breakthroughs, we could identify the people who can do this better than others. Then we could ask these people to take a second look at some of the "crazy" ideas that other people reject.

USING SEMIAUTOMATED TOOLS TO EVALUATE POSSIBILITIES

The hardest—but also potentially the most valuable—thing computers can do in this process is automatically evaluating possibilities. Evaluating ideas about business strategy often requires the kind of soft knowledge that is very hard to formalize in computers because it's related to the kind of general intelligence that people have and computers don't. But as we saw in the Foldit system, if you *can* do automatic evaluation of possibilities, that allows the whole problem-solving process to operate far faster.

Spreadsheets, Simulations, and Bayesian Networks

Perhaps the most obvious way to automate part of the evaluation process is to use spreadsheets and other kinds of computer software that can simulate real-world outcomes. For instance, if the people who submit proposed strategies for all the parts of your business include revenue and expense projections, then spreadsheets (or other simple programs) can do a good job of estimating the consolidated earnings for your whole company. Or if you've already done enough market research to have good automated models of how different customers respond to price changes, then you could use those models to estimate your revenue at different price points.

For instance, Amazon has done vast amounts of data-science work to develop detailed models of many parts of its business: how customers respond to prices, ads, and recommendations; how supply-chain costs vary with inventory policies, delivery methods, and warehouse locations; and how load balancing and server purchases affect software and hardware costs.[6] With tools like these, computers can do much of the work by "running the numbers," and people can then use their general intelligence to do a higher level of analysis.

Another interesting way of simulating what might happen in the real world is to use Bayesian networks like those we saw in our discussion of predicting terrorist attacks in chapter 14. For instance, a major recession in the next two years could affect many of the factors P&G would evaluate for potential new products, including the cost of raw materials and consumer demand. But if purchasing specialists separately estimate whether materials costs would be acceptable with a recession and without one, and if marketers do the same for sales volume, then a Bayesian network could automatically combine all these estimates with separate projections by economists about the probability of a recession. The result would thus be an integrated prediction that draws upon expertise from economists, purchasing specialists, and marketers, all automatically combined by computers.

Of course, we're still a long way from having anything like complete computer models of even a single company, much less the whole economy. Such models would have to take into account the vagaries of human behavior, political changes, market fads, and all the other complexities of the real world. So even though automated simulations can be incredibly helpful for making and combining predictions, they're not enough. People—who aren't perfect at predicting these things, either—will probably still need to use their best judgment to make final decisions after computer simulations have done what they can.

Automating Rules from Experts
Another way computers can be helpful is by applying rules experts have previously specified. For instance, if each person who creates a strategy proposal for P&G checks a box to specify what type of generic strategy his or her proposal embodies (e.g., low-cost, differentiated, or niche), then simple programs can check whether a given proposal is consistent with the overall P&G corporate strategy. Even if the people who create proposals don't specify the type of strategy explicitly, today's natural-language-understanding programs could probably do a pretty good job of figuring it out.

Using Machine Learning to Recognize Patterns
Another intriguing possibility is to use "learning loops" like those we saw in chapter 16. The process could start with human experts doing evaluations manually and then gradually automating more and more of the work over time as the machines get better at predicting what human experts would do.

For instance, instead of an expert explicitly telling a programmer to write a rule for filtering out low-cost products, a machine-learning program might just recognize that experts often do this and start automatically suggesting this action in the future. If the expert agrees with the suggestion enough times, then the program might stop asking and just do the filtering automatically.

A CYBER-HUMAN STRATEGY MACHINE

You might call the kind of system I've just described a *cyber-human strategy machine.*[7] Given how complex such a system could be and how generic much of the work would be, it seems unlikely that each company in the world would want to develop its own system to do all these things. Instead I expect that today's strategy consulting firms (or their future competitors) will provide much of this functionality as a service. Such a strategy-machine company, for instance, could have a stable of people — at many levels of expertise — on call to rapidly generate and evaluate various strategic possibilities. They could also use software to automate some parts of the process and help manage the rest.

In the long run, such a strategy machine would use a combination of people and computers to generate and evaluate millions of possible strategies for a single company. Over time, computers would do more and more of the work, but people would still be involved in parts of the process. The end result would be a handful of the most promising options from which the human managers of the company would make their final choices.

The system we've just seen is focused on strategic decision making, but what we've really seen is an architecture for a general-purpose problem-solving machine. As we saw in chapter 13, this type of problem-solving machine is more like a combination of markets (such as the supply chain for manufacturing cars) than it is like a traditional hierarchy. It is a kind of ecosystem supermind that combines markets (the contests), communities (for proposing ideas), democracies, and hierarchies (for evaluating ideas). And it lets a large group of people and machines apply many more kinds of knowledge and explore many more possibilities than traditional hierarchical problem-solving processes do.

As new technologies make it easier to coordinate the activities of much larger groups of people and machines, I suspect we'll see many more examples of this approach to solving all kinds of business and societal problems—not just plans for dealing with climate change and corporate strategy but also designs for new houses, smartphones, factories, cities, educational systems, antiterrorism approaches, medical treatment plans, and a virtually unlimited number of other possibilities.

CHAPTER 18

Climate Change

The next problem we'll analyze is the focus of Climate CoLab: What can we humans do about climate change? At the time I am writing this (in mid-2017), many people around the world believe that *climate change is real, humans are part of the cause,* and *bad things will happen if we don't do something about it.*[1] But in the United States, especially, there is substantial disagreement about these beliefs, both in the public and in the government.

My own view on these questions is partly based on my reading of the scientific literature, but more important, it is based on conversations with my MIT colleagues who are among the world's leading scientific experts on the subject. They believe that the scientific evidence supporting these assumptions is overwhelming. That's my belief, too, and that's the point of view from which we will analyze the problem. Sensible people can certainly differ on what we should *do* about climate change, but these basic assumptions about the existence, cause, and likely effects of climate change are extremely well supported scientifically.

Here's a more precise statement of the problem we will analyze: What can we humans do to minimize the human suffering caused by climate change without causing other problems that would be even worse? That's a difficult question, but this framing of the problem is enough to start thinking about how different superminds could help solve it.

REDUCING EMISSIONS

The primary way humans affect the climate is by burning fossil fuels (like coal and gasoline) and by doing other activities that emit carbon dioxide and other "greenhouse gases" into the atmosphere. So a big part of solving the problem is figuring out how to reduce these emissions.

Of course, having cost-effective technologies for generating electricity, like solar, wind, and nuclear power, could certainly help reduce these emissions. So could having affordable, efficient technologies for powering cars, heating buildings, and many other human activities. But these technologies alone would almost certainly not be enough to really solve the problem. From a collective-intelligence point of view, the key question is: What kinds of superminds could best choose when and how to use new technologies—along with other methods—for reducing emissions?

Community Norms

One possibility would be to rely on community norms to do this. For instance, in many communities, large numbers of consumers have voluntarily replaced their incandescent lightbulbs with energy-saving fluorescent bulbs, in part because that is socially encouraged among their friends. This is certainly a useful thing to do, and if the changes in norms are large enough (as, for example, they might be in the China Dream plan, described in chapter 12), this could help a lot. But I suspect that in many cases, changes like this would not motivate enough people to make a real difference.

More important, vague community norms like this provide very little information people can use when they're making choices between reducing carbon emissions and getting other things they want. For instance, I like taking long, hot showers every morning. If I like these showers so much that I would be willing to forgo one airplane trip per year to make up for them, would that be a good trade-off? My community's norms don't help me much in figuring this out because they aren't nearly detailed and quantitative enough. Because of this, I think it's clear that changes in community norms alone would not be a very good way of solving the climate-change problem.

Hierarchical Government Regulations

Another possibility would be to use regulations by hierarchical governments to reduce emissions. For example, the United States government has, for many years, required manufacturers of cars and light trucks to ensure that the vehicles they sell meet certain average fuel-economy standards. These mandatory requirements certainly do some good in reducing emissions, but they are a very blunt instrument that isn't very good at facilitating detailed trade-offs between alternative ways of reducing emissions.

For instance, my daily commute to work is less than two miles each way, so it doesn't really matter very much how fuel-efficient my vehicle is. I usually commute in an electric car, and that helps me feel good about myself according to the norms of my community. But maybe the world would be better off if I bought an old gas-guzzler for my short commute from someone with a much longer commute who could then buy a more fuel-efficient car. Perhaps a hierarchical government could make up a complicated set of rules to cover situations like this, but in general, a hierarchical method for managing all the emission-reduction choices an economy needs to make is not a very good way of solving the problem, either.

Markets

In theory, the most promising type of supermind for managing all these detailed decisions about reducing emissions is a market. As we've already seen, markets provide a very effective way of making a huge number of detailed decisions in our world, so they are well suited to managing the kinds of detailed decisions we've just been discussing.

But there's a big problem: most of the costs of high emissions today will be paid by people who live on our planet in future decades, so most of those costs aren't included in the prices for the things we buy today. What's worse, the benefits of any investments I voluntarily make in reducing emissions (like changing my lightbulbs) are averaged over everyone else on earth, and I won't personally get any noticeable benefit from my own investment.

In other words, this is a classic example of what economists call an *externality*. People who cause the emission of greenhouse gases create costs for everyone on the planet, but they have to pay only a tiny fraction of those costs themselves. And since these costs are not included in today's markets, markets essentially ignore them when they make their decisions.

But economists know that there is an obvious solution to this problem. There are various ways of adding the costs that greenhouse-gas emissions will cause in the future into the prices that people have to pay today. This is called *internalizing* these costs, and as soon as that happens, markets can do what they do best: efficiently make all kinds of detailed decisions about different ways to reduce emissions with today's technologies and to invest in better technologies for the future.

Internalizing the Costs of Carbon Emissions

One of the best ways to include the costs of emissions in today's prices is for the government to require people who generate emissions to pay the costs that result from those emissions. For instance, this could be done by adding a carbon tax to the sales of products whose manufacture or use generates carbon emissions. When you buy a car, for example, you would pay (directly or indirectly) a carbon tax on all the emissions that were generated to make the car. When you buy gasoline, you would pay for all the emissions that will be generated when you use it.

The same goal could also be accomplished with what are called cap-and-trade systems, in which governments set a limit (cap) on the emissions that a given company (or other entity) can cause. Companies can then buy and sell (trade) these emission allowances among themselves. For instance, if Ford can easily reduce its emissions but Walmart can't, then Ford can sell some of its emission allowances to Walmart for whatever price they both agree upon.

The European Union has used an emissions-trading system like this, as has the state of California. But one of the most interesting examples of this approach will probably be in China. Even though China still has many state-owned enterprises and thus is not yet officially considered a market economy, it announced plans to start using a large-scale emissions-trading system in 2017.[2]

The United States does not have any plans for large-scale pricing of carbon emissions, and the current political environment in the country does not seem at all conducive to legislation that would provide this framework. As the world's second-largest carbon emitter (after China), the United States is critical to solving the world's climate-change problem. So what can be done?

What Could Cause the US Government to Internalize Emissions Costs?

If you don't have direct control of a powerful supermind (like the US Congress), but you want that supermind to do something, then you can try to influence it in various ways, like lobbying and making political donations. Perhaps developing novel policies could also help. For example, a number of conservatives support a revenue-neutral carbon tax, revenues from which would be used to offset other taxes.

But perhaps the most powerful way to influence the US Congress is to change the views of the voters who elect them. This basically means changing the shared values of the communities to which people belong. Some of this can be done via markets with advertising and professional news and entertainment, like television shows and movies that highlight the importance of doing something about climate change.

Online communities can also be influential. For instance, last year's winning proposal in the Climate CoLab contest "Shifting Behavior for a Changing Climate" was for a project called DearTomorrow.[3] In this project, anyone can contribute open online letters, photos, and videos for their loved ones to see in the year 2050. The project plans to archive the material until then and in the meantime to promote some of the most powerful items widely on social media and elsewhere. Behavioral research by one of the founders of the project and numerous testimonials from users suggest that the simple act of writing such a letter significantly increases people's donations to climate-related causes. In general, I think there are lots of opportunities like this for creative ways of changing cultural attitudes in communities.

Are There Other Ways of Internalizing Emissions Costs?

If it's not possible to convince a government to legally require carbon emitters to pay the true cost of their emissions, is there another way of internalizing these costs? Yes, it's always possible for people to voluntarily pay for the costs of their emissions, even if no government requires them to.

For example, some people and businesses have been buying "carbon offsets" to compensate for their own emissions for years. If you fly from Boston to Paris, for instance, your share of the emissions caused by the flight might be about four metric tons of carbon dioxide. So you could also buy, at the same time, a carbon offset that would save four metric tons of emissions by using solar energy instead of coal to generate electricity in Brazil. This approach is limited, however, by the number of people who want to voluntarily reduce their emissions in this way.

It might also be possible to create additional financial incentives for people to reduce their emissions. For example, several Climate CoLab proposals have suggested using digital currencies (like bitcoin) to buy and sell emission rights.[4] It is common for the value of these digital currencies to increase very substantially over time. The value of a bitcoin, for instance, has increased from about $0.30 in 2011 to over $1,200.00 in 2017, and there are structural reasons to expect that such increases may continue.[5] In this case, early participants in a voluntary emissions-trading program with a digital currency might receive an initial allocation of emission rights. Then, if they didn't use all these rights, they would potentially stand to make substantial profits later.

Sensing, Remembering, and Learning

All the ideas about climate change we've discussed so far involve ways of using superminds to make *decisions* about reducing emissions. But there are also other roles superminds could play. For instance, we hope that over time Climate CoLab will also serve as a repository of best practices and other good ideas for dealing with climate change. In that sense, it is helping a global community *remember* things that it has already learned.

It's also easy to imagine using online communities like Climate CoLab to speed up our global *learning* about what methods actually work for reducing emissions. For instance, we could do something like the experiments about what helps kids learn better that we saw in chapter 16. With climate change, for example, different cities might test different methods to encourage mass-transit usage. Some might try advertising campaigns, others new schedules, and others might replace subways with buses running every five minutes. As long as there is a way of *sensing* the changes in emissions and other variables that might affect mass-transit usage, you could use machine-learning techniques to detect what seems to be working and what doesn't. Then, later, you might do more controlled experiments to be confident of the results.

ADAPTING TO THE RESULTS OF CLIMATE CHANGE

Most climate-change experts believe that even if we radically reduce our greenhouse-gas emissions tomorrow, the gases already in the atmosphere will cause a variety of changes on our planet. These changes include increasing average temperatures, rising sea levels, and more intense storms. How can superminds help deal with these changes? Let's think about two examples related to coastal flooding: *reducing the risks* and *improving the responses*.

Reducing Risks of Coastal Flooding

It seems obvious, but it's worth saying that one way to reduce the risks of coastal flooding is to have fewer vulnerable buildings in areas that might flood. One way to accomplish this goal would be for hierarchical governments to use zoning laws to forbid people from creating or occupying buildings in flood zones.

But as we've already seen, it would be very difficult for regulations to deal with all the potential special cases. For instance, what about temporary buildings whose loss would be of minimal economic consequence? What about buildings that are specially designed to float on water so as not to be damaged in a flood?

Perhaps a better solution would be for governments and markets to work together, each doing what it does best, within a larger supermind. For instance, governments can (and sometimes already do) require owners of coastal property to have insurance, just as they already require automobile owners to have insurance. Then insurance companies can use detailed underwriting methods to determine how much to charge in different situations. As a result, it would likely become prohibitively expensive to own buildings on vulnerable coastal real estate, and market forces would influence owners to convert the land to less risky uses (such as beaches and parks).

Anticipating and Responding to Coastal Floods

Another way to use superminds in dealing with sea-level rise is to improve the warning and response systems for severe floods. For instance, it's easy to imagine using many of the techniques we saw previously (such as prediction markets) to improve the accuracy and timeliness of coastal-flood warnings.

It should also be possible to use all kinds of information technology tools to help respond to floods. For instance, a nonprofit company named Ushahidi (Swahili for "testimony") has developed software tools for use in crisis mapping. These tools help emergency responders and others deal with crisis situations by crowdsourcing much of the *sensing* that needs to happen. The software allows anyone to submit eyewitness reports via e-mail, text message, or Twitter, and these reports are then shown on a consolidated map of the disaster area. After the Haiti earthquake in 2010, for instance, reports included "Chantal Landrin is stuck under the rubble at a house in Turjo!" and "Route 9 is access point into [Port-au-Prince] but still precarious." Individually, these reports might not have been very useful, but when mapped together, they give a constantly updated view of the whole situation.[6]

CREATING A NEW KIND OF GLOBAL COMMUNITY

One of the most intriguing ways of dealing with the climate-change problem might be to create a new kind of governance mechanism—a new supermind—for dealing with it. Since the problem is global by nature, one obvious possibility would be a global hierarchical government or perhaps a global democracy of some sort. The United Nations is the closest thing we have to such a global government, and its success in brokering the Paris climate agreement of 2015 is evidence of its potential for helping solve the problem. But for various historical and other reasons, the UN's power to compel action is much more limited than a typical hierarchy's. Even the Paris Agreement was essentially a voluntary agreement among the global community of nations. So although the UN may play an important role, it is likely to be more of an organizer of communities rather than a hierarchical or democratic decision maker.

Another possibility would be a global market. Markets are certainly powerful and increasingly global in scale, but as we've seen, today's markets rarely account for the costs of carbon emissions, and it seems politically unlikely that all the world's governments will agree to a global market for carbon emissions anytime soon. Of course, it's also theoretically possible that a powerful actor in the global ecosystem (such as a military superpower) might force everyone else in the world to reduce carbon emissions, but this seems even more unlikely (not to mention undesirable for other reasons).

Perhaps the most promising near-term approach uses the only type of supermind left: communities. In this case, we're not talking about people in your neighborhood switching lightbulbs. We're talking about all the governments, businesses, and organizations in the world constituting a kind of global community. None completely controls all the others, but they can certainly influence one another. They generally share certain norms, care what others think of them, and can punish or reward one another with trade agreements, economic sanctions, and wars.

But as we've seen earlier, it is very hard for a community, with its loose consensus decision making, to effectively deal with many aspects of this complex problem. Perhaps there is a way, however. Perhaps we could use the consensus decision making of the global community augmented by much more powerful evaluation capabilities than communities usually have. The basic idea would be to use something like the strategic-planning system we saw in the previous chapter but focused on climate-change strategies for the world.

Here's what such an endeavor might look like, framed in the context of the Paris climate agreement. In signing the Paris Agreement, almost every country in the world specified voluntary goals for emission reductions and other climate-related actions. If a country doesn't meet its goals, it will be subject to disapproval—and perhaps other kinds of pressure—from other countries.

But how do we know that the combination of all the goals countries specified will be enough? It turns out that, according to most scientists who've analyzed the situation, even if all the countries meet their goals from the Paris Agreement, that still won't be nearly enough to avoid the worst risks of climate change.[7] So at a minimum, the attention of the world community needs to be focused on how to achieve even more ambitious goals.

But there's a harder problem. On a worldwide level, it's hard to estimate the overall results of actions taken by different countries. You can't just add up, say, the emission-reduction goals of all the participating countries because the actions of one country may substantially affect what happens in other countries.

It's even harder to do this within a single country. It's far more complicated than just adding up the total emission-reduction effects of actions by state governments, city governments, businesses, other organizations, and individual consumers. There are many opportunities for double-counting emission reductions or ignoring other kinds of interdependencies, so it takes serious quantitative expertise to make credible estimates of the combined effects of many actions within a country. And to really evaluate whether all these proposed actions are realistic, we also need to gauge whether they are feasible in technical, economic, political, and other ways.

Fortunately, as we saw in the previous chapter, there is a way to tackle this kind of complex problem. We could use contest webs, augmented by a network of people and computers with many different kinds of expertise, to evaluate the overall results of the various combinations of proposals. That way, the social pressure and consensus decision making of the world community could be much more precisely targeted toward specific combinations of actions that would be most useful.

Not every country (or organization) in the world would need to participate in this community for it to be effective. Even if only a critical mass of the largest carbon-emitting countries, cities, and businesses participate, that might be enough to make very significant progress.

In fact, as I write this, we are developing a plan to implement something very much like this using Climate CoLab as a foundation and working with many other groups at MIT and elsewhere. By the time you read these pages, our plans may have changed substantially, but this general approach still illustrates a powerful way of thinking about how superminds can solve big problems.

Is this guaranteed to work? Of course not. But our hope is that this approach will help bring together scientists, policy makers, businesspeople, and many others to develop—and gain support for—more effective climate-related actions than anything the world would have done otherwise.

CHAPTER 19

Risks of Artificial Intelligence

Will a robot take your job? Will superintelligent computers someday take over the world? If you've been reading newspapers and magazines in recent years, you may be worried about these things. In this chapter, we'll see how a collective-intelligence perspective can shed some light on these questions and show us that there is probably less to worry about than you might think.

WILL A ROBOT TAKE YOUR JOB?

Since long before the Industrial Revolution, we humans have been inventing machines that do things humans used to do. And for at least the past 200 years, people have worried about these machines taking away human jobs. In the early 1800s, as power looms eliminated jobs previously held by human weavers, industrial activists called Luddites burned factories and destroyed machinery in protest.[1] In the 1960s, as computers eliminated large numbers of clerical jobs in the back offices of banks and insurance companies, President Lyndon Johnson created a National Commission on Technology, Automation, and Economic Progress to study the problem.[2] And in the 2010s, Erik Brynjolfsson and Andrew

McAfee (see page 65) have warned about the risks of artificial intelligence putting many humans out of work, not just in blue-collar and clerical jobs but in white-collar jobs, too.[3]

But people have consistently underestimated the ability of the superminds we call markets to adapt to changes like these. In every past case where technology destroyed jobs, markets eventually created even more new jobs. For instance, in 1900, 41 percent of the US workforce was employed in agriculture. By 2000, it was only 2 percent, since new farm technologies like tractors, cotton pickers, and sprinkler systems allowed a tiny number of farm workers to feed all the rest of us.[4]

I've seen this in my own life. When I was a kid, the farm I grew up on, in New Mexico, employed up to 15 people full-time and another 30 to 40 people seasonally. In the same place today, five people—and lots of machines—farm about three times as many acres of land and produce far more cotton, alfalfa, and other crops per acre. In other words, when machines could produce things more cheaply than people, markets decided to eliminate those human jobs.

But here's the thing: many of the farm-worker jobs of 1900 were replaced by new jobs that those farm workers would never have imagined.[5] If you had told my grandfather in the early 1930s, when he moved to the farm, that someday his grandchildren's friends would have jobs like software developer, website designer, and online community manager, he would not have had any idea what you were even talking about, much less believed you.

Is it possible that this time will be different—that the jobs eliminated by artificial intelligence will never be replaced? Yes, it's at least theoretically possible. But I think the burden of proof is extremely high for anyone who argues that the outcome this time will be different from all the other times technologies have eliminated jobs in the past 200 years. I think it's much more likely that someday our grandchildren, too, will work in jobs that we can barely imagine today.

What will these new jobs look like? Of course, we don't know for sure. But I think we can make some good guesses based on three observations about how market superminds are likely to decide to use human labor to give us what we want:

- *People will do what machines can't.*
- *People will do more of the things that machines make cheaper to do.*
- *People will do things just because we want people to do them.*

People Will Do What Machines Can't

The first—and most common—way of guessing what jobs people will do more of in the future is by looking at what people can do that machines can't. For the foreseeable future, this includes three important capabilities:

- *general intelligence* (not just the various kinds of specialized intelligence that machines will more easily master),
- *interpersonal skills* (beyond the simple ones machines will have), and
- *certain physical skills* (like operating in unpredictable environments).

Even when computers can do some *parts* of today's jobs, other parts will still require some or all of these capabilities.[6] For instance, if machines can do much of the routine legal research that today's law-firm associates do, there will still be a need for human attorneys to manage relationships with clients and make decisions that require general intelligence that computers don't have.

Here are a few more examples of workers whose jobs will require various combinations of human skills for the foreseeable future: physicians, teachers, social workers, investment bankers, plumbers, electricians, carpenters, fitness coaches, and child-care workers. In fact, a study by the McKinsey consulting firm estimates that even though about 50 percent of the *activities* people are paid to do could be automated with current technology, only about 5 percent of today's *occupations* could be fully replaced.[7] Whether this leads to a net increase or decrease in total jobs depends on other factors, as we'll see below.

Interpersonal skills may be even more important than we think. I think one of the most overlooked human capabilities that machines will not fully replace anytime soon is interpersonal skills. This opinion is partly based on the research I described in chapter 2, where we found that the collective intelligence of groups depended as much on the social intelligence of the group members as on their cognitive intelligence. It's also consistent with my own personal observation that the people who succeed in life often seem to be the ones with the most social intelligence, not necessarily the most cognitive intelligence.

Now, computers are certainly making progress with their interpersonal skills. For example, my colleagues Roz Picard and Cynthia Breazeal, at the MIT Media Lab, have done fascinating research on how computers can both detect and influence human emotions.[8] But I suspect that computers are likely to make much faster progress on cognitive tasks than emotional and interpersonal ones.

That means there will be a market opportunity for humans to do the interpersonal things that computers can't. Here's a surprising example that illustrates the point: In 1970, automated teller machines (ATMs) were introduced, and by 2010, there were about 400,000 of them in the United States. You might think that the number of bank-teller jobs in that period would have gone down, but in fact it increased slightly, from 500,000 to 550,000 over the years between 1980 and 2010. Of course, there were other things (like bank deregulation and changes in transaction volume) going on during that period, but one of the most interesting explanations for this result is that bank tellers moved from being the equivalent of checkout clerks who just gave people their money to being salespeople who built relationships with customers.[9]

In other words, ATM technology increased the value of interpersonal skills in bank tellers. I think the same phenomenon is likely to occur for lots of other kinds of workers—such as salespeople, nurses, and party planners—whose interpersonal skills are at least as important as their cognitive ones.

I think it's also likely that lots of new jobs will be created that primarily involve interpersonal skills. In the early 1900s, most people would have found it hard to believe that there would someday be large numbers of full-time jobs like personal trainer, psychotherapist, and online community manager. I'm not sure what the equivalent new social-skill jobs will be in the coming decades, but I think there will be a lot of them.

Home health aides. As a specific example of jobs likely to grow, I am particularly aware of the need for workers who can use their interpersonal skills to help care for elderly people in their homes. While writing this book, I've been responsible for arranging such care for my 90-year-old mother. I can tell you from personal experience that finding people with the right combination of interpersonal skills and general intelligence for this job is not easy and is incredibly important for the health, comfort, and happiness of people we love.

And soon there will be many more of us needing this kind of care. My MIT colleague Paul Osterman estimates that by 2040, there will be a shortage of at least 350,000 paid care providers for the elderly in the United States.[10] Today, in part because of limitations on allowing nonmedical personnel to administer medication and do other medical tasks, this profession is relatively low paying and often doesn't receive the respect it probably deserves. But I suspect that as the need grows, many more of these jobs will be created and that the career path for these workers and their managers will increase in status and level of compensation.

People Will Do More of the Things That Machines Make Cheaper to Do

When the printing press was invented, around 1440, it eliminated the need for human scribes to spend their days laboriously copying books by hand. But since text could then be copied far more cheaply, people wanted much more of it, and that's what markets gave them. By reducing the cost of copying text, the printing press created huge new economic opportunities for writing and distributing books, newspapers, scientific articles, and many other kinds of text. This dramatic expansion of the publishing industry also created vastly more jobs—for authors, editors, typesetters, librarians, and others—than were eliminated for scribes.

In the same way, IT is eliminating part or all of the jobs of some humans whose work can now be done more cheaply by computers. For instance, Google's search service has presumably reduced the amount of time reference librarians spend helping library patrons look up material in card catalogs. But Google's service has also enabled a vast new industry of advertising-supported online search that employs software developers, advertising salespeople, search-engine optimization specialists, and huge numbers of others.

Of course, this doesn't always happen with new technologies. Whether the net effect of a new technology on employment is positive or negative depends on what economists call *elasticities of supply, demand, and substitution* for the different products and services involved. But it seems very likely that IT will continue to enable the creation of at least as many new jobs as it destroys.[11]

For instance, in many of the examples throughout this book, we've seen places where people can specialize in relatively narrow tasks, like generating part of a strategic plan for a company, making a prediction about a geopolitical or business event, or writing a piece of text. I suspect that specialized information-based tasks like these may someday account for a substantial portion of the global workforce.

All these tasks require the ability to do things that computers can't yet do, like conversing naturally with another person or using some other kind of general intelligence. Some of the tasks can be done by anyone who speaks English; others require expertise about topics like business strategy, economics, or political science. Almost all these tasks can be done remotely from anywhere in the world.

Since many of these jobs don't require full-time work for a single customer, many people will do them as independent contractors. In a 1997 *Harvard Business Review* article, my colleague Rob Laubacher and I coined the term *e-lancers*—short for "electronically connected freelancers"—to describe these workers.[12] Today many people use the term *gig economy* to describe essentially the same phenomenon. Many of the tasks so far in the gig economy are physical tasks, like driving for Uber, but almost all of them rely on electronic matching of workers to jobs. And I think cheap communication will create many more opportunities for e-lancers to do whatever work they do best from anywhere in the world.

People Will Do Things Just Because We Want People to Do Them

Sometimes the best way to get insight into a phenomenon is to imagine its most extreme form. So in that spirit, let's imagine that someday machines can do everything humans can do today. Not only that, but the machines can do these things better and more cheaply than humans can.[13] I don't think this is likely anytime soon, but if we ever reach that point, what would happen to the market demand for human workers?

First of all, if everything we buy today could be made much more cheaply in the future, then the cost of living would fall precipitously.

But if people could no longer get jobs doing all the things machines do, where would they get the money to buy even the much cheaper food, clothes, and other essentials?

We'll see some other possibilities later in this chapter, but here's one that seems quite plausible to me: we will pay humans to do some of the things that machines could do more cheaply just because we will want people to do them instead of machines.

Now, this may seem silly to you, but we humans already do lots of things like this today. For instance, we pay to hear live musicians at rock concerts and parties, even though we can easily hear mechanically recorded music of similar or better quality for less money. We pay to see live actors in theaters when we could watch the same production in a movie more cheaply. We pay to watch human athletes, not machines, play football. Even though various kinds of football-playing machines could certainly move the ball down the field better than humans can, there's just something different—and interesting—about watching humans do it.

Might we pay humans to do even more of these kinds of things in the future? I think so. If all our physical needs can be easily and cheaply taken care of by machines, one obvious place to spend our money is on entertainment. And if it's more entertaining for us to watch or interact with other humans than machines, then there will be more jobs for humans in the entertainment industries.

We already pay more for handmade sweaters and furniture than we do for similar products made in factories, not necessarily because they're of higher quality (although they often are) but because it's cool to have something made by the charming young woman you met at the crafts fair. Might we also pay to have humans create art or poetry, even if machines could do so just as well, because there's something special about having a human do it? I think so. Might we pay to send humans to explore other planets even if machines could do it more cheaply? I think so. Might we want human judges to make the final decisions about sentencing criminals instead of letting an algorithm's recommendation be final? I think so.

We also pay a lot for status symbols. For instance, many people I know today buy houses that are far larger than they actually need for their daily lives—not because the extra space is terribly useful but because our community norms of what a respectable house size is have changed, and people have to keep up. So if all the physical things we need become much cheaper, we'll find other kinds of status symbols to compete about.

Maybe, for instance, most businesses will have human receptionists, even if a machine could do the same function more cheaply. Maybe many restaurants will have human servers, not because a human does it better than a robot could but because having a real human is an important sign of a high-quality restaurant.

Of course, it's hard to predict which of these—or other—possibilities will actually become a reality. And if I had a time machine that could show us our true future, you might not believe it any more than my grandfather would have believed the IT-enabled jobs his grandchildren's friends actually have today. But just because we can't imagine it doesn't mean it won't happen.

In any case, for the foreseeable future, many of the goods and services we use will require humans to help produce them, so there will still be work for humans to do. And even if, in the distant future, machines can give us everything we have today more cheaply, markets will probably figure out ways of giving us things we didn't know we wanted, including goods and services produced by humans—just because they're human.

What Happens During the Transition?

So far, we've talked about how markets are very likely to create new jobs to replace the jobs that are eliminated by technology. But it's worth noting that eliminating the old jobs will probably take longer than many people today expect. Even after new technologies are developed in the laboratory, it can take years to commercialize them and often even longer for them to spread through the economy. Amazon, for example, successfully commercialized the technology for online retailing when it launched its first website in 1995, but it took over 20 years for this technology to spread through the economy enough to have a major impact on the number of retail jobs.

The faster old jobs are eliminated, however, the harder the transition will be for people who lose their old jobs but aren't well-suited for the new ones. Even if, in the long run, enough new jobs will be created to employ their children, that doesn't help the workers who lose their jobs today very much. So what can superminds do to help with this?

One obvious possibility is to help people learn to do the new jobs by offering traditional courses in schools and elsewhere. But I think we often underestimate the potential of another approach: learning on the job.

Traditional methods of education require students to be in a classroom, often far away from their actual workplaces, with a bunch of other students and a teacher. But new technologies now make it possible for education to come to you wherever you are. We've seen the beginnings of this already with various forms of online courses, and I think we'll get much better at figuring out how to combine online learning with actual work experience.

For instance, in many of the intellectual e-lancing jobs we saw above (like evaluating strategic options for businesses or predicting geopolitical events), there is often a lot of redundancy built into the system. In some cases, many people compete for the same job; in others, several people's answers are averaged or combined in some other way. This means that, like apprentices, people who are learning to do a job can often contribute value, even if they aren't very good at the beginning.

Who Will Pay?

An obvious question about educating a new workforce is who will pay for the time and educational services people use when learning new jobs. In some cases, workers may be able to finance their educations themselves, but what about when they can't? There are at least two intriguing possibilities, both of which make use of markets.

Investors. One possibility is that investors could pay to retrain workers in return for a share of the workers' future incomes. For instance, Purdue University announced plans to offer its students something called income share agreements (ISAs).[14] Under these agreements, an investor (or a university) could invest, say, $10,000 in a student's college education and in return get 5 percent of the student's income for the first five years after graduation. If the student does well financially, the investor could earn a very good return; if the student can't find work or decides to work in a low-paying career, the investor might lose money. This idea was first proposed by economist Milton Friedman in the 1950s, and it has mostly been discussed in the context of financing college educations. But it also seems like a very promising way that markets could finance programs for unemployed workers to learn the skills they need to find new work, regardless of what life stage they are in at the time.

Worker associations. Another possibility is that associations of workers could pay to retrain their own members. For instance, in work I did with my colleague Rob Laubacher, we suggested that independent contractors (like Uber drivers) could form associations (which we called guilds) to provide many of the benefits that might otherwise come from long-term employers (like training, health care, retirement plans, and a place to socialize).[15] Some of these guilds might be based on occupation (like unions and professional associations), and others on where you went to college or where you live.

A very important benefit the guilds could provide would be a kind of unemployment insurance. In return for a percentage of your income in good times, for instance, your guild could guarantee you a minimum income in bad times. That means it would clearly be in your guild's interest to help you learn new, marketable skills if your old job were eliminated. For instance, if driverless cars took away your job as an Uber driver, your guild might pay for you to learn to participate in online markets where you identify signs of cancer in mammograms or predict voter behavior.

In any case, if your fellow guild members felt that you weren't trying hard enough to learn new skills and find new work, they could do something government unemployment insurance programs never could: they could exert social pressure on you. In other words, the guild, as a community, could help motivate its members to find work using its social norms as leverage.

What Can Governments Do?

So far, we've talked mostly about ways markets can deal with the problems of people whose jobs are eliminated by new technologies. But what if these market mechanisms aren't enough to solve the problem? What can other superminds—like governments—do?

Tax incentives for job creation. As we've seen elsewhere in this book, hierarchical governments can often do things that markets can't do alone, and that's the case here, too. At a simple level, governments could step in and pay for the retraining programs needed by unemployed workers.

But here's a subtler possibility: if a government thinks its citizens would be better off if there were more jobs, then the government can provide financial incentives for businesses to create jobs. For instance, a "new jobs tax credit" was used in the United States in 1977 and 1978 and, according to one study, was responsible for adding 700,000 jobs to the economy.[16] Like putting a price on carbon, this is an example of governments establishing a goal and then letting markets figure out the details of how to achieve it.

Redistribution of income. Perhaps the most extreme way governments can deal with this problem is with direct redistribution of income. Many countries do this already with progressive income taxes and various forms of social benefits (such as welfare payments and subsidized medical care). There could certainly be special programs established to support people who can't recover financially after losing their jobs to automation. Whatever methods are used, it's clear that hierarchical governments can intervene in various ways to solve the job-transition problems that markets don't solve on their own.

If it becomes common for income to be decoupled from employment, then we might, as a society, put more emphasis on other kinds of contributions to our communities. For instance, in chapter 9, we saw how cyber-socialism—an extreme version of this—might use new technologies to track many kinds of contributions people make to their communities—like creating art, providing entertainment, and being a good neighbor—without requiring them to have conventional jobs.

In summary, I'm not as worried as many people are about AI destroying jobs. First, I think that markets will adapt to this much more effectively than most people realize. Second, if markets don't entirely solve the problem themselves, there are lots of ways that governments, communities, and other superminds can intervene to do what markets can't.

WILL SUPERINTELLIGENT COMPUTERS TAKE OVER THE WORLD?

Along with the worries about robots taking away human jobs, it has long been popular to worry about the risks of superintelligent artificial intelligence systems taking over the world. From *R.U.R.: Rossum's*

Universal Robots—the 1920 play that introduced the word *robot* to the English language[17]—to the film *The Terminator* and its sequels, stories of human creations turning against their creators have been a staple of science fiction. Even though these examples are pure fantasy, they have made it very easy for us to imagine this actually happening.

But with recent progress in AI, some very smart people, including Stephen Hawking, Elon Musk, and my MIT colleague Max Tegmark, have begun to believe that the risks of this actually happening are large enough for us to take them seriously. In fact, Hawking, Tegmark, and others have formed the Future of Life Institute to study these and other existential risks to humanity.[18]

One of the most complete and carefully reasoned descriptions of the problem is in the book *Superintelligence*, by Nick Bostrom.[19] Bostrom carefully analyzes various ways that artificially intelligent systems (AIs) could eventually reach human-level intelligence. Even though, as we've seen, this is not likely to happen for decades or perhaps centuries, he observes that once it does happen, these machines will be able to use their intelligence to keep improving themselves. So it's possible that soon after they reach human-level intelligence, they will rapidly become much, much more intelligent. Bostrom concludes that the implications of this are serious enough that we should worry.

First, he observes—correctly—that superintelligent AIs (which we'll call SAIs) could plausibly control vast resources. For instance, computers are already intimately involved in controlling everything from electrical power grids to the world's money-transfer network to home heating systems. With security lapses and help from friendly humans, it's certainly possible that SAIs could gain effective control over many of these resources. In fact, our militaries are already creating semi-intelligent drones and other weapons that could, in principle, be hijacked by SAIs. So it seems clear that SAIs could plausibly have the *means* to take over the world at some point in the (presumably distant) future.

The next question is: Would they have a *motive* to do so? I don't think the common science fiction trope—that robots rebel against their creators because, well, that's what robots do—is all that plausible. Perhaps there's something about human nature that makes it likely for us to rebel against oppressive authority figures, but I don't see any particular reason to think that robots would behave the same way.

However, it's not hard to imagine a single human or a group of humans intentionally designing an SAI as an all-powerful weapon to take over the world on their behalf. Then they might somehow lose control of it, and the nature of its programming as a destructive machine might lead it to continue wreaking havoc, perhaps even killing its own creators as a side effect.

But Bostrom, intriguingly, points out that there are many other scenarios in which computers might *accidentally* destroy the world while pursuing other goals. For instance, in one memorable example, he imagines that someone might program an SAI to make paper clips and, through an oversight in programming, fail to completely specify all the things *not* to do while making paper clips. In this case, a well-intentioned but extremely powerful SAI might end up destroying the earth and all its inhabitants just to get more raw materials with which to make as many paper clips as possible.

How Can We Deal with This Risk?

So it seems there is a plausible risk that SAIs might someday cause great harm to humanity. A key question Bostrom raises, therefore, is: How can we reduce the risk of this happening? And the question for us is: How can a collective-intelligence perspective help us think about this problem? Let's think about the strengths and weaknesses of each type of supermind in preventing an SAI from taking over the world.

First, since the individuals in a pure *ecosystem* have no way of cooperating to control an SAI that becomes more powerful than they are, ecosystems are not a good approach for reducing these risks. Second, even though *communities* could try to reduce the threat of a rogue SAI, their enforcement mechanisms (such as public shaming) are almost certainly too weak to prevent highly motivated—or simply careless—actors from creating harmful SAIs.

Third, *democracies*, like communities, could agree to try to stop SAIs, but their enforcement capabilities are even more limited than those of communities. It certainly wouldn't make sense for citizens to vote individually on each possible decision about how to find individuals perpetrating risky actions and force them to stop. Fourth, even though *markets* could give financial incentives *not* to develop SAIs, this would allow an obvious form of extortion: the closer I get to creating an SAI, the more you would be willing to pay me to stop, so I would have incentives to get as close as possible to creating a dangerous SAI.

That leaves us only one possibility: *hierarchies*. Hierarchies can decide to prevent dangerous AI work, and they have the power to enforce their decisions. But hierarchies have the same problem here that they have in managing an economy: without some kind of oversight, they may serve the narrow interests of whoever is at the top of the hierarchy rather than the broader interests of all members of a society. An obvious solution to that problem is to do what most modern societies do: let a democracy oversee the hierarchy that monitors and regulates AI development.

But that leads to another problem: like climate change, the potential for a dangerous AI is a truly global problem. An SAI could be developed anywhere on the planet and still grow powerful enough to affect us all. If one hierarchical government outlawed or regulated certain kinds of AI activity, then someone who wanted to do that kind of work could just move to a country without such laws or work in international waters, where they aren't subject to any country's laws.

The closest we have now to the kind of global supermind that's needed is the United Nations. But as we saw in the previous chapter, its complex set of voting rules and veto rights limit its power to make and enforce the kind of rules that would be important in controlling an SAI.

But I still don't think there's reason to panic. If we assume (as I do) that we are probably at least decades away from anything approaching human-level AI, it's quite possible that our methods for global governance may have developed sufficiently before we actually need them.

What Can We Do in the Meantime?

In the meantime, I think there are at least three things we can—and should—do. All three will help us prepare for a possible future in which superintelligence presents an immediate threat, and all three will also provide substantial benefit long before then.

Legal responsibility for actions by automated systems. First, I think it would be highly desirable to have greater legal clarity about who is responsible for the actions of automated systems such as personal shopping agents, self-driving cars, and autonomous weapons.[20] Is it the manufacturer of the system? The owner? Or someone else?

For instance, if you own an armed security-guard robot, and if you tell the robot to kill your spouse's lover and the robot does it, should you be guilty of murder? I think so. Or what if your security-guard robot accidentally kills an innocent person it thinks is an intruder? Should you be guilty of murder then? Probably not. But perhaps you should be guilty of something like involuntary manslaughter.

One approach to thinking about these issues would be to use the way current US law deals with liability for the actions of animals.[21] If you own a domesticated animal, like a dog, you are only liable for damages caused by the dog when they result from your own negligence. But if you own a dangerous wild animal, like a tiger, you are liable for whatever the tiger does, even if you haven't been negligent at all.

Should some automated systems (such as armed robots) be treated legally as wild animals and others (such as shopping agents) as domesticated animals? Whatever answers we choose will be helpful in ensuring that our hierarchical legal systems can exercise control over the actions of automated systems long before such systems pose an existential threat to humanity.

Should international attacks by automated systems be war crimes? Even if there are clear lines of legal responsibility for automated systems, attacks that cross national borders are often beyond the reach of customary law-enforcement methods. For example, hackers in North Korea who attack American businesses can't be prosecuted by American law enforcement, and the operators of weaponized American drones that kill people in Pakistan are beyond the reach of the Pakistani judicial system.[22]

Reasonable people can differ about exactly what legal lines to draw in situations like these, but it seems to me that, in at least some cases, automated international attacks should be treated like attacks with biological weapons or other actions we consider war crimes. For instance, autonomous killer drones could someday do huge damage to civilians in foreign countries, just as biological weapons could.

Today, most people in the developed world don't seem too worried about these possibilities. But I suspect these risks will seem much more real to people when attacks from such systems occur in their own countries. And I think that treaties and other forms of international law can provide another useful way to help control dangerous automated systems long before they become existential threats.

Human-computer synthesis. The two measures we've just seen will strongly encourage something that we should certainly do anyway: thinking carefully about how to include human intelligence in systems that are largely automated. Before deploying any automated systems (from credit-approval systems to armed robots), we should think hard about what could go wrong and how human intelligence could help deal with these situations. When we are tempted to develop automated systems that can override human judgment (like safety measures in semiautonomous vehicles), we should carefully consider whether and how humans can override the overrides.

And in all cases, we should think especially hard about how humans can start and stop automated systems and how they determine what the systems' goals should be. Doing all these things will be useful long before there is any chance of SAIs running amok, and it will help keep that from ever happening.

What Does This Leave Out?

There is one type of risk for which we haven't yet considered a solution. If some individual or small group were able to create an SAI in secret much sooner than the community expected, then Bostrom's worst fears might be realized. Is this a theoretical possibility? Yes. But it seems to me that this very theoretical risk is substantially smaller than several other existential threats that humanity faces today, such as nuclear war, pandemics, and climate change.

In general, I think that markets, communities, and other superminds have a good chance of dealing effectively with many of the risks of computers taking away people's jobs or taking over the world. In many ways, the same technologies that create these risks in the first place can also help increase the intelligence of the superminds that need to deal with them.

Part VII

Where Are We Headed?

CHAPTER 20

Hello, Internet, Are You Awake?

Throughout this book, we've seen many examples of how super-minds can be intelligent. But can they be conscious, too?

In the world of biological organisms, the phenomenon we call intelligence and the one we call consciousness are frequently linked. We recognize them both most strongly in our fellow human beings, and if you think of an animal—like your cat or dog—as intelligent, you probably think of that animal as conscious, too. Changes in consciousness also often cause changes in intelligence. If you are fully awake and conscious, you generally act more intelligently than when you are groggy, anesthetized, or asleep.

We also sometimes talk about groups as if they are conscious. For instance, people sometimes say things like, "The stock market was jittery after Monday's sell-off" or "America was traumatized by the attacks of September 11." Are these just anthropomorphic metaphors that make for a dramatic story line? Or could groups like "the stock market" and "America" actually have something like feelings and consciousness in a more literal sense?

To answer questions like these, of course, we need to define what we mean by "consciousness" in the first place. And if intelligence is hard to define, consciousness is even harder. But we'll see in this chapter that we can build a definition of consciousness by drawing on studies of consciousness in the fields of philosophy, psychology, and neuroscience. And we'll see that there are many important senses in which groups can, indeed, be conscious.

WHAT IS CONSCIOUSNESS?

One reason consciousness is so hard to define is that it is inherently subjective. Even though you experience something in your own mind that you call consciousness, you never really know for sure whether other people—much less other kinds of entities in the world— experience the same thing. For all you know, all the other people in the world could be alien robots who simulate the behaviors that make you think they are conscious even though they are actually just going through the motions without really feeling anything at all.

But if we can define consciousness in a more abstract way, we can then ask more interesting questions about whether other kinds of entities can be conscious, too. Unfortunately, there is no general scientific or philosophical consensus about what such an abstract definition of consciousness might be. But there are a number of common themes in the ways scholars have tried to define the concept.[1] Here's a representative list of five of the most common ways of defining consciousness, starting with the ones that are probably easiest to satisfy:

1. *Awareness: an entity is conscious if it reacts to stimuli in the world.* By this definition, an entity is conscious if it acts differently depending on its environment. This is the sense of consciousness we use when we say you regain consciousness when you wake up from sleep or anesthesia. Taken broadly, this definition would allow you to say that all living things are conscious because they react to environmental changes. You could also say that many nonliving

things, such as home burglar alarms that sound whenever there is movement inside your house, are conscious for the same reason.

2. *Self-awareness: an entity is conscious if it reacts to—and can tell others about—changes in itself.* When you are conscious, you are usually aware of how you feel—whether you are hungry, puzzled, or afraid—and you can tell others about that. Depending on how we define the ability to "tell others," many nonhuman entities might qualify as conscious as well. Is your dog self-aware when he wags his tail to show he's happy? Or your cat when she purrs? Is your car conscious if it knows—and can tell you—where it is, how fast it's going, and whether any of its internal components are showing signs of failure?

3. *Goal-directed behavior: an entity is conscious if it takes intentional action to achieve goals.* If you drive to work every day, you probably aren't usually very conscious of your driving. But if there is a big accident on your regular route one morning, you will probably think very consciously about taking a different route to work that day. Depending on how we define "intentional actions," we might also say that lots of other animals are conscious, since they pursue goals like food and sex. And in a trivial sense, you might even say that the thermostat in your house is conscious when it turns your furnace on and off to achieve the goal of keeping your house at 70 degrees.

4. *Integrated information: an entity is conscious if it integrates many kinds of information.* Neuroscientists have found that different parts of your brain specialize in doing different kinds of things—one part interprets visual signals; another moves muscles. But the behaviors we consider conscious usually involve combining information from many parts of the brain simultaneously.[2] If on your morning commute, for example, you see cars pulling over and hear a siren coming toward you, you will probably integrate this new information with things you already know about the world to consciously conclude that an ambulance, police car, or fire engine is coming, and

you will pull your car over, too. Like the other definitions, this one can be interpreted very broadly. For instance, is a blade of grass conscious when it integrates information about sunlight, moisture, and soil nutrients to "decide" how fast to grow? Is a group of Wikipedia editors conscious when it integrates information from all over the world into a single article?

5. *Experience: an entity is conscious if there is something "it is like" to be that entity.* You know very well what it is like to be you, and by extrapolating from your own experience, you probably feel you have some understanding of what it's like to be another person. Maybe you even have an understanding of what it's like to be your dog or cat. But what is it like to be a bat?[3] Or a fish or an ant? Is it "like" anything at all to be a rock, or Beyoncé's shoe, or an iPhone? To the degree that we think an entity has the experience of what it is like to be that thing, we probably feel that thing is conscious.

That last one is perhaps the most difficult of these definitions to apply. Since experience is subjective, it's not clear how we could ever tell whether another entity is having an experience without simply using our imagination or empathy. Explaining how and why any system could have a subjective experience is what the philosopher David Chalmers calls the hard problem of consciousness.[4] It's hard, in part, because it brings up the classic "mind-body problem," which has haunted Western philosophy at least since Descartes said, "I think, therefore I am." Is it your physical brain that is conscious? Or is it some nonphysical entity called a mind? If the two are different, how do they influence each other?

Fortunately, we don't have to solve the mind-body problem in order to make progress on deciding whether groups can be conscious. First we will use what philosophers call a materialist approach. That is, we'll assume it's possible—at least in principle—to understand consciousness scientifically, in terms of physical objects (like neurons) and other measurable physical properties (like electrical currents). In other words, we'll assume that consciousness is something that occurs in the physical world, not something that involves nonmaterial entities like souls and spirits.[5]

We'll also assume that whether we call something conscious or not is a somewhat subjective decision; we can do so fairly confidently in some situations but not in others. In particular, we will say that we can be more confident in calling an entity conscious when it satisfies more than one of the five definitions above, and the more definitions it satisfies, the more confident we can be, especially when the definitions apply in more complex ways.

For instance, when you look at your new baby's face, feel yourself overcome with love, and reach out to hug her, you are exhibiting complex versions of all the above definitions of consciousness: awareness, self-awareness, goal-directed behavior, integrated information, and experience. But when your thermostat senses a temperature change in the baby's room and turns on the furnace, it is exhibiting only the simplest versions of awareness and goal-directed behavior. So even though we could say that in a certain limited sense your thermostat might be conscious, we can be much more confident about saying that you were conscious when you hugged your baby.

Now, with this approach, we can proceed to the core question of the chapter.

CAN GROUPS BE CONSCIOUS?

Let's get one thing out of the way immediately. If you take a materialist perspective, the answer to the question of whether groups can be conscious is almost certainly yes. According to any reasonable definition of consciousness—including all those we've just seen—I think you would agree that *you* are conscious. And, continuing to assume a materialist perspective, you'd say that your consciousness is occurring in some physical place, most probably your brain. You'd also agree that your brain is a group of neurons.

If your own brain is an example of a conscious group of neurons, it follows that at least *some* groups can be conscious. The harder questions involve how confidently we can call different kinds of groups conscious in different kinds of situations. One particularly interesting version of the question is whether groups that include *people* can be conscious.

To explore this question, let's consider a very specific example of a human group: Apple, Inc.

IS APPLE CONSCIOUS?

First, let's define the supermind called Apple as including all the employees of Apple, Inc., along with all the machines, buildings, and other resources the employees use to do their work. Is this group conscious according to the definitions above?

Awareness

Apple certainly reacts to stimuli in the outside world. If you buy a song on iTunes, Apple will make it available for you to download. If you walk into an Apple store, someone will greet you and try to help you buy an Apple product. In 2007, Apple responded to a variety of changes in the markets for mobile phones, computers, and their components by introducing a widely acclaimed new product called the iPhone. In 2011, after Samsung introduced products that Apple believed infringed on its iPhone patents, Apple sued Samsung in various countries around the world.

For some of these actions, like responding to customers entering an Apple store, Apple is only "awake" at certain hours of the day. For others, like responding to iTunes orders, Apple is always awake. All these responses are much more complex than something like a thermostat turning a furnace off and on.

Now, you may be thinking that all these different kinds of responses Apple makes to the world are really the work of individual people (or, in the case of iTunes, computers)—that maybe it's not really Apple that is conscious but just the individual people in it. There are at least two problems with this argument. First, even though individual people are certainly involved in these actions, none could have happened without the rest of the group. Second, and even more important, this line of reasoning would lead you to conclude that your own brain is not really conscious—only the individual neurons in it. I don't think that is a conclusion you would welcome. So at least in the sense of being aware of and responsive to its environment, I think we would have to conclude that Apple is indeed conscious.

Self-Awareness

Apple is certainly aware of many aspects of itself and its corporate identity. From financial statements to market-share data, it constantly monitors many measures of its own performance. Apple executives (especially the late Steve Jobs) have not been shy about sharing Apple's self-image as a company that makes "insanely great" products, and Apple's advertising and public relations efforts are remarkably sophisticated and effective in reporting to the world at least some aspects of how Apple sees itself.

I will probably never forget, for instance, Apple's iconic "1984" Super Bowl commercial, which I showed to the first class I ever taught at MIT, in February 1984. In this commercial, a young female athlete smashes a huge television screen on which a Big Brother–like figure is addressing a crowd of soulless drones. The commercial ends by announcing the Apple Macintosh and saying that this new computer is why the year 1984 won't be like the dystopian novel *1984*. Most people interpreted the commercial as symbolizing how the countercultural ethos of Apple and its new computer would destroy IBM's dominance of the computer industry, and that self-image—the one Apple portrayed to the world—helped propel its growth in the following decades.

Perhaps one of the most sophisticated ways Apple is self-aware is exemplified by Apple University, led by Joel Podolny, former dean of the Yale School of Management. The goal of this secretive internal training facility is to teach Apple managers the company's proprietary way of managing, which Steve Jobs felt was quite different from what is taught in traditional MBA programs. For instance, course work at Apple University includes lessons in how Apple formulated its own retail strategy from scratch and how it took an unusual approach to commissioning factories in China.[6]

Given all these factors, it's clear that in a variety of sophisticated ways, Apple is conscious in the sense of being self-aware.

Goal-Directed Behavior

Like any for-profit corporation, Apple needs to make a profit to survive. It's clear that Apple does many intentional things to achieve this goal and that it has succeeded admirably in doing so.

In fact, Apple is unusual in having another goal beyond merely making a profit: the company strives to make innovative products, not just as a way of making money but also as a goal in itself. Here's how Jonathan Ive, Apple's design chief, summarized this idea: "Steve's talked about the goal of Apple, and the goal of Apple is not to make money but to make really nice products, really great products. That is our goal and as a consequence if they are good, people will buy them and we'll make money."[7]

In fact, not only does Apple *say* it is intentionally pursuing this goal, it has also structured itself in an unusual way that makes this more likely. As Adam Lashinsky reports in his book *Inside Apple*, when

Steve Jobs was CEO, only Jobs himself and the chief financial officer were responsible for the profit-and-loss statement. Other managers were rarely pressed for any kind of financial analysis. In fact, one former marketing executive said, "I can't recall one discussion when the conversation was about dollars or expenses."[8] Instead much of Apple's attention was focused on making innovative products.

So there's lots of evidence to suggest that Apple is conscious in the sense of intentionally trying to achieve goals, both financial and nonfinancial.

Integrated Information

Does Apple integrate information from a variety of sources in anything like the same sense that a conscious human brain does? Absolutely. Just as a human brain integrates many kinds of sensory information and knowledge to make conscious decisions, Apple integrates many kinds of business information—about factors like sales, product development, supplier relationships, and new technologies—to make its decisions.

In fact, Apple does this in a more centrally integrated way than most large companies do. Apple organizes the whole company along functional lines: executives responsible for functions like hardware engineering, software engineering, marketing, retail stores, and operations all report directly to the CEO. In most large companies, there are separate divisions for different products, and the functional managers for each product report to the product-division heads. But in Apple's organizational structure, the only place all the different functional points of view come together is at the very top, which leads to an unusually centralized form of information integration.

And, as Lashinsky reports, much of the company's information integration is accomplished at the weekly executive team meetings, held on Monday mornings. "Because Apple has so few products, the executive team is able to review all of them over the course of two weekly meetings...Teams throughout the company are in a constant state of preparing their boss or their boss's boss to present at an executive-team meeting."[9]

Are the details of how information gets integrated for decision making the same in Apple as they are in your brain? Of course not. The kinds of information that get integrated, the methods of integration, and the amount of information integrated are clearly different. But both your brain and Apple depend on a kind of centralized information integration to function, and thus in this sense, both qualify as conscious.

Experience

At this point, you may be thinking something like, "This is all well and good. I agree that Apple has a number of the same characteristics as conscious humans. But I don't think these characteristics really capture what consciousness means. I know from my own experience what it's like to be conscious, and I just can't believe that Apple—as a whole—is conscious in the same way."

Of course, you're free to have your own intuitions about whether it would be "like" anything at all to be Apple. And, of course, you'll never really know what it's like to be Apple any more than you will really know what it's like to be your mother or your dog or Marilyn Monroe. But just as you can speculate what it would be like to be other people and animals, you can at least speculate about what it might be like to be Apple.

For instance, people can't live without eating food, and if they don't get enough, they feel hungry. Apple can't live without making money, and if it doesn't get enough, perhaps it feels something like hunger, too. In 1997, when Steve Jobs returned to Apple as CEO, for example, Apple had only about 90 days of cash left, and perhaps the company felt something like deep hunger pangs, perhaps even panic, at that point.

But if Apple sometimes feels hunger for profits, I think it probably feels something closer to lust for creating innovative products. Even when the company is well fed with profits, it seems driven by its desire to change the world by spreading its products all over the planet. This seems analogous, in some ways, to an individual human's sex drive.

To speculate even further, I think that if I were Apple, I would have experienced something like deep sadness or pain when Steve Jobs died. Of course, many of the individual people in Apple grieved for the person they had known so well. But maybe Apple itself felt something like the pain and disorientation you might feel if you lost a leg or had a heart transplant.

Of course, we'll never know for sure what it's like to be Apple. But it seems to me pretty shortsighted—and perhaps just plain prejudiced against nonhuman entities—to claim that Apple *couldn't* have some kinds of conscious experiences that are in some ways similar to those we humans have. Thus in this sense, too, Apple may be conscious.

In summary, therefore, the supermind called Apple is certainly aware, self-aware, goal-directed, and integrated in complex—not just trivial—ways. And depending on how empathetic we're willing to be, it seems likely that Apple may even have experiences analogous to the experiences we humans have.

So is Apple conscious? In many important senses, I think we'd have to say yes. Whether these senses capture the essence of what consciousness means to you is something only you can say. But it seems to me that we are justified in saying that Apple is conscious in a way that is closer to being literally true than just metaphorical.

By the way, here's one more piece of evidence: When Apple's CEO, Tim Cook, spoke at MIT's commencement, I told him I was writing a book that included the example you've just read. When I asked him whether he thought Apple was conscious, he considered the question very thoughtfully. Then, over the course of several minutes, he said he thought Apple was an organism like a person with values and goals and that, of course, it was conscious. You may not view this as conclusive evidence, but I think it's a very interesting perspective from someone with a uniquely privileged view of the company.

CAN OTHER TYPES OF SUPERMINDS BE CONSCIOUS?

Is the reasoning we've just been through unique to Apple? Of course not. Apple is an unusual company, but all companies satisfy—in different ways—the same definitions of consciousness that Apple does. And thus we can view them all as entities that are—in important senses—conscious.

And, of course, this doesn't apply just to companies. For instance, the analysis of Apple we've just seen was inspired, in part, by contemporary philosopher Eric Schwitzgebel's fascinating article called "If Materialism Is True, the United States Is Probably Conscious."[10] The article concludes, as we did about Apple, that under a very reasonable set of assumptions, we should regard the United States as being at least as conscious as a rabbit. For instance, the United States is a massive information-processing entity that is goal-directed and self-preserving and that responds to opportunities and threats. As Schwitzgebel picturesquely describes it:

> When Al Qaeda struck New York, the United States responded in a variety of ways, formally and informally, in many branches and levels of government and in the populace as a whole. Saddam Hussein shook his sword and the United States invaded Iraq. The U.S. acts in part through its army, and the army's movements involve perceptual or quasi-perceptual responses to inputs: The army moves around the mountain, doesn't crash into it. Similarly, the spy networks of the CIA detected the location of Osama bin Laden, whom the U.S. then killed. The United States monitors space for asteroids that might threaten

Earth. Is there less information, less coordination, less intelligence than in a hamster? The Pentagon monitors the actions of the Army, and its own actions. The Census Bureau counts us. The State Department announces the U.S. position on foreign affairs. The Congress passes a resolution declaring that we hate tyranny and love apple pie. This is self-representation. Isn't it? The United States is also a social entity, communicating with other entities of its type. It wars against Germany then reconciles then wars again. It threatens and monitors Iran. It cooperates with other nations in threatening and monitoring Iran. As in other linguistic entities, some of its internal states are well known and straightforwardly reportable to others (who just won the Presidential election, the approximate unemployment rate) while others are not (how many foreign spies have infiltrated the CIA, the reason Elvis Presley sells more albums than Ella Fitzgerald).[11]

Of course, there's nothing unique about the United States in this regard. If the United States is conscious in these ways, other countries are, too.

So what are the limits of group consciousness? Is it potentially useful to regard all groups as conscious? To help us think about this, let's consider the different species of superminds: hierarchies, democracies, markets, communities, and ecosystems. How well does each type of supermind meet our five definitions of consciousness?

First, are all these types of superminds *aware* of their environments and responsive to them? It's possible, but not all that easy, to imagine an isolated supermind that, once started, receives no further input from the outside world but produces, say, brilliant mathematical proofs. In practice, however, all the examples of superminds we've seen in this book respond to changes in their environments. Voters in democracies change how they will vote when they hear a candidate speak. If there's a freeze in Florida that destroys all the orange crops, then the market price of orange juice in Minneapolis will probably go up. Since mobile phones have made it easier for teenagers to connect with each other, teenage communities have evolved dating customs that are different from those of their parents, who had to rely on land-line phones to arrange meetings.

Some of these superminds—like the market on the floor of the New York Stock Exchange—only "wake up" at certain times of the day and week. Other superminds—like the ecosystem of hierarchies, markets, and communities in the emergency room of Massachusetts General Hospital, in Boston—never sleep. Either way, essentially all the superminds we see around us are conscious in the sense that they are aware of their environments.

Next, are these different types of superminds *self-aware*? In most cases, the answer is almost certainly yes. For instance, markets often keep track of statistics like price changes, and a market's reactions to rising or falling prices sometimes lead to booms and busts. Democracies usually report the results of voting, and even between official votes, people are often influenced by polls showing how other people say they are planning to vote. An important activity of communities like Rotarians or the Occupy Wall Street protesters is trying to articulate their norms and values. And the Mass General emergency room knows whether it is mostly empty, normally busy, or completely overloaded. In all these cases, I think we would have to agree that these superminds are all aware of themselves.

So are these different types of superminds *intentionally goal-directed*? Here things begin to get a little more complicated. For some superminds, like the business and governmental hierarchies we saw above, the answer is clearly yes, since these groups are pursuing goals that their leaders explicitly articulate. But for others, like some markets and ecosystems, the answer is less clear, because the "goals" they are pursuing may never be articulated by any individual in the supermind itself. Outside observers can evaluate a market, for instance, on how well it is achieving the goal of optimally allocating societal resources. But if none of the market participants ever articulates this goal, then we have to make a subjective judgment about whether the market was *intentionally* goal-directed.

According to the definition of superminds in chapter 1, we have to attribute a goal to a supermind to consider it intelligent in the first place. In the same way, we can also decide whether to view a supermind's actions as *intentional* or not. In this sense of consciousness, therefore, some superminds are conscious, and some probably aren't.

Next we can ask whether these different types of superminds involve *integrated information*. Here I think the answer would be yes in almost all cases. In hierarchies, information is integrated at the top of an organization and usually at many intermediate levels. In democracies, voting integrates information from all participants. In markets, price changes in one part of a market spread to many other places, eventually integrating information throughout the whole market. Communities integrate information by informal consensus decision making and by norms that are shared throughout the community's members. In ecosystems, all the interactions among participants lead to an overall allocation of resources. For instance, the complex ecosystem we call the United States allocates resources like power, money, prestige, and marriage partners among its participants.

Finally, do these different types of superminds *experience* anything? All we can really do to answer this question is try to empathize and speculate. For instance, we saw above what it might be like to be Apple, and you can easily imagine how other hierarchical organizations might have similar feelings. But what might it be like to be some other kind of supermind, like a democracy or a market?

Perhaps, as in human brains, much of the processing goes on at an unconscious level. Maybe a democracy, for instance, has only a vague sense of something happening during an election but isn't consciously aware of much until the votes are counted and a winner is announced. And perhaps a market, like a good athlete, feels its "muscles" operating smoothly as lots of negotiating, buying, and selling take place but is only fully conscious of the final allocation of goods and services. And maybe markets and democracies both feel some kind of drive to satisfy as many people as possible, even though they do this in very different ways.

Another possibility is that superminds consciously experience many more things simultaneously than human brains. Perhaps, for instance, a market is, in some sense, consciously aware of all the negotiations and transactions going on within it at any time. And maybe a market "feels" something like excitement in boom times and something like depression in, well, depressions.

Of course, these are all pure speculations. We will probably never really know what it's like to be a market. Skeptics might argue that these speculations are so unintuitive and so ungrounded in anything observable that it's a waste of time to even contemplate them.

But I think it would be a mistake to dismiss these speculations out of hand. Just because something seems unintuitive at one time doesn't mean it will remain so forever. In fact, many of our most important intellectual advances have involved accepting ideas that once seemed obviously wrong to almost everyone: the earth is round, not flat; the earth moves around the sun, not vice versa; germs—not evil spirits—cause disease.

We've already seen that many groups satisfy many sensible definitions of consciousness. And perhaps someday our cultural notions of consciousness will change in such a way that it becomes common sense to think that many kinds of human groups are actually conscious.

For now, however, one of the most important difficulties with all these philosophical arguments about whether groups can be conscious is that ultimately we are just relying on our own intuitions and imaginations. As philosopher Bryce Huebner writes: "It is hard to imagine that collectivities can be conscious; but it is just as hard to imagine that a mass of neurons, skin, blood, bones, and chemicals can be...conscious."[12] Lots of things in science—like quantum mechanics—are hard to imagine, but that doesn't mean they're false.

In many branches of science, we long ago stopped needing to rely on purely subjective, intuitive assessments of things like weight and temperature. Instead we developed systematic, objective ways of measuring these things. And, as we saw in chapter 2, the same thing happened with intelligence about 100 years ago, when we developed systematic ways of measuring it.

What if we could do something similar for consciousness? What if there were objective ways of measuring consciousness that corresponded to our intuitive sense of consciousness in the most typical cases (such as when a person is awake or asleep) and also gave us a systematic way of measuring the consciousness of other entities (such as groups of people) when our intuitions were less clear?

CAN WE MEASURE GROUP CONSCIOUSNESS?

There is not yet any broad scientific consensus about how to systematically measure consciousness, but there have been some very intriguing attempts. Probably the best known and best developed such attempts have been made by the neuroscientist Giulio Tononi and his colleagues. They call their theory of consciousness integrated information theory.[13]

What Is Integrated Information?

Underlying this approach is the idea that consciousness isn't just something you either have or don't. Instead Tononi considers consciousness a property that a system can have in varying degrees. This approach, therefore, is like the scientific approach we use today for measuring temperature. According to our everyday, intuitive experience, some things are hot, some are cold, and some are in between. But after centuries of scientific progress, scientists now say that physical objects have varying amounts of heat, and even the coldest things we encounter still have some relatively small amount of heat.[14]

In a similar way, the integrated information theory of consciousness says that different systems can have different degrees of consciousness. And even though it's possible for a system to have no consciousness at all, many systems that we might intuitively think of as not conscious (like a thermostat) could still have some small level of consciousness.

The core claim of integrated information theory is that consciousness is associated with something called *integrated information* (represented by phi, the Greek letter Φ). Tononi and others have developed detailed mathematical techniques for measuring integrated information, but loosely speaking, it is the amount of information a whole system generates that is more than just the sum of what its parts generate. The mathematical definitions of integrated information calculate this by splitting the system into subparts and then calculating how much information is generated when considering the system as a whole but not when looking at the subparts separately.

For instance, a black-and-white digital camera with a million dots (pixels) can generate a million "bits" of information, or $2^{1,000,000}$ possible pictures from the combination of all the dots. But each of those pixels is independent of the others, so the total information in the camera's image sensor is just the sum of the information in all the different pixels. The camera has no *integrated* information at all.

But the moment you look at the camera's viewfinder and see that it is showing a beautiful sunset on a beach, you have created some new information that required you to integrate information from throughout the whole image. In doing this, you have created some integrated information, and the system that includes both you and the camera has more integrated information than just the camera alone.

In fact, Tononi and his colleagues would say that your conscious perception of *anything* generates integrated information. For instance, when you consciously perceive a red triangle, you don't see "a triangle but no red, plus a red patch but no triangle." Instead you have a single, integrated experience that includes both color and shape.[15]

In general, for a system to have a great deal of consciousness—in the sense of integrated information—it must have many parts that can be in different states. For instance, a brain with many neurons, each of which could be active or not, can generate much more information than a brain with only one neuron. In addition, the states of some parts need to depend, in complex ways, on the states of others. For example, if a brain is divided into different regions, and the neurons in each region only affect others in the same region, then the brain produces less *integrated* information than one in which neurons affect others all over the brain.

There is still considerable debate among researchers about whether integrated information actually measures consciousness,[16] but that interpretation is consistent with a number of observations about the neuroscience of human brains. For example, in one set of experiments, scientists magnetically stimulated the brains of healthy, conscious people as well as those of people who were unconscious because they were asleep, anesthetized, or brain-damaged. When the brains of conscious people were stimulated, they responded with complex patterns of neural activity that were both widespread across the brain (integrated) and highly variable (informationally complex). But when the brains of unconscious people were stimulated, their neural responses were either very local to one part of the brain (not integrated) or very simple (not informationally complex).[17]

Can We Measure the Integrated Information of a Group?

So what would happen if we were to actually measure integrated information, or phi, for human groups? Would the measures of phi correspond to anything that is intuitively related to consciousness? To answer these questions, my former postdoctoral associate David Engel and I studied three kinds of groups: (1) the four-person work groups whose collective intelligence we measured in chapter 2, (2) ad hoc groups of up to 150 people who edited Wikipedia articles together, and (3) a sample from more than one million people and computers communicating via the Internet over a six-year period.[18]

The definition of phi was originally formulated to analyze groups of neurons, each of which is sometimes active (sending an electrical signal) and sometimes not. So to analyze our groups, we simply measured, at each point in time, whether or not each individual in the group was active—sending a message or talking. Then we used this information to calculate a value of phi for each group. What we found was consistent with the idea that phi was a measure of something like the consciousness of the groups.

In humans, when people are more wide awake and alert—that is, more conscious—they generally perform better on many kinds of tasks than when they're not. We found the same thing with our first two kinds of groups. The laboratory work groups with higher measured phi were more collectively intelligent, on average, than those with lower measured phi. They performed better on the wide range of tasks used in our collective-intelligence tests. And the groups of Wikipedia editors with higher measured phi also produced higher-quality articles.

In the third kind of groups—people and computers communicating over the Internet—we didn't have a specific measure of performance. But you might expect that the Internet would become more conscious as it grows larger and more complex over time. And that is exactly what we found: the measured value of phi for the Internet grew significantly over the six-year period we studied, from 2008 to 2014.

In other words, this data is consistent with the idea that the group of people and computers communicating via the Internet may be "waking up," becoming more conscious over time. We'll talk more in the following chapter about what this might mean, but for now, it's interesting to observe that even though many people have speculated about this possibility for years,[19] this is the first detailed data of which I am aware that provides a kind of scientific support for the speculation that the Internet might be waking up.

Do these results *prove* that the Internet and other human groups can be conscious? Of course not. As we've seen throughout this chapter, that is ultimately a philosophical question that depends on how you define consciousness in the first place. But these results do lend more credibility to the idea that the concept of consciousness could be sensibly applied to groups that include humans.

Does this mean you have to agree that groups are conscious in order to understand and take advantage of the kinds of collective intelligence we've discussed throughout this book? No, you don't. But especially as new information technologies allow us to build more and more intelligent combinations of people and computers, I think it will become more and more useful to think of many kinds of superminds as conscious, too.

CHAPTER 21

The Global Mind

In Robert Wright's fascinating book *Nonzero*, he describes what he calls the "logic of human destiny."[1] He shows how, at every stage of human development, there has been a tendency—not an absolute law, but a general tendency—for humans to form larger and larger groups that lead to a net improvement in human welfare. In a sense, Wright's logic of human destiny is a profound example of the principle of evolutionary utilitarianism in action: societal evolution moves in the direction of the greatest good for the greatest number. We've seen this pattern over and over, from the hunting-and-gathering communities of the first humans to the kingdoms of the agrarian world to the vast global markets of today.

Each time these transitions occurred, new technologies enabled larger groups of people to communicate with each other more easily. As we've seen throughout this book, today's communication technologies have already enabled far more connectivity than we have figured out how to use. And as these technologies continue to improve, it seems very likely that there will be many more opportunities for realizing benefits from ever larger scales of organization using all the different types of superminds we've seen.

It's not absolutely inevitable that this will happen. A global catastrophe such as a pandemic, a nuclear war, or massive disruptions from climate change could certainly delay or prevent such progress. And even if there isn't a catastrophe, humans don't always make progress in straight lines. For instance, even though there has been a general trend toward more democratic government over the past two millennia, there have been plenty of ups and downs along the way. Democracies were probably invented in ancient Greece about 2,500 years ago, but they weren't widely used until after the American and French Revolutions many centuries later. Democratic governments are sometimes overthrown by dictators, and in some cases—such as with Hitler in Germany—democracies elect leaders who later become dictators.[2]

But in the long run, as Robert Wright says, there is "a direction, an arrow…in human history" in which technologies arise that enable "new, richer forms of non-zero-sum interaction"—that is, interactions in which all participants are better off from having interacted.[3] I am persuaded by Wright's argument, and I think it is very likely that we will continue to see movement toward what you might think of as the end point of this process: global-scale integration of all the people, computers, and other forms of intelligence on our planet.

A good name for this vast global supermind is the global mind. Other writers, like Peter Russell and Howard Bloom, have called it the global brain.[4] Pierre Teilhard de Chardin, the renegade Catholic paleontologist and philosopher, called it the noosphere. He used this term, analogous to the word *biosphere*, to mean the global web of minds all over the planet, and he viewed the emergence of this "mind sphere" as the end point of evolution on earth.[5]

To many people, phrases like *global mind* and *global brain* sound like science fiction or maybe vague mysticism. But if we define the global mind simply as the combination of all the forms of intelligence on our planet, then by definition it exists whenever there is any intelligence at all on the planet.

Thus in a certain sense, the global mind existed at least 3.5 billion years ago, when colonies of bacteria developed a kind of intelligent division of labor among their different cells. Some cells specialized in photosynthesis, storing the sun's energy in complex molecules, while others specialized in consuming the potentially poisonous wastes that resulted from this process.[6] Later, the global mind grew as colonies of ants, schools of fish, and packs of wolves created their own forms of social organization. And the global mind became increasingly visible as humans developed language, writing, and advanced forms of social organization, including all the different types of superminds we've discussed in this book.

HOW WILL THE GLOBAL MIND CHANGE WITH NEW INFORMATION TECHNOLOGIES?

For most of its existence, the global mind operated so slowly and with such weak connections among its many parts that we could be forgiven for not noticing it was there at all. But starting about 200 years ago, with the invention of the telegraph and continuing with the radio, telephone, television, and Internet, the global mind has become far more connected than ever before. The number, speed, and capacity of connections in the global mind has exploded in the last two centuries.

This hyperconnectivity is making the global mind harder and harder to ignore. When terrorists attacked a restaurant in Paris, people all over the planet reacted to it almost instantly. When the United States elected a new president, it immediately affected the prices of stocks and currencies around the world. If a medical researcher in Boston discovers a new treatment for lung cancer, it will soon affect physicians and patients everywhere else in the world, too.

The global mind is also growing dramatically larger every decade. Not only is the human population of the planet increasing, the computer population is, too. Of course, none of these individual computers has the general intelligence that a human does. But just as individual neurons in a human brain—which aren't very intelligent by themselves—contribute to the overall intelligence of the brain, so, too, will these individual computers contribute to the overall intelligence of the global mind. As we've seen throughout this book, the combination of all the people and computers in the global mind will be increasingly effective at solving problems in business, government, science, and society in ways that would have been unimaginable even a few decades ago.

DOES THE GLOBAL MIND REALLY EXIST?

The global mind isn't something that either exists or doesn't. Instead, like collective intelligence and superminds, it is a *perspective*—a way of looking at the world. If you choose to look at the world this way, then the global mind exists by definition. And as more and more intelligent individuals become more and more closely connected, this perspective will become more and more useful.

Of course, you don't have to look at the world this way—it's possible to understand the world by separately analyzing the individual parts of the global mind. But if you don't focus on the big picture, you'll find it increasingly hard to understand some of the most important things that are happening.

To see why, think about this analogy: You could, in principle, explain why I choose to eat vanilla ice cream instead of mocha by describing a complex sequence of chemical and electrical processes involving neurons in my brain. But for most purposes, it would be much simpler and more useful to just say that I like vanilla and not mocha.

In the same way, you could explain the rate at which semiconductor technologies have developed over the last few decades by describing a detailed set of processes involving scientific discoveries, engineering prototypes, and commercial products. But it would be much more useful to use a simpler, higher-level explanation. For instance, you could refer to Moore's law, which says that the cost performance of integrated circuit technology doubles roughly every 18 months. Even though Moore's law is not a law of nature, it has been a surprisingly accurate description of the combined actions of all the scientific communities, corporate hierarchies, and technology markets involved in the worldwide ecosystem of the semiconductor industry. Thus, in a very real sense, Moore's law describes the actions of the global mind as a whole, not just the elements it contains.

In general, whether you are analyzing how the world addresses climate change, how it feeds its people, or how it decides what movies to watch, you need to take into account complex worldwide interactions among governments, businesses, markets, democracies, and many other groups all over the planet. In other words, no matter what you call it, what you are really analyzing is the global supermind.

WHAT DOES THE GLOBAL MIND WANT?

As we've seen throughout this book, there are many ways in which the global mind can get smarter. But if being smart means being effective at achieving goals, what are the global mind's goals? What does the global mind "want"?

The global mind is an ecosystem, so it wants whatever the most powerful actors in the ecosystem want. As we've seen, the most powerful actors on our planet today are mostly groups of humans organized in superminds, such as governments, businesses, markets, democracies, and communities. All these superminds want to survive and reproduce. To do that, as we saw in chapter 10, they usually need to provide their members with whatever *they* want. And who are the members of these superminds? We are, of course.

If what we really want are more gas-guzzling cars, iPhones, and entertaining videos, that's what the global mind will do its best to give us. Or if what we really want is richer and more satisfying relationships with our families and friends, then the global mind will try to give us that, too.

At one level, we might say that all human desires are equally valid, and the global mind doesn't take sides about what we should or should not want. But many people would say that it's better to want some things than others—perhaps even that it's *wiser* to want some things than others.

WHAT WOULD A WISE GLOBAL MIND WANT?

You could say that to be *intelligent* you need to be good at getting whatever it is you want. But to be *wise*, you also need to want the right things. So if we want our global mind to be wise, what are the right things for it to want? Of course, philosophers and others have discussed versions of this question for millennia, and there are many ways of answering the question. But there are two that are particularly relevant for our purposes here.

The Greatest Good for the Greatest Number

One answer comes from the utilitarian philosophers. As we saw earlier, according to utilitarianism, the right thing for a supermind (or any mind) to want is whatever provides the greatest good for the greatest number of people.[7] This is still a popular view in the modern world, and it is consistent with how economists analyze the ways resources are allocated in societies. It also seems sensible to say that a wise global mind would make choices to provide the greatest good to the greatest number of people.

But even this straightforward-seeming approach leaves many questions unanswered. What is "good" in the first place? Is it just individual happiness or something "deeper"? Who decides what's good? How do we balance something that is really good for one person and only a little bit bad for several others?

Perhaps an even more basic question is: How should we determine whose interests count when determining the greater good? In most modern societies, for instance, we usually say we believe that all humans count, but there are still some disagreements. For example, when does an unborn embryo count as a human?

Just as it's clear today that previous societies were wrong to believe that slaves didn't count as humans, some would argue that our current conceptions of who counts are still too narrow. For instance, there's an increasing feeling that we are unconscionably cruel to many animals, and perhaps a wise global mind should consider the welfare of animals, too. Courts in India, New Zealand, and Ecuador have even recognized the legal rights of personhood for glaciers, rivers, and entire ecosystems.[8]

Others might say that computers will someday be intelligent enough—and conscious enough—that their welfare should also be considered by a wise global mind. And, as we have seen in this book, superminds have a kind of intelligence and perhaps even a kind of consciousness. Maybe their welfare should be considered, too.

I'm not yet ready to argue that the welfare of animals, nature, computers, and superminds should always count in determining what wise choices are. But I find these possibilities plausible and intriguing.

In any case, all superminds need to make these kinds of choices, even if the choices are somewhat arbitrary. But there is another way of thinking about wise choices that has particular resonance for the global mind. Perhaps a wise global mind shouldn't just serve the desires of its own members; perhaps it should serve some larger purpose.

Serving a Purpose Larger Than Yourself

As writers like Abraham Maslow, Viktor Frankl, and many others have observed, people often have a kind of hunger for meaning in their lives. One common way for people to find that meaning is by helping to achieve some purpose larger than themselves. Some version of this theme is essentially universal in all major religious and spiritual traditions,[9] and it can just as easily be secular. Take John F. Kennedy's famous quotation "Ask not what your country can do for you; ask what you can do for your country."

Of course, different people have different ideas about what larger goals are worth pursuing. For some, worthy goals might include advancing our scientific understanding of the universe or enriching the body of artistic responses to the human condition. Others might focus on doing God's will or promoting social justice. For still others, larger goals might be saving lives with medicine, defending innocent people from military attack, or helping friends and neighbors in need.

In the face of many plausible higher-level goals, one of the most important challenges for a wise global mind is figuring out how to choose which goals to pursue. In a sense, of course, the overall choices the global mind makes will be determined by the individual choices of some (or all) of its members. So perhaps the most important way we as individuals can help the global mind make wise choices is to make wise choices ourselves.

But how can we do that? Many of us feel like we already have some kind of moral intuition that helps us make wise choices.[10] But intriguing suggestions about how to develop a better moral intuition also come—in different forms—from many spiritual traditions.

My favorite summary of the surprising commonalities among all the world's major religious and spiritual teachings comes from Aldous Huxley's book *The Perennial Philosophy*.[11] To paraphrase Huxley: To be able to sense what is right—or wise—to do in a given situation, we need to develop ourselves. We need to become less attached to our own personal desires and our own egos. There are many ways to do this—some that involve organized religious traditions and others that don't. But when we are able to detach from our own desires, we become better able to sense what the situation calls for and what would be the right and wise thing to do.

For instance, the British philosopher Alan Watts, in interpreting Eastern philosophy for Western audiences, said that "the prevalent sensation of oneself as a separate ego, enclosed in a bag of skin, is a hallucination."[12] In other words, we—especially in the West—usually view the world as if we are separate individuals when in reality we are all inextricable parts of a much larger whole. For example, some people are deeply inspired by the idea that we are all part of the global ecosystem (sometimes called Gaia) and that caring for our planetary environment is a wise and important thing for us to do.

The Sufi teacher Idries Shah, quoting another Sufi teacher, says, "What we have to do is detach from both intellect and emotion… [T]here is a level below this, which is a single, small, but vital one…This true intellect is the organ of comprehension, existing in every human being."[13] In other words, we may never be able to figure out what is the wise thing to do by using only our intellect and emotions. Instead we need to develop, through proper practice and experience, a deeper, intuitive sense of what is right.

Mindfulness meditation techniques, which have become popular in many secular communities, like Silicon Valley high-tech firms, involve methods for observing one's own thoughts and feelings much more systematically and objectively than we usually do. Practitioners of these techniques report that they are often better able to detach from the emotions and fixed mental models that prevent them from accurately seeing the larger contexts in which they are operating.

In any case, if we—as individuals—develop our own abilities to wisely influence the superminds to which we belong, it seems quite plausible that a wise global mind could undertake ambitious goals that go far beyond our personal desires. For instance, it seems to me that exploring space, advancing science and art, developing intelligent machines, and exploring new forms of collective human consciousness could all be worthy goals for a wise global mind.

It also seems plausible that many individuals within the global mind will derive a vital sense of meaning in their lives from pursuing such worthy goals and harmonizing with the superminds that make them possible. In fact, it even seems plausible that new human religions will emerge that attribute some form of ultimate value to endeavors like these.

WILL WE EVER REALLY UNDERSTAND THE GLOBAL MIND?

A single neuron in a brain can't begin to "understand" how the whole brain works. A single ant in a colony can't really understand how the colony searches for food. But humans have enough intelligence as individuals that we are often able to understand quite a bit about how the superminds to which we belong work. If that weren't true, I wouldn't have been able to write this book, and you wouldn't have been able to understand it.

But as superminds get larger and more complex, it becomes harder and harder for individuals to really understand the problems a supermind faces and the choices it makes. For instance, even in a large hierarchical company like Apple—where you can ask key decision makers why they made choices like what size screens to use in the new iPhones—it may be hard to figure out exactly why a specific decision was made. And in large markets, democracies, or ecosystems, where the key decisions result from interactions among vast numbers of individuals, it can be harder still to understand why these choices are made.

Why, for instance, did Donald Trump win the US presidential election in 2016? Of course, we can come up with theories. By the time you read this book, there may be one or two simple theories that most people accept as "explanations" for the result. But those theories will, necessarily, be simplifications of a much more complex reality.

How, then, can we ever hope to really understand the choices that the global mind makes today? How will our descendants ever understand the "universal mind" that may someday arise when they settle other planets or interact with extraterrestrial life forms?

The answer is that, just as a one-year-old human can't really understand quantum physics, individual humans will probably never be able to truly understand superminds at high levels of complexity. We may be able to have simplified theories that help us understand them to some degree. And if our natural biological intelligence is augmented by enough computational or other enhancements, we may be able to understand much more. But then we will essentially become more complex superminds ourselves.

In the meantime, however, we will have to make do with a partial understanding of all the complex superminds around us. If you are a scientific materialist, you may say that understanding all this complexity is a good goal for our future science. If you are spiritually inclined, you may think of this complexity as God's will or Fate and try to harmonize your own actions with it.

In any case, I think it's hard not to be impressed—even inspired—by the possibilities ahead as we humans build ever richer connections among ourselves and the computer technologies we have created.

Will our global mind someday conceive and carry out vast projects that engage huge numbers of humans and that would be hard for us to even imagine today? Almost certainly.

Will our computational descendants someday—probably many decades from now—supersede the biological humans who created them? Perhaps.

Will our global mind make choices that are not just smart but also wise? I very much hope so.

Is developing such a global mind our destiny? I think it is.

Acknowledgments

Many people contributed to the writing of this book. I would especially like to thank my editor, Tracy Behar, whose experience, intelligence, and very detailed comments helped make this book much better than it would otherwise have been. I would also like to thank my agent, John Brockman, who saw the potential for this book before I did and encouraged me to write it.

And I am very grateful to the friends and colleagues who commented on earlier versions of the manuscript. Bob Gibbons provided extensive comments on the comparisons of different species of superminds in chapter 11; Randy Davis gave me detailed comments on technical (and many other) issues in numerous chapters; and all of the following provided other useful comments: Rob Laubacher, Patrick Winston, Erik Duhaime, Jeff Cooper, Ian Straus, Vint Cerf, Judy Olson, Mel Blake, Mark Klein, Anita Woolley, David Engel, and Laur Fisher.

I am also grateful to four people whose work influenced this book more than is reflected in citations alone. First, Douglas Engelbart (1925–2013), who invented the computer mouse and did other pioneering work on interactive computing environments, is perhaps more than any other single person responsible for the idea that groups of people and computers—together—can be more intelligent than either can alone. Second, I was very inspired by the history of life on earth and the provocative speculations about its future in Robert Wright's book *Nonzero*. While my arguments here are different from his, I might never have attempted this work without his example. Third, the argument in the introduction that the intelligence of human groups—not individual humans—led to human success is based largely on the insights in Yuval Harari's book *Sapiens*. And finally, the insight that collective intelligence isn't just a property of a group but also a kind of group that has this property was crystallized for me in a conversation with Benjamin Kuipers in 2011. I asked Ben to write about that idea so I could cite him. He did, I did (in chapters 1 and 10), and eventually I realized that a good name for these groups would be...superminds.

I would also like to thank computer industry analyst and investor Esther Dyson and science fiction writer Vernor Vinge for a remarkable dinner in 2005. In a sense, they are responsible for this book because, by the end of that dinner, I had the feeling not that I had *decided* what my next main research topic would be, but that I had finally *admitted to myself* something I had already known unconsciously: that my next research topic would be what I now call "superminds."

The work reported here has been supported by a number of sponsors over the years, including the US National Science Foundation (grant numbers IIS-0963285, ACI-1322254, IIS-0963451, IIS-1442887, IIS-1144663, IIS-0968321, IIS-1047567, IIS-1302522, IIS-1211084, IIS-1422066, CCF-1442887, and CCF-1442840), the US Army Research Office (grant numbers 56692-MA, 64079-NS, W911NF-15-1-0577, and W911NF-13-1-0422), the Swiss National Science Foundation (project 200021-143411), the V. Kann Rasmussen Foundation, the Argosy Foundation, the MIT Sloan School of Management, the MIT Solve Initiative, the MIT Sustainability Initiative, the MIT Energy Initiative, and Cisco Systems, Inc., as well as other sponsors of the MIT Center for Collective Intelligence.

I also want to thank the two very able administrative assistants who helped me in many ways during the writing of this book: Liz McFall and Richard Hill (with special thanks to Liz for formatting the references!).

And most important, I want to thank my wife, Joan, for supporting me during the many times while writing this book that it must have seemed to her I was almost married to the book!

Notes

PREFACE

1. *Collins English Dictionary*, s.v. "supermind," accessed April 30, 2017, https://www.collinsdictionary.com/us/dictionary/english/supermind.

INTRODUCTION

1. Timothy Gowers and Michael Nielsen, "Massively Collaborative Mathematics," *Nature* 461, no. 7266 (2009): 879–81, doi:10.1038/461879a; Justin Cranshaw and Aniket Kittur, "The Polymath Project: Lessons from a Successful Online Collaboration in Mathematics," in *Proceedings of the SIGCHI Conference on Human Factors in Computing Systems* (New York: Association for Computing Machinery, 2011), 1,865–74, doi:10.1145/1978942.1979213.
2. Timothy Gowers, "Is Massively Collaborative Mathematics Possible?" *Gowers's Weblog*, January 27, 2009, http://gowers.wordpress.com/2009/01/27/is-massively-collaborative-mathematics-possible/.
3. D. H. J. Polymath, "Density Hales-Jewett and Moser Numbers," preprint, submitted February 2, 2010, https://arxiv.org/abs/1002.0374; D. H. J. Polymath, "A New Proof of the Density Hales-Jewett Theorem," preprint, submitted October 20, 2009, https://arxiv.org/abs/0910.3926.
4. Cranshaw and Kittur, "The Polymath Project."
5. Yuval Noah Harari, *Sapiens: A Brief History of Humankind* (New York: HarperCollins, 2015), 11.
6. The dimension on which humans excel is called the *encephalization quotient*. See M. D. Lieberman, *Social: Why Our Brains Are Wired to Connect* (New York: Crown, 2013), 29; Gerhard Roth and Ursula Dicke, "Evolution of the Brain and Intelligence," *Trends in Cognitive Sciences* 9, no. 5 (2005): 250–57, http://dx.doi.org/10.1016/j.tics.2005.03.005; Robin I. M. Dunbar, "Neocortex Size as a Constraint on Group Size in Primates," *Journal of Human Evolution* 22, no. 6 (1992): 469–93, doi:10.1016/0047-2484(92)90081-J; Robin I. M. Dunbar, "Coevolution of Neocortical Size, Group Size and Language in Humans," *Behavioral and Brain Sciences* 16, no. 4 (1993): 681–94, https://doi.org/10.1017/S0140525X00032325; Robin I. M. Dunbar, *Grooming, Gossip, and the Evolution of Language* (Cambridge, MA: Harvard University Press, 1998); Robin I. M.

Dunbar and Susanne Shultz, "Evolution in the Social Brain," *Science* 317, no. 5,843 (2007): 1,344–47, doi:10.1126/science.1145463.

7. Dunbar, "Neocortex Size as a Constraint."

8. Dunbar, *Grooming, Gossip, and the Evolution of Language*, 17–18.

    Dunbar gives several examples of primates acting in groups to defend against predators. But if you are a stickler for the historical plausibility of hypothetical examples, you may be wondering whether lions and mangoes ever existed together in ancient times as I posited here. The answer is: they probably did. Lions were common in Africa, and so were African mangoes. See Wikipedia, s.v. "lion," accessed February 11, 2018, https://en.wikipedia.org/wiki/Lion; "Historic vs Present Geographical Distribution of Lions," *Brilliant Maps*, April 26, 2016, http://brilliantmaps.com/distribution-of-lions/; Wikipedia, s.v. "Irvingia gabonensis," accessed February 11, 2018, https://en.wikipedia.org/wiki/Irvingia_gabonensis.

    It is less likely that lions would have been in a rainforest, since they typically inhabit grasslands and savannas. But perhaps the imaginary scenarios described here took place near the edge of a rainforest or involved unusual lions who liked rainforests. See Wikipedia, s.v. "lion"; Jeremy Hance, "King of the Jungle: Lions Discovered in Rainforests," *Mongabay*, August 13, 2012, https://news.mongabay.com/2012/08/king-of-the-jungle-lions-discovered-in-rainforests/.

9. Harari, *Sapiens*, 36.

10. Ibid., 20–21.

11. Large animals are defined as species weighing 100 pounds or more. See detailed reference in Harari, *Sapiens*, 65n2.

    Recent research suggests that humans may have been in Australia for 5,000 to 18,000 years before the megafauna went extinct, but humans are still prime suspects in their death. See Nicholas St. Fleur, "Humans First Arrived in Australia 65,000 Years Ago, Study Suggests," *New York Times*, July 19, 2017, https://www.nytimes.com/2017/07/19/science/humans-reached-australia-aboriginal-65000-years.html.

12. For population estimates used here and in the rest of this section, see Max Rosner and Esteban Ortiz-Ospina, "World Population Growth," *Our World in Data*, April 2017, https://ourworldindata.org/world-population-growth/.

13. Lingling Wei, "China's Response to Stock Rout Exposes Regulatory Disarray," *Wall Street Journal*, August 4, 2015, http://www.wsj.com/articles/chinas-response-to-stock-rout-exposes-regulatory-disarray-1438670061; Keith Bradsher and Chris Buckley, "China's Market Rout Is a Double Threat," *New York Times*, July 5, 2015, http://www.nytimes.com/2015/07/06/business/international/chinas-market-rout-is-a-double-threat.html.

14. Peter Russell, *The Global Brain: Speculations on the Evolutionary Leap to Planetary Consciousness* (Los Angeles: J. P. Tarcher, 1983); Howard Bloom, *Global Brain: The Evolution of Mass Mind from the Big Bang to the 21st Century* (New York: Wiley, 2000); Abraham Bernstein, Mark Klein, and Thomas W. Malone, "Programming the Global Brain," *Communications of the ACM* 55, no. 5 (May 2012): 41–43, doi:10.1145/2160718.2160731.

CHAPTER 1

1. Kenneth J. Arrow and Gérard Debreu, "Existence of an Equilibrium for a Competitive Economy," *Econometrica* 22, no. 3 (1954): 265–90, doi:10.2307/1907353.
2. The basic concept of supermind used here is a generalization of the concept of "corporate entity" as defined by Benjamin Kuipers in "An Existing, Ecologically-Successful Genus of Collectively Intelligent Artificial Creatures," presented at the Collective Intelligence Conference, MIT, Cambridge, MA, April 2012, https://arxiv.org/pdf/1204.4116.pdf.

     The detailed definition of a supermind is based on the definition of collective intelligence in Thomas W. Malone and Michael S. Bernstein, *Handbook of Collective Intelligence* (Cambridge, MA: MIT Press, 2015), 1–13.

     Of course, this is not the only way to define collective intelligence, and many authors have defined it in other ways. A sample of other definitions and a history of how the term has been used previously is also included in Malone and Bernstein, *Handbook*, 10.

     Starr Roxanne Hiltz and Murray Turoff, for example, define collective intelligence as "a collective decision capability [that is] at least as good as or better than any single member of the group." See Hiltz and Turoff, *The Network Nation: Human Communication via Computer* (Reading, MA: Addison-Wesley, 1978).

     John B. Smith defines it as "a group of human beings [carrying] out a task as if the group, itself, were a coherent, intelligent organism working with one mind, rather than a collection of independent agents." See Smith, *Collective Intelligence in Computer-Based Collaboration* (Hillsdale, NJ: Lawrence Erlbaum, 1994).

     Pierre Levy defines it as "a form of universally distributed intelligence, constantly enhanced, coordinated in real time, and resulting in the effective mobilization of skills." See Levy, *L'intelligence collective: Pour une anthropologie du cyberspace* (Paris: Editions La Decouverte, 1994). Translated by Robert Bononno as *Collective Intelligence: Mankind's Emerging World in Cyberspace* (Cambridge, MA: Perseus Books, 1997).

     And Douglas Engelbart defines the closely related term *collective IQ* as a community's "capability for dealing with complex, urgent problems." See Engelbart, "Augmenting Society's Collective IQ," presented at the Association of Computing Machinery Conference on Hypertext and Hypermedia, Santa Cruz, CA, August 2004, doi:10.1145/1012807.1012809.

     Each of these definitions provides useful insights, but as we'll see, the broader definition used here allows us to derive insights by comparing and contrasting very different forms of collective intelligence.
3. We are taking here a *pragmatic* view in two different philosophical senses: the pragmatic view of scientific theories and the philosophical tradition of pragmatism. See Rasmus Grønfeldt Winther, "The Structure of Scientific Theories," in *Stanford Encyclopedia of Philosophy* (Winter 2016 edition), ed. Edward N. Zalta (Stanford, CA: Stanford University, 2016), https://plato.stanford.edu/archives/win2016/entries/structure-scientific-theories/;

Christopher Hookway, "Pragmatism," in *The Stanford Encyclopedia of Philosophy*, https://plato.stanford.edu/archives/sum2016/entries/pragmatism/.

In other words, we are saying that a scientific theory (such as our theory of superminds) includes how the theory is interpreted in practice and whether these interpretations are useful.

This means, from our point of view, that it doesn't really make sense to ask whether a supermind *exists*. What matters is whether a particular interpretation of the world that includes that supermind is *useful*. One could similarly say that theoretical concepts in physics (like force and energy) and in economics (like supply and demand) exist only in the context of how they are interpreted by observers in particular situations and how useful those interpretations are.

4. *Encyclopedia Britannica*, s.v. "intelligence" (cited by Shane Legg and Marcus Hutter, "A Collection of Definitions of Intelligence," technical report no. IDSIA-07-07, IDSIA, Manno, Switzerland, 2007, https://arxiv.org/pdf/0706.3639.pdf); Howard Gardner, *Frames of Mind: Theory of Multiple Intelligences* (New York: Basic Books, 1983).

5. Linda S. Gottfredson, "Mainstream Science on Intelligence: An Editorial with 52 Signatories, History, and Bibliography," *Intelligence* 24, no. 1 (1997): 13–23.

CHAPTER 2

1. The first person to document this was Charles Spearman, and it is arguably one of the most replicated results in all of psychology. See Spearman, " 'General Intelligence,' Objectively Determined and Measured," *American Journal of Psychology* 15 (1904): 201–93.

2. Ian J. Deary, *Looking Down on Human Intelligence: From Psychometrics to the Brain* (New York: Oxford University Press, 2000).

3. Christopher Chabris, "Cognitive and Neurobiological Mechanisms of the Law of General Intelligence," in *Integrating the Mind: Domain General Versus Domain Specific Processes in Higher Cognition*, ed. Maxwell J. Roberts (Hove, UK: Psychology Press, 2007), 449–91; Earl Hunt, *Human Intelligence* (Cambridge, UK: Cambridge University Press, 2011), 91*ff.*; Gilles E. Gignac, "The WAIS-III as a Nested Factors Model: A Useful Alternative to the More Conventional Oblique and Higher-Order Models," *Journal of Individual Differences* 27, no. 2 (2006): 73–86.

4. Robert R. McCrae and Paul T. Costa, "Validation of the Five-Factor Model of Personality Across Instruments and Observers," *Journal of Personality and Social Psychology* 52, no. 1 (1987): 81–90; John M. Digman, "Personality Structure: Emergence of the Five-Factor Model," in *Annual Review of Psychology* 41, ed. Mark R. Rosenzweig and Lyman W. Porter (Palo Alto, CA: Annual Reviews, Inc., 1990): 417–40.

   Some researchers have proposed that there may be a "general factor" for personality, as there is for intelligence (e.g., Janek Musek, "A General Factor of Personality: Evidence for the Big One in the Five-Factor Model," *Journal of Research in Personality* 41, no. 6 [2007]: 1,213–33), but there is not yet a consensus in the field that this is true. If there comes to be a general consensus that there *is* a general personality factor, the point made in the main text is still valid: it's certainly not *preordained* that there would be a general factor, either for intelligence or for personality.

5. Deary, *Looking Down on Human Intelligence*, 22–23.

6. Howard Gardner, *Frames of Mind: Theory of Multiple Intelligences* (New York: Basic Books, 1983); Howard Gardner, *Multiple Intelligences: New Horizons* (New York: Basic Books, 2006).

7. John E. Hunter and Ronda F. Hunter, "Validity and Utility of Alternative Predictors of Job Performance," *Psychological Bulletin* 96 (1984): 72–98.

8. Anita Williams Woolley, Christopher F. Chabris, Alex Pentland, Nada Hashmi, and Thomas W. Malone, "Evidence for a Collective Intelligence Factor in the Performance of Human Groups," *Science* 330, no. 6,004 (October 29, 2010): 686–88, http://science.sciencemag.org/content/330/6004/686, doi:10.1126/science.1193147.

9. Joseph Edward McGrath, *Groups: Interaction and Performance* (Englewood Cliffs, NJ: Prentice Hall, 1984).

10. Simon Baron-Cohen, Sally Wheelwright, Jacqueline J. Hill, Yogini Raste, and Ian Plumb, "The 'Reading the Mind in the Eyes' Test Revised Version: A Study with Normal Adults, and Adults with Asperger Syndrome or High-Functioning Autism," *Journal of Child Psychology and Psychiatry* 42, no. 2 (2001): 241–51, doi:10.1017/S0021963001006643; Simon Baron-Cohen, Therese Jolliffe, Catherine Mortimore, and Mary Robertson, "Another Advanced Test of Theory of Mind: Evidence from Very High Functioning Adults with Autism or Asperger Syndrome," *Journal of Child Psychology and Psychiatry* 38, no. 7 (1997): 813–22. Figure reproduced with author's permission.

11. An adapted version of this figure was published in Anita Williams Woolley and Thomas W. Malone, "Defend Your Research: What Makes a Team Smarter? More Women," *Harvard Business Review* 89, no. 6 (June 2011): 32–33.

    The collective intelligence scores are normalized with 0 as the average across all scores.

12. David Engel, Anita Williams Woolley, Lisa X. Jing, Christopher F. Chabris, and Thomas W. Malone, "Reading the Mind in the Eyes or Reading Between the Lines? Theory of Mind Predicts Effective Collaboration Equally Well Online and Face-to-Face," *PLOS One* 9, no. 12 (2014), http://www.plosone.org/article/info%3Adoi%2F10.1371%2Fjournal.pone.0115212, doi:10.1371/journal.pone.0115212.

13. Ishani Aggarwal, Anita Williams Woolley, Christopher F. Chabris, and Thomas W. Malone, "Cognitive Diversity, Collective Intelligence and Learning in Teams," presented at the 2015 European Academy of Management Conference, Warsaw, Poland, June 17–20, 2015.

14. Maria Kozhevnikov, "Cognitive Styles in the Context of Modern Psychology: Toward an Integrated Framework," *Psychological Bulletin* 133 (2007): 464–81.

15. Aggarwal, "Cognitive Diversity"; John B. Van Huyck, Raymond C. Battalio, and Richard O. Beil, "Tacit Coordination Games, Strategic Uncertainty, and Coordination Failure," *The American Economic Review* 80, no. 1 (1990): 234–48; Cary Deck and Nikos Nikiforakis, "Perfect and Imperfect Real-Time

Monitoring in a Minimum-Effort Game," *Experimental Economics* 15, no. 1 (2012): 71–88.

16. Figure from Aggarwal, "Cognitive Diversity," 2015. Reprinted by permission of authors.

17. David Engel, Anita Williams Woolley, Ishani Aggarwal, Christopher F. Chabris, Masamichi Takahashi, Keiichi Nemoto, Carolin Kaiser, Young Ji Kim, and Thomas W. Malone, "Collective Intelligence in Computer-Mediated Collaboration Emerges in Different Contexts and Cultures," *Proceedings of the SIGCHI Conference on Human Factors in Computing Systems* (New York: Association for Computing Machinery, 2015), doi:10.1145/2702123.2702259 (conference held in Seoul, South Korea, April 18–23, 2015).

18. Young Ji Kim, David Engel, Anita Williams Woolley, Jeffery Yu-Ting Lin, Naomi McArthur, and Thomas W. Malone, "What Makes a Strong Team? Using Collective Intelligence to Predict Team Performance in League of Legends," *Proceedings of the ACM Conference on Computer-Supported Cooperative Work and Social Computing*, (New York: Association for Computing Machinery, 2017), http://dx.doi.org/10.1145/2998181.2998185 (conference held in Portland, OR, February 25–March 1, 2017).

19. Steve Schaefer, "The First 12 Dow Components: Where Are They Now?" *Forbes*, July 15, 2011, http://www.forbes.com/sites/steveschaefer/2011/07/15/the-first-12-dow-components-where-are-they-now.

20. Martin Baily, Charles Hulten, and David Campbell, "Productivity Dynamics in Manufacturing Plants," *Brookings Papers on Economic Activity: Microeconomics* (1992): 187–267, doi:10.2307/2534764; Eric Bartelsman and Phoebus Dhrymes, "Productivity Dynamics: U.S. Manufacturing Plants, 1972–1986," *Journal of Productivity Analysis* 9, no. 1 (1998): 5–34, doi:10.1023/A:101838362; Eric Bartelsman and Mark Doms, "Understanding Productivity: Lessons from Longitudinal Microdata," *Journal of Economic Literature* 38, no. 3 (2000): 569–94, doi:10.1257/jel.38.3.569.

21. Baily et al., "Productivity Dynamics," 187–267.
    The statistics reported here count plants *weighted by their employment numbers*. The more workers plants employed, the more heavily they were weighted.

CHAPTER 3

1. The Google statistics are from Craig Smith, "270 Amazing Google Statistics and Facts (August 2017)," *DMR*, modified August 13, 2017, http://expandedramblings.com/index.php/by-the-numbers-a-gigantic-list-of-google-stats-and-facts/.
    If there are 1.17 billion monthly unique searchers and a world population of about 7.4 billion (see United States Census Bureau, "U.S. and World Population Clock," accessed September 21, 2017, https://www.census.gov/popclock/), this means that about one in seven people in the world do a search each month. One hundred billion searches per month means about three per user per day.

2. See http://damnyouautocorrect.com.

3. H. James Wilson, Paul Daugherty, and Prashant Shukla, "How One Clothing Company Blends AI and Human Expertise," *Harvard Business Review*, November 21, 2016, https://hbr.org/2016/11/how-one-clothing-company-blends-ai-and -human-expertise.

4. "WatsonPaths," IBM, accessed August 17, 2016, https://www.research.ibm .com/cognitive-computing/watson/watsonpaths.shtml?cmp=usbrb&cm =s&csr=watson.site_20140319&cr=work&ct=usbrb301&cn=s1healthcare.

5. Shai Wininger, "The Secret Behind Lemonade's Instant Insurance," Lemonade, November 23, 2016, https://stories.lemonade.com/the-secret -behind-lemonades-instant-insurance-3129537d661.

6. Wikipedia, s.v. "Wikipedia:Bots," accessed August 18, 2016, https://en.wikipedia .org/wiki/Wikipedia:Bots.

7. Aniket Kittur, Boris Smus, Susheel Khamkar, and Robert E. Kraut, "CrowdForge: Crowdsourcing Complex Work," in *Proceedings of the ACM Symposium on User Interface Software and Technology* (New York: ACM Press, 2011), http://smus.com/crowdforge/crowdforge-uist-11.pdf.

8. Figure from Kittur A., Smus, B., Khamkar, S., Kraut, R.E., "CrowdForge: Crowdsourcing Complex Work." *UIST 2011: Proceedings of the ACM Symposium on User Interface Software and Technology*. New York: ACM Press, http:doi.acm .org/10.1145/2047196.2047202. © 2011 Association for Computing Machinery, Inc. Reprinted by permission.

9. Simple English Wikipedia, accessed October 21, 2017, https://simple.wikipedia .org/wiki/Main_Page.

10. Marshall McLuhan, *Understanding Media* (New York: McGraw-Hill, 1964).

11. James H. Hines, Thomas W. Malone, Paulo Gonçalves, George Herman, John Quimby, Mary Murphy-Hoye, James Rice, James Patten, and Hiroshi Ishii, "Construction by Replacement: A New Approach to Simulation Modeling," *System Dynamics Review* 27, no. 1 (July 28, 2010): 64–90, http://onlinelibrary .wiley.com/doi/10.1002/sdr.437/abstract, doi:10.1002/sdr.437.

12. Aubrey Colter, Patlapa Davivongsa, Donald Derek Haddad, Halla Moore, Bruan Tice, and Hiroshi Ishii, "SoundFORMS: Manipulating Sound Through Touch," in *Proceedings of the 2016 CHI Conference Extended Abstracts on Human Factors in Computing Systems* (New York: Association for Computing Machinery, 2016), 2,425–30.

   The photograph is from the above paper and is available online at https:// tangible.media.mit.edu/project/soundform, where you can also see a fascinating video of the system in operation. Photograph © Tangible Media Group, MIT Media Lab. Reprinted with permission.

13. Erico Guizzo and Evan Ackerman, "How Rethink Robotics Built Its New Baxter Robot Worker," *IEEE Spectrum*, September 18, 2012, http://spectrum .ieee.org/robotics/industrial-robots/rethink-robotics-baxter-robot-factory -worker.

14. Robert Lee Hotz, "Neural Implants Let Paralyzed Man Take a Drink," *Wall Street Journal*, May 21, 2015, http://www.wsj.com/articles/neural-implants-let -paralyzed-man-take-a-drink-1432231201; Tyson Aflalo, Spencer Kellis,

Christian Klaes, Brian Lee, Ying Shi, Kelsie Shanfield, Stephanie Hayes-Jackson, et al., "Decoding Motor Imagery from the Posterior Parietal Cortex of a Tetraplegic Human," *Science* 348, no. 6,237 (May 22, 2015): 906–910, http:// science.sciencemag.org/content/348/6237/906.full, doi:10.1126/science.aaa5417.

CHAPTER 4

1. Stuart Russell and Peter Norvig, *Artificial Intelligence: A Modern Approach* (New York: Prentice Hall, 1995).
2. Alan Turing, "Computing Machinery and Intelligence," *Mind* 59 (1950): 433–60.
3. Wikipedia, s.v. "artificial intelligence," accessed August 8, 2016, https://en .wikipedia.org/wiki/Artificial_intelligence.
4. Rodney Brooks, "Artificial Intelligence Is a Tool, Not a Threat," *Rethink Robotics*, November 10, 2014, http://www.rethinkrobotics.com/blog/artificial -intelligence-tool-threat.
5. David Ferrucci, e-mail message to the author, August 24, 2016. Ferrucci was the leader of the IBM team that developed the Watson technology.
6. See, for example, a review of this literature in Russell and Norvig, *Artificial Intelligence*, chapter 26.
7. Hubert L. Dreyfus, *What Computers Still Can't Do: A Critique of Artificial Reason* (Cambridge, MA: MIT Press, 1992); John R. Searle, "Minds, Brains, and Programs," *Behavioral and Brain Sciences* 3, no. 3 (1980): 417–24.
8. Edsger W. Dijkstra, "The Threats to Computing Science," presented at the ACM South Central Regional Conference, Austin, TX, November 1984.
9. Russell and Norvig, *Artificial Intelligence*, 1,021.
10. Erik Brynjolfsson and Andrew McAfee, *The Second Machine Age: Work, Progress, and Prosperity in a Time of Brilliant Technologies* (New York: W. W. Norton, 2014); Martin Ford, *Rise of the Robots: Technology and the Threat of a Jobless Future* (New York: Basic Books, 2015).
11. Brooks, "Artificial Intelligence Is a Tool"; Rodney Brooks, "The Seven Deadly Sins of AI Predictions," *MIT Technology Review*, October 6, 2017, https://www .technologyreview.com/s/609048/the-seven-deadly-sins-of-ai-predictions/.
12. Stuart Armstrong and Kaj Sotala, "How We're Predicting AI — or Failing To," in *Beyond AI: Artificial Dreams*, ed. Jan Romportl, Pavel Ircing, Eva Zackova, Michal Polak, and Radek Schuster (Pilsen, Czech Republic: University of West Bohemia, 2012): 52–75, https://intelligence.org/files/PredictingAI.pdf.
13. Nick Bostrom, *Superintelligence: Paths, Dangers, Strategies* (Oxford, UK: Oxford University Press, 2014).
14. Stuart Madnick, "Understanding the Computer (Little Man Computer)," unpublished teaching note, MIT Sloan School of Management, Cambridge, MA, June 10, 1993. Based on the 1979 version. The figure shown here was drawn by Rob Malone, and is adapted from this teaching note with permission of Stuart Madnick.
15. Rachel Potvin and Josh Levenberg, "Why Google Stores Billions of Lines of Code in a Single Repository," *Communications of the ACM* 59, no. 7 (2016): 78–87, doi:10.1145/2854146.

16. Full disclosure: in addition to having known Doug Lenat for over 30 years, I am a member of the advisory board of Lucid, a company that is commercializing his research.

17. Will Knight, "An AI with 30 Years' Worth of Knowledge Finally Goes to Work," *MIT Technology Review*, March 14, 2016, https://www.technology review.com/s/600984/an-ai-with-30-years-worth-of-knowledge-finally-goes -to-work.

18. Melvin Johnson, Mike Schister, Quoc V. Lee, Maxim Krikun, Yonghui Wu, Zhifeng Chen, Nikhil Thorat, et al., "Google's Multilingual Neural Machine Translation System: Enabling Zero-Shot Translation," preprint, submitted November 14, 2016, https://arxiv.org/abs/1611.04558; Justin Bariso, "The Artificial Intelligence Behind Google Translate Recently Did Something Extraordinary," *Inc.*, November 28, 2016, https://www.inc.com/justin-bariso/ the-ai-behind-google-translate-recently-did-something-extraordinary.html.

19. Quoc V. Le, Marc'Aurelio Ranzato, Rajat Monga, Matthieu Devin, Kai Chen, Greg S. Corrado, Jeff Dean, and Andrew Y. Ng, "Building High-Level Features Using Large Scale Unsupervised Learning," in *Proceedings of the 29th International Conference on Machine Learning*, ed. John Langford and Joelle Pineau (Edinburgh, Scotland: Omnipress, 2012), http://static.googleusercontent.com/external_content/ untrusted_dlcp/research.google.com/en/us/pubs/archive/38115.pdf; John Markoff, "How Many Computers to Identify a Cat? 16,000," *New York Times*, June 25, 2012, http://www.nytimes.com/2012/06/26/technology/in-a-big-network-of-computers -evidence-of-machine-learning.html.

20. James Randerson, "How Many Neurons Make a Human Brain? Billions Fewer Than We Thought," *Guardian*, February 28, 2012, https://www.theguardian .com/science/blog/2012/feb/28/how-many-neurons-human-brain; Federico A. C. Azevedo, Ludmila R. B. Carvalho, Lea T. Grinberg, Jose Farfel, Renata E. L. Ferretti, Renata E. P. Leite, Wilson Jacob Filho, Roberto Lent, and Suzana Herculano-Houzel, "Equal Numbers of Neuronal and Nonneuronal Cells Make the Human Brain an Isometrically Scaled-Up Primate Brain," *Journal of Comparative Neurology* 513, no. 5 (2009): 532–41, https://www.researchgate.net/ profile/Lea_Grinberg/publication/24024444_Equal_numbers_of_neuronal _and_nonneuronal_cells_make_the_human_brain_an_isometrically_scaled-up _primate_brain/links/0912f50c100f1e72ba000000.pdf.

21. Don Monroe, "Neuromorphic Computing Gets Ready for the (Really) Big Time," *Communications of the ACM* 57, no. 6 (2014): 13–15, http://cacm.acm.org/ magazines/2014/6/175183-neuromorphic-computing-gets-ready-for-the-really -big-time/fulltext.

22. Marvin Minsky, *Society of Mind* (New York: Simon and Schuster, 1988).

23. David A. Ferrucci, "Introduction to 'This Is Watson,'" *IBM Journal of Research and Development* 56, no. 3.4 (April 3, 2012): 1–1, doi:10.1147/JRD.2012.2184356.

24. Lukas Biewald, "Why Human-in-the-Loop Computing Is the Future of Machine Learning," *Computerworld*, November 13, 2015, https://www.computerworld.com/ article/3004013/robotics/why-human-in-the-loop-computing-is-the-future-of -machine-learning.html.

CHAPTER 5

1. Stuart J. Russell, "Rationality and Intelligence," *Artificial Intelligence* 94, nos. 1–2 (July 1997): 57–77, doi:10.1016/S0004-3702(97)00026-X; Stewart J. Russell, "Defining Intelligence: A Conversation with Stuart Russell," *Edge*, February 7, 2017, https://www.edge.org/conversation/stuart_russell-defining-intelligence.

CHAPTER 6

1. Edward O. Wilson, *Sociobiology: The New Synthesis* (Cambridge, MA: Harvard University Press, 2000), 282ff.
2. Yuval Noah Harari, *Sapiens: A Brief History of Humankind* (New York: HarperCollins, 2015), chapter 2.
3. Robert F. Freeland and Ezra W. Zuckerman, "The Problems and Promise of Hierarchy: Voice Rights and the Firm" (unpublished manuscript, November 11, 2014), https://ssrn.com/abstract=2523245.
4. Thomas W. Malone, *The Future of Work: How the New Order of Business Will Shape Your Organization, Your Management Style, and Your Life* (Boston, MA: Harvard Business School Press, 2004).
5. Alvin Toffler, *Future Shock* (New York: Random House, 1970); Warren Bennis, *The Temporary Society* (New York: Harper & Row, 1968); Henry Mintzberg, *The Structuring of Organizations: A Synthesis of the Research* (Englewood Cliffs, NJ: Prentice Hall, 1979).
6. Valve Corporation, *Valve: Handbook for New Employees* (Bellevue, WA: Valve Corporation, 2012). Figure is adapted from page 4 and reprinted here with permission of Valve Corporation.
7. Philippa Warr, "Former Valve Employee: 'It Felt a Lot Like High School,'" *Wired*, July 9, 2013, http://www.wired.com/2013/07/wireduk-valve-jeri-ellsworth.

CHAPTER 7

1. Nicolas de Condorcet, *Essay sur l'Application de l'Analyse à la Probabilité des Décisions Rendue à la Pluralité des Voix* (Paris, 1785); Christian List and Robert E. Goodin, "Epistemic Democracy: Generalizing the Condorcet Jury Theorem," *Journal of Political Philosophy* 9 (2001): 277–306, doi:10.1111/1467-9760.00128.
2. Thomas W. Malone, *The Future of Work: How the New Order of Business Will Shape Your Organization, Your Management Style, and Your Life* (Boston, MA: Harvard Business School Press, 2004).
3. Bryan Ford, "Delegative Democracy Revisited," *Bryan Ford's Blog*, November 16, 2014, http://bford.github.io/2014/11/16/deleg.html; Malone, *The Future of Work*, 65n21.
4. Sven Becker, "Web Platform Makes Professor Most Powerful Pirate," *Spiegel Online*, March 2, 2012, http://www.spiegel.de/international/germany/liquid-democracy-web-platform-makes-professor-most-powerful-pirate-a-818683.html; Wikipedia, s.v. "Pirate Party," accessed February 20, 2017, https://en.wikipedia.org/wiki/Pirate_Party.
5. Steve Hardt and Lia C. R. Lopes, "Google Votes: A Liquid Democracy Experiment on a Corporate Social Network," *Technical Disclosure Commons*, June 5, 2015, http://www.tdcommons.org/dpubs_series/79.

6. "The Story So Far," Galaxy Zoo, accessed October 21, 2017, https://www
   .galaxyzoo.org/?_ga=1.247761351.1568972630.1472315428#/story.

7. "About Eyewire, a Game to Map the Brain," Eyewire, accessed February 20,
   2017, http://blog.eyewire.org/about/.

8. Barbara Mellers, Eric Stone, Pavel Atanasov, Nick Rohrbaugh, S. Emlen Metz,
   Lyle Ungar, Michael Metcalf Bishop, et al., "The Psychology of Intelligence
   Analysis: Drivers of Prediction Accuracy in World Politics," *Journal of
   Experimental Psychology: Applied* 21, no. 1 (2015): 1; Barbara Mellers, Lyle Ungar,
   Jonathan Baron, Jamie Ramos, Burcu Gurcay, Katrina Fincher, Sydney E.
   Scott, et al., "Psychological Strategies for Winning a Geopolitical Forecasting
   Tournament," *Psychological Science* 25, no. 5 (2014): 1,106–15; Barbara Mellers,
   Eric Stone, Terry Murray, Angela Minster, Nick Rohrbaugh, Michael Bishop,
   Eva Chen, et al., "Identifying and Cultivating Superforecasters as a Method of
   Improving Probabilistic Predictions," *Perspectives on Psychological Science* 10, no.
   3 (2015): 267–81; Pavel Atanasov, Phillip Rescober, Eric Stone, Samuel A. Swift,
   Emile Servan-Schreiber, Philip Tetlock, Lyle Ungar, and Barbara Mellers,
   "Distilling the Wisdom of Crowds: Prediction Markets vs. Prediction Polls,"
   Management Science 63, no. 3 (2016), http://dx.doi.org/10.1287/mnsc.2015.2374.

9. Atanasov et al., "Distilling the Wisdom"; Philip Tetlock and Dan Gardner, *Super-
   forecasting: The Art and Science of Prediction* (New York: Random House, 2016), 91.

10. Ibid.

11. David Ignatius, "More Chatter Than Needed," *Washington Post*, November 1,
    2013, https://www.washingtonpost.com/opinions/david-ignatius-more-chatter
    -than-needed/2013/11/01/1194a984-425a-11e3-a624-41d661b0bb78_story
    .html?utm_term=.e54b9bf0b8f5.

    This interpretation of the Ignatius quotation comes from Tetlock and
    Gardner, *Superforecasting*, 91.

CHAPTER 8

1. Cristina Gomes and Christophe Boesch, "Wild Chimpanzees Exchange Meat
   for Sex on a Long-Term Basis," *PLOS One* 4, no. 4 (2009), doi:10.1371/journal
   .pone.0005116.

2. Kenneth J. Arrow and Gérard Debreu, "Existence of an Equilibrium for a
   Competitive Economy," *Econometrica* 22 (1954): 265–90.

3. Daniel Kahneman, *Thinking, Fast and Slow* (New York: Macmillan, 2011),
   chapter 21.

4. Yiftach Nagar and Thomas W. Malone, "Making Business Predictions by
   Combining Human and Machine Intelligence in Prediction Markets,"
   Proceedings of the International Conference on Information Systems, Shanghai,
   China, December 5, 2011, http://web.mit.edu/ynagar/www/papers/Nagar
   _Malone_MakingBusinessPredictionsbyCombiningHumanandMachine
   Intelligence.ICIS2011.pdf; Yiftach Nagar and Thomas W. Malone,
   "Combining Human and Machine Intelligence for Making Predictions"
   (working paper no. 2011-002, MIT Center for Collective Intelligence,
   Cambridge, MA, 2011), http://cci.mit.edu/publications/CCIwp2011-02.pdf.

5. Justin Wolfers and Eric Zitzewitz, "Prediction Markets," *Journal of Economic Perspectives* 18, no. 2 (2004): 107–26.

6. Justin Wolfers and Eric Zitzewitz, "Interpreting Prediction Market Prices as Probabilities" (working paper no. W12200, National Bureau of Economic Research, Cambridge, MA, 2006).

CHAPTER 9

1. Note that this definition of community is different from the technical definitions of this term in some fields. Instead of focusing on the decision-making process for a group (as we do here), other fields focus on other dimensions.

   For instance, ecologists define community as "an association of interacting species inhabiting some defined area." See Manuel Molles, *Ecology: Concepts and Applications* (New York: McGraw-Hill Higher Education, 2015), 353.

   Similarly, one definition of community in sociology is a "collectivity the members of which share a common territorial area as their base of operations for daily activities." See Talcott Parsons, *The Social System* (London: Routledge & Kegan Paul, 1951), 91.

2. Brent Simpson and Robb Willer, "Beyond Altruism: Sociological Foundations of Cooperation and Prosocial Behavior," *Annual Review of Sociology* 41 (2015): 43–63, doi:10.1146/annurev-soc-073014-112242; Matthew Feinberg, Robb Willer, and Michael Schultz, "Gossip and Ostracism Promote Cooperation in Groups," *Psychological Science* 25 (2014): 656–64, doi:10.1177/09567 97613510184; Brent Simpson, Robb Willer, and Cecilia L. Ridgeway, "Status Hierarchies and the Organization of Collective Action," *Sociological Theory* 30, no. 3 (2012): 149–66, doi:10.1177/0735275112457912.

3. The story of Wikipedia's beginnings has been recounted in numerous places. See Wikipedia, s.v. "history of Wikipedia," accessed July 6, 2016, https://en .wikipedia.org/wiki/History_of_Wikipedia; Larry Sanger, "The Early History of Nupedia and Wikipedia: A Memoir," *Slashdot*, April 18, 2005, https:// features.slashdot.org/story/05/04/18/164213/the-early-history-of-nupedia -and-wikipedia-a-memoir; Marshall Poe, "The Hive: Can Thousands of Wikipedians Be Wrong? How an Attempt to Build an Online Encyclopedia Touched off History's Biggest Experiment in Collaborative Knowledge," *Atlantic Monthly*, September 2006, 86–94, http://www.theatlantic.com/ magazine/archive/2006/09/the-hive/5118.

4. Jean Lave and Etienne Wenger, *Situated Learning: Legitimate Peripheral Participation* (Cambridge, UK: Cambridge University Press, 1991); Etienne Wenger, *Communities of Practice: Learning, Meaning, and Identity* (Cambridge, UK: Cambridge University Press, 1998).

5. Julian E. Orr, *Talking About Machines: An Ethnography of a Modern Job* (Ithaca, NY: Cornell University Press, 1996).

6. John Seely Brown and Paul Duguid, "Balancing Act: How to Capture Knowledge Without Killing It," *Harvard Business Review* 78, no. 3 (2000): 73–80.

7. Sherry Turkle, *Reclaiming Conversation: The Power of Talk in the Digital Age* (New York: Penguin Press, 2015).

8. John Herrman, "Inside Facebook's (Totally Insane, Unintentionally Gigantic, Hyperpartisan) Political-Media Machine: How a Strange New Class of Media Outlet Has Arisen to Take Over Our News Feeds," *New York Times Magazine*, August 24, 2016, https://www.nytimes.com/2016/08/28/magazine/inside -facebooks-totally-insane-unintentionally-gigantic-hyperpartisan-political -media-machine.html.

9. Monroe C. Beardsley, *Practical Logic* (New York: Prentice Hall, 1950); Stephen E. Toulmin, *The Uses of Argument*, rev. ed. (1958; repr., New York: Cambridge University Press, 2003); Werner Kunz and Horst W. J. Rittel, "Issues as Elements of Information Systems," (working paper no. 131, Institute of Urban and Regional Development, University of California, Berkeley, July 1970, reprinted May 1979).

10. Mark Klein, "How to Harvest Collective Wisdom for Complex Problems: An Introduction to the MIT Deliberatorium" (working paper no. 2012-004, MIT Center for Collective Intelligence, Cambridge, MA, spring 2012), http://cci .mit.edu/docs/working_papers_2012_2013/kleinwp2013.pdf. The following two figures are adapted from this paper with permission of Mark Klein.

11. Mark Klein, Paolo Spada, and Rafaele Calabretta, "Enabling Deliberations in a Political Party Using Large-Scale Argumentations: A Preliminary Report," presented at the International Conference on the Design of Cooperative Systems from Research to Practice: Results and Open Challenges, Marseilles, France, May 29, 2012, https://www.researchgate.net/publication/263307756 _Enabling_Deliberations_in_a_Political_Party_Using_Large-Scale _Argumentation_A_Preliminary_Report.

12. Jeffrey Conklin, *Dialogue Mapping: Building Shared Understanding of Wicked Problems* (Chichester, UK: Wiley, 2006); Jeffrey Conklin, Albert Selvin, Simon Buckingham Shum, and Maarten Sierhuis, "Facilitated Hypertext for Collective Sensemaking: 15 Years on from gIBIS," in *Proceedings of the 12th ACM Conference on Hypertext and Hypermedia* (New York: Association for Computing Machinery, 2001), 123–24; Paul A. Kirschner, Simon J. Buckingham-Shum, and Chad S. Carr, eds., *Visualizing Argumentation: Software Tools for Collaborative and Educational Sense-making* (London: Springer Science & Business Media, 2012).

13. David Brin, "Disputation Arenas: Harnessing Conflict and Competitiveness for Society's Benefit," *Ohio State Journal on Dispute Resolution* 15 (1999): 597, http://www.davidbrin.com/disputation.html.

14. David G. Lowe, "Synview: The Design of a System for Cooperative Structuring of Information," in *Proceedings of the 1986 ACM Conference on Computer-Supported Cooperative Work* (New York: Association for Computing Machinery, 1986).

15. Karl Marx and Friedrich Engels, *The Communist Manifesto* (New York: Penguin, 2002); Friedrich Engels, *The Origin of the Family, Private Property, and the State* (1884), https://www.marxists.org/archive/marx/works/download/pdf/ origin_family.pdf.

16. Richard B. Lee, "Primitive Communism and the Origin of Social Inequality," in *Evolution of Political Systems: Sociopolitics in Small-Scale Sedentary Societies*, ed. Steadman Upham (New York: Cambridge University Press, 1990), 225–46.

17. E. E. Evans-Pritchard, *Kinship and Marriage Among the Nuer* (Oxford, UK: Clarendon Press, 1951), 132.

18. W. Paul Cockshott and Allin Cottrell, *Towards a New Socialism* (Nottingham, UK: Spokesman, 1993), http://ricardo.ecn.wfu.edu/~cottrell/socialism_book/new_socialism.pdf.

19. Josh Chin and Gillian Wong, "China's New Tool for Social Control: A Credit Rating for Everything," *Wall Street Journal*, November 28, 2016, http://www.wsj.com/articles/chinas-new-tool-for-social-control-a-credit-rating-for-everything-1480351590.

CHAPTER 10

1. Note that in some fields, the definition of *ecosystem* is different from the definition used here. In biology, an ecosystem is defined as "all the organisms that live in an area and the physical environment with which those organisms interact." In other words, this definition explicitly includes the physical environment in which the individuals interact. See Manuel Molles, *Ecology: Concepts and Applications* (New York: McGraw-Hill Higher Education, 2015), 6.

   In the field of business strategy, it is common to talk about "business ecosystems" that include a number of companies cooperating and competing to satisfy customer needs. Unlike the ecosystems described in this book, business ecosystems, in this sense, often have a leader and substantial amounts of cooperation among the ecosystem members. For example, both Apple and Microsoft are leaders in their respective ecosystems of IT companies. See James F. Moore, "Predators and Prey: A New Ecology of Competition," *Harvard Business Review* (May–June 1993): 75–86.

2. Erin Griffith, "Why Uber CEO Travis Kalanick's Resignation Matters," *Fortune*, June 21, 2017, http://fortune.com/2017/06/21/uber-ceo-travis-kalanick-why-it-matter.

3. Charles Darwin, *On the Origin of Species by Means of Natural Selection* (London: John Murray, 1859).

4. Richard R. Nelson and Sidney G. Winter, *An Evolutionary Theory of Economic Change* (Cambridge, MA: Harvard University Press, 1982); Michael T. Hannan and John Freeman, *Organizational Ecology* (Cambridge, MA: Harvard University Press, 1993); Andrew W. Lo, *Adaptive Markets: Financial Evolution at the Speed of Thought* (Princeton, NJ: Princeton University Press, 2017).

5. Richard Dawkins, *The Selfish Gene*, 2nd ed. (New York: Oxford University Press, 1989), 192.

6. There is a very large—and controversy-filled—literature on sociobiology, behavioral ecology, group selection, and other concepts that are related to the points made here. However, almost all this other literature focuses on how group behavior evolves through the biological evolution of individual organisms in these groups. The discussion in this book is at a different level.

Here we focus on the groups themselves, not their biological members, and we focus on the evolution that occurs through transmitting ideas and behaviors socially, not via biological genes. See Edward O. Wilson, *Sociobiology: The New Synthesis* (Cambridge, MA: Harvard University Press, 1975); Edward O. Wilson, *The Social Conquest of Earth* (New York: W. W. Norton, 2012); Steven Pinker, "The False Allure of Group Selection," in *The Handbook of Evolutionary Psychology*, ed. David M. Buss (Hoboken, NJ: Wiley, 2015).

7. Zeynep Ton, *The Good Jobs Strategy: How the Smartest Companies Invest in Employees to Lower Costs and Boost Profits* (Seattle, WA: Amazon Publishing / New Harvest, 2014).

8. Robert Michels, *Political Parties: A Sociological Study of the Oligarchical Tendencies of Modern Democracy* (1911; repr., New York: Collier, 1962).

9. Benjamin Kuipers, "An Existing, Ecologically-Successful Genus of Collectively Intelligent Artificial Creatures," presented at the Collective Intelligence Conference, MIT, Cambridge, MA, April 2012, https://arxiv.org/pdf/1204 .4116.pdf.

10. Marshall Sahlins, *Stone Age Economics* (New York: Taylor & Francis, 1972); Jared Diamond, *Guns, Germs, and Steel: The Fates of Human Societies* (New York: W. W. Norton, 1997), chapters 4 and 6; Yuval Noah Harari, *Sapiens: A Brief History of Humankind* (New York: HarperCollins, 2015), chapter 5.

11. Diamond, *Guns, Germs, and Steel*, 112.

12. Ibid., 105.

13. John Stuart Mill, *Utilitarianism*, ed. Roger Crisp (1861; repr., Oxford, UK: Oxford University Press, 1998); Jeremy Bentham, *An Introduction to the Principles of Morals and Legislation* (1789; repr., Oxford, UK: Clarendon Press, 1907); Julia Driver, "The History of Utilitarianism," in *Stanford Encyclopedia of Philosophy* (Winter 2014 edition), ed. Edward N. Zalta (Stanford, CA: Stanford University, 2014), https://plato.stanford.edu/archives/win2014/entries/ utilitarianism-history; Yuval Noah Harari, *Homo Deus: A Brief History of Tomorrow* (New York: HarperCollins, 2017), chapter 1.

14. It is not novel to make a connection between evolution and ethics. Others, including Charles Darwin and Herbert Spencer, have done so. But the point I am making here differs from points made by earlier writers in at least two ways. First, as I explained in note 6 above, I am talking only about evolution at the level of superminds, not biological evolution. Second, I am not claiming that something is good *because* that is what evolution produces. I am merely noting the surprising coincidence between what evolution produces and what moral philosophers have argued, for various reasons, is good. For overviews of some of the philosophical issues here, see Doris Schroeder, "Evolutionary Ethics," *Internet Encyclopedia of Philosophy*, accessed August 9, 2017, http://www.iep.utm .edu/evol-eth; and David Weinstein, "Herbert Spencer," *Stanford Encyclopedia of Philosophy* (Spring 2017 edition), ed. Edward N. Zalta (Stanford, CA: Stanford University, 2017), https://plato.stanford.edu/archives/spr2017/entries/spencer.

The principle of evolutionary utilitarianism was inspired by and, in a sense, generalizes the argument in Robert Wright's *Nonzero: The Logic of Human*

Destiny (New York: Pantheon, 2000). This evolutionary principle, however, also provides a concise summary of the basic mechanism behind Wright's logic. That means it can explain other possible results of the same mechanism, such as the evolution of smaller or simpler forms of social organization in situations where that leads to more benefits for more people.

CHAPTER 11

1. Friedrich August Hayek, "The Use of Knowledge in Society," *American Economic Review* 35, no. 4 (1945): 519–30; Ronald H. Coase, "The Nature of the Firm," *Economica* 4, no. 16 (1937): 386–405; Oliver E. Williamson, *Markets and Hierarchies* (New York: Free Press, 1975); Oliver Hart, *Firms, Contracts, and Financial Structure* (London: Oxford University Press, 1995); Oliver Hart and Bengt Holmstrom, "The Theory of Contracts," in *Advances in Economic Theory*, ed. Truman F. Bewley (Cambridge, UK: Cambridge University Press, 1987), 71–155.

2. For a comparison of two perspectives on the question of why markets can sometimes be higher cost and sometimes lower cost than hierarchies, see Robert Gibbons, Richard Holden, and Michael Powell, "Organization and Information: Firms' Governance Choices in Rational-Expectations Equilibrium," *Quarterly Journal of Economics* 127, no. 4 (2012): 1,813–41.

3. John Locke, *Two Treatises of Government and a Letter Concerning Toleration* (New Haven, CT: Yale University Press, 2003); Thomas Hobbes, *Leviathan*, ed. C. B. Macpherson (London: Penguin Books, 1985); Jean-Jacques Rousseau, *The Basic Political Writings*, translated by Donald A. Cress (Indianapolis: Hackett Publishing Company, 1987); John Rawls, *A Theory of Justice* (Cambridge, MA: Harvard University Press, 1971).

4. Garrett Hardin, "The Tragedy of the Commons," *Science* 162, no. 3,859 (1968): 1,243–48; Robert L. Trivers, "The Evolution of Reciprocal Altruism," *Quarterly Review of Biology* 46 (1971): 35–57, doi:10.1086/406755; Christopher Stephens, "Modelling Reciprocal Altruism," *British Journal for the Philosophy of Science* 47, no. 4 (1996): 533–51, doi:10.1093/bjps/47.4.533.

5. I believe it would be possible (and highly desirable) to formalize arguments like those given here in a more precise mathematical form, and I hope that I or others will do that in the future. Here, however, I describe the basic arguments in an intuitive way that I hope will be both understandable to general readers and useful for future academic work. A key message for academic readers is that it is *possible* to systematically compare this wide range of superminds that have mostly been studied in separate disciplines and that it would be *desirable* to improve on the simple forms of comparison described here.

6. Richard B. Lee and Richard Daly, eds., *Cambridge Encyclopedia of Hunters and Gatherers* (New York: Cambridge University Press, 1999), 1–19.

7. Friedrich August Hayek, "The Use of Knowledge in Society," *The American Economic Review* 35, no. 4 (1945): 526–27. Reprinted with permission of publisher.

8. Coase, "The Nature of the Firm," 386–405; Williamson, *Markets and Hierarchies*; Hart, *Firms, Contracts*; Sanford J. Grossman and Oliver D. Hart, "The Costs and Benefits of Ownership: A Theory of Vertical and Lateral

Integration," *Journal of Political Economy* 94, no. 4 (1986): 691–719, doi:10.1086/261404; Hart, "Theory of Contracts," 71–155.

    For a comparison of the two perspectives on why markets can sometimes be more expensive and sometimes less expensive than hierarchies, see Gibbons, "Organization and Information," 1,813–41.

9. Hobbes, *Leviathan*, XIII.9.
10. Hardin, "The Tragedy of the Commons."
11. Trivers, "The Evolution of Reciprocal Altruism"; Stephens, "Modelling Reciprocal Altruism."
12. See a useful summary of work on this topic in Christian List, "Social Choice Theory," in *Stanford Encyclopedia of Philosophy* (Winter 2013 edition), ed. Edward N. Zalta (Stanford, CA: Stanford University, 2013), http://plato .stanford.edu/archives/win2013/entries/social-choice.
13. Lee and Daly, *Cambridge Encyclopedia of Hunters and Gatherers.*
14. Ibid.
15. For instance, democracies had more potential benefits of group decision making (high instead of medium), but they were more expensive to operate (high instead of medium), so they weren't used for most decisions. Markets had better distribution of benefits (high instead of medium), but they created fewer benefits (medium- instead of medium), and they may have been more expensive to operate (medium+/- instead of medium). So markets were used for certain kinds of trades, but most group decisions weren't made this way. Hierarchies had the potential to create more benefits (high instead of medium), but they didn't distribute these benefits as effectively (low instead of medium). So hierarchies were used for certain kinds of decisions (perhaps what to do in battle when fighting another band), but not for many others.

    In general, the theory summarized by our table wouldn't be enough to *predict* which types of superminds would have been used by primitive human groups if you didn't already know. But it does help us systematically *explain* what we know from anthropologists about what actually happened.
16. Siqi Han and Susan Chan Shifflett, "Infographic: Interlinked U.S.-China Food Trade," Wilson Center, China Environment Forum, September 22, 2014, https://www.wilsoncenter.org/article/infographic-interlinked-us-china -food-trade.
17. Josh Constine, "How Facebook News Feed Works," *TechCrunch*, September 6, 2016, https://techcrunch.com/2016/09/06/ultimate-guide-to-the-news-feed.

CHAPTER 12

1. Climate CoLab, accessed October 22, 2017, https://climatecolab.org/.

    Until October 2010, the system was called the Climate Collaboratorium. The project has involved many people over the years, including the following (all from MIT except where noted): Rob Laubacher, Laur Fisher, Josh Introne, Patrick de Boer, Jenn Perron, Gary Olson (University of California at Irvine), Jeff Nickerson (Stevens Institute of Technology), Mark Klein, John Sterman, Hal Abelson, Jim Herbsleb (Carnegie Mellon University), Johannes Bachhuber,

Carlos Botelho, Nancy Taubenslag, Erik Duhaime, Yiftach Nagar, Ben Towne (Carnegie Mellon University), Yue Han (Stevens Institute of Technology), Annalyn Bachmann.

See summaries of the project in Thomas W. Malone, Jeffrey V. Nickerson, Robert Laubacher, Laur Hesse Fisher, Patrick de Boer, Yue Han, and W. Ben Towne, "Putting the Pieces Back Together Again: Contest Webs for Large-Scale Problem Solving," *Proceedings of the ACM Conference on Computer-Supported Cooperative Work and Social Computing* (New York: Association for Computing Machinery, 2017), 1,661–74 (conference held in Portland, OR, February 25–March 1, 2017), https://ssrn.com/abstract=2912951; and Thomas W. Malone, Robert Laubacher, and Laur Hesse Fisher, "How Millions of People Can Help Solve Climate Change," *NOVA Next*, January 15, 2014, http://www.pbs.org/wgbh/nova/next/earth/crowdsourcing-climate-change-solutions.

2. Rex E. Jung and Richard J. Haier, "The Parieto-Frontal Integration Theory (P-FIT) of Intelligence: Converging Neuroimaging Evidence," *Behavioral and Brain Sciences* 30, no. 2 (2007): 135–54. Suzana Herculano-Houzel, "The Human Brain in Numbers: A Linearly Scaled-Up Primate Brain," *Frontiers in Human Neuroscience* 3 (2009): 31, https://www.ncbi.nlm.nih.gov/pmc/articles/PMC2776484/.

3. Erik Duhaime, Gary M. Olson, and Thomas W. Malone, "Broad Participation in Collective Problem Solving Can Influence Participants and Lead to Better Solutions: Evidence from the MIT Climate CoLab," (working paper no. 2015-02, MIT Center for Collective Intelligence, Cambridge, MA, June 2015), http://cci.mit.edu/working_papers_2012_2013/duhaime%20colab%20wp%206-2015%20final.pdf.

4. Lyndsey Gilpin, "The Woman Who Turned Her High School Science Fair Project into a Global Solar Nonprofit," *Forbes*, October 28, 2015, http://www.forbes.com/sites/lyndseygilpin/2015/10/28/the-woman-who-turned-her-high-school-science-project-into-a-global-solar-nonprofit/#641eee956591).

5. For more detailed descriptions of these and other winning Climate CoLab ideas, see "Contest Winners and Awardees," Climate CoLab, accessed July 13, 2016, http://climatecolab.org/web/guest/resources/-/wiki/Main/Climate+CoLab+Contest+Winners.

6. John C. Tang, Manuel Cebrian, Nicklaus A. Giacobe, Hyun-Woo Kim, Taemie Kim, and Douglas "Beaker" Wickert, "Reflecting on the DARPA Red Balloon Challenge," *Communications of the ACM* 54, no. 4 (2011): 78–85, https://cacm.acm.org/magazines/2011/4/106587-reflecting-on-the-darpa-red-balloon-challenge/fulltext.

7. Galen Pickard, Wei Pan, Iyad Rahwan, Manuel Cebrian, Riley Crane, Anmol Madan, and Alex Pentland, "Time-Critical Social Mobilization," *Science* 334, no. 6,055 (2011): 509–12.

8. Alex Rutherford, Manuel Cebrian, Sohan Dsouza, Esteban Moro, Alex Pentland, and Iyad Rahwan, "Limits of Social Mobilization," *Proceedings of the National Academy of Sciences* 110, no. 16 (2013): 6,281–86.

9. James Surowiecki, *The Wisdom of Crowds* (New York: Doubleday, 2004).

10. Andrew J. King and Guy Cowlishaw, "When to Use Social Information: The Advantage of Large Group Size in Individual Decision Making," *Biology Letters* 3, no. 2 (2007): 137–39, http://rsbl.royalsocietypublishing.org/content/3/2/137?i jkey=f4eb55e0f4b8eda962eb8f930301e30d9eeda600&keytype2=tf_ipsecsha, doi:0.1098/rsbl.2007.0017; Albert Kao and Iain D. Couzin, "Decision Accuracy in Complex Environments Is Often Maximized by Small Group Sizes," *Proceedings of the Royal Society B* 281, no. 1,784 (2014): 20133305, http://rspb .royalsocietypublishing.org/content/281/1784/20133305.full#ref-list-1.

11. Jan Lorenz, Heiko Rauhut, Frank Schweitzer, and Dirk Helbing, "How Social Influence Can Undermine the Wisdom of Crowd Effect," *Proceedings of the National Academy of Sciences* 108, no. 22 (2011): 9,020–25, http://www.pnas.org/ content/108/22/9020.full.pdf, doi:10.1073/pnas.1008636108; Erik B. Steiner, "Turns Out the Internet Is Bad at Guessing How Many Coins Are in a Jar," *Wired*, January 6, 2015, http://www.wired.com/2015/01/coin-jar-crowd -wisdom-experiment-results.

12. Lorenz et al., "How Social Influence."

13. Leonard E. Read, "I, Pencil: My Family Tree as Told by Leonard E. Read," (1958; repr., Irvington-on-Hudson, NY: Foundation for Economic Education, 1999), http://www.econlib.org/library/Essays/rdPncl1.html; Stephen J. Dubner, "How Can This Possibly Be True?" *Freakonomics*, February 18, 2016, http://freakonomics.com/podcast/i-pencil/.

14. "InnoCentive Solver Develops Solution to Help Clean up Remaining Oil from the 1989 Exxon Valdez Disaster," November 7, 2007, https://www.innocentive .com/innocentive-solver-develops-solution-to-help-clean-up-remaining-oil -from-the-1989-exxon-valdez-disaster; Cornelia Dean, "If You Have a Problem, Ask Everyone," *New York Times*, July 22, 2008, http://www.nytimes .com/2008/07/22/science/22inno.html.

15. Lars Bo Jeppesen and Karim R. Lakhani, "Marginality and Problem-Solving Effectiveness in Broadcast Search," *Organization Science* 21, no. 5 (2010): 1,016–33, http://pubsonline.informs.org/doi/pdf/10.1287/orsc.1090.0491, doi:10.1287/ orsc.1090.0491.

16. Duhaime, Olson, and Malone, "Broad Participation."

17. Scott E. Page, *The Difference: How the Power of Diversity Creates Better Groups, Firms, Schools, and Societies* (Princeton, NJ: Princeton University Press, 2008).

18. Benjamin M. Good and Andrew I. Su, "Games with a Scientific Purpose," *Genome Biology* 12, no. 12 (2011): 1.

19. Seth Cooper, Firas Khatib, Adrien Treuille, Janos Barbero, Jeehyung Lee, Michael Beenen, Andrew Leaver-Fay, David Baker, and Zoran Popović, "Predicting Protein Structures with a Multiplayer Online Game," *Nature* 466, no. 7,307 (2010): 756–60; Firas Khatib, Frank DiMaio, Seth Cooper, Maclej Kazmierczyk, Miroslaw Gilski, Szymon Krzywda, Helena Zabranska, Iva Pichova, James Thompson, Zoran Popović, Mariusz Jaskolski, and David Baker, "Crystal Structure of a Monomeric Retroviral Protease Solved by Protein Folding Game Players," *Nature Structural and Molecular Biology* 18, no. 10 (2011): 1,175–77.

20. John Bohannon, "Gamers Unravel the Secret Life of Protein," *Wired*, April 20, 2009, http://www.wired.com/2009/04/ff-protein.

21. Khatib et al., "Crystal Structure."

22. Ivan D. Steiner, *Group Process and Productivity* (New York: Academic Press, 1972).

23. Occupy Wall Street NYC General Assembly, "GA-Consensed Documents," accessed July 17, 2016, archived at https://web.archive.org/web/20170328075306/http://www.nycga.net:80/resources/documents/.

CHAPTER 13

1. Portions of the opening and "Hyperspecialization" sections of this chapter are adapted from Thomas W. Malone, Robert Laubacher, and Tammy Johns, "The Age of Hyperspecialization," *Harvard Business Review* 89 (July–August 2011): 56–65.

2. Wikipedia, s.v. "the Turk," accessed October 10, 2017, https://en.wikipedia.org/wiki/The_Turk. Image is in the public domain.

3. Mary L. Gray and Siddharth Suri, "The Humans Behind the AI Curtain," *Harvard Business Review*, January 9, 2017, https://hbr.org/2017/01/the-humans-working-behind-the-ai-curtain.

4. Jonathan Zittrain, "The Internet Creates a New Kind of Sweatshop," *Newsweek*, December 7, 2009, http://www.newsweek.com/internet-creates-new-kind-sweatshop-75751; Fiona Graham, "Crowdsourcing Work: Labour on Demand or Digital Sweatshop?" BBC News, October 22, 2010, http://www.bbc.com/news/business-11600902; Ellen Cushing, "Amazon Mechanical Turk: The Digital Sweatshop," *Utne Reader*, January/February 2013, http://www.utne.com/science-and-technology/amazon-mechanical-turk-zm0z13jfzlin.

5. Miranda Katz, "Amazon's Turker Crowd Has Had Enough," *Wired*, August 23, 2017, https://www.wired.com/story/amazons-turker-crowd-has-had-enough.

6. This comparison was suggested by David Nordfors, "The Untapped $140 Trillion Innovation for Jobs Market," *TechCrunch*, February 21, 2015, https://techcrunch.com/2015/02/21/the-untapped-140-trillion-innovation-for-jobs-market.

7. For specific algorithms, see Pinar Donmez, Jamie G. Carbonell, and Jeff Schneider, "Efficiently Learning the Accuracy of Labeling Sources for Selective Sampling," in *Proceedings of the 15th ACM SIGKDD International Conference on Knowledge Discovery and Data Mining* (New York: Association for Computing Machinery, 2009), http://www.cs.cmu.edu/~pinard/Papers/rsp767-donmez.pdf; Pinar Donmez, Jamie G. Carbonell, and Jeff Schneider, "A Probabilistic Framework to Learn from Multiple Annotators with Time-Varying Accuracy," presented at the SIAM Conference on Data Mining, Columbus, OH, April 29–May 1, 2010, http://www.cs.cmu.edu/~pinard/Papers/280_Donmez.pdf.

   For a more general overview of various approaches, see Daniel S. Weld, Mausam, Christopher H. Lin, and Jonathan Bragg, "Artificial Intelligence and Collective Intelligence," in *The Collective Intelligence Handbook*, ed. Thomas W. Malone and Michael S. Bernstein (Cambridge, MA: MIT Press, 2015).

8. Adam Cohen, *The Perfect Store: Inside eBay* (New York: Little, Brown / Back Bay, 2002), 1–5.

9. David Nordfors and Vint Cerf, *Disrupting Unemployment* (Kansas City, MO: Ewing Marion Kauffman Foundation, 2016).

10. For more details on this view of coordination, see Thomas W. Malone, Kevin Crowston, Jintae Lee, Brian Pentland, Chrysanthos Dellarocas, George Wyner, John Quimby, Charles S. Osborn, Abraham Bernstein, George Herman, Mark Klein, and Elissa O'Donnell, "Tools for Inventing Organizations: Toward a Handbook of Organizational Processes," *Management Science* 45, no. 3 (March 1999): 425–43; Thomas W. Malone, Kevin Crowston, and George A. Herman, eds., *Organizing Business Knowledge: The MIT Process Handbook* (Cambridge, MA: MIT Press, 2003); Thomas W. Malone and Kevin Crowston, "The Interdisciplinary Study of Coordination," *ACM Computing Surveys* 26, no. 1 (March 1994): 87–119.

    For other views of coordination, see James D. Thompson, *Organizations in Action* (New York: McGraw-Hill, 1967); and Andrew H. Van de Ven, Andre L. Delbecq, and Richard Koenig, Jr., "Determinants of Coordination Modes within Organizations," *American Sociological Review* 41, no. 2 (1976): 322–38.

11. Haoqi Zhang, Edith Law, Robert C. Miller, Krzysztof Z. Gajos, David C. Parkes, and Eric Horvitz, "Human Computation Tasks with Global Constraints," *Proceedings of the SIGCHI Conference on Human Factors in Computing Systems* (CHI 2012) (New York: Association of Computing Machinery, 2012), 217–26 (conference held in Austin, TX, May 5–10, 2012), http://users.eecs.northwestern.edu/~hq/papers/mobi.pdf.

12. Portions of this section are adapted from Thomas W. Malone, Jeffrey V. Nickerson, Robert Laubacher, Laur Hesse Fisher, Patrick de Boer, Yue Han, and W. Ben Towne, "Putting the Pieces Back Together Again: Contest Webs for Large-Scale Problem Solving," *Proceedings of the ACM Conference on Computer-Supported Cooperative Work and Social Computing*, (New York: Association for Computing Machinery, 2017), 1,661–74 (conference held in Portland, OR, February 25–March 1, 2017), https://ssrn.com/abstract=2912951.

13. Ellen Christiaanse and Kuldeep Kumar, "ICT-Enabled Coordination of Dynamic Supply Webs," *International Journal of Physical Distribution & Logistics Management* 30, no. 3/4 (2000): 268–85.

14. Figure is adapted from Thomas Malone et al., "Putting the Pieces Back Together," with permission of the authors. Special thanks to Yue Han who prepared both the original and adapted versions of the figure.

15. For more details, see Malone et al., "Putting the Pieces Back Together."

CHAPTER 14

1. Donald G. McNeil, Jr., Simon Romero, and Sabrina Tavernise, "How a Medical Mystery in Brazil Led Doctors to Zika," *New York Times*, February 6, 2016, http://www.nytimes.com/2016/02/07/health/zika-virus-brazil-how-it-spread-explained.html; Sarah Boseley, "On the Frontline in Brazil's War on Zika: 'I Felt Like I Was in a Horror Movie,'" *Guardian*, April 12, 2016, https://www.theguardian.com/global-development/2016/apr/12/on-front-line-brazil-war-zika-virus-i-felt-horror-movie-no-cure.

2. Boseley, "On the Frontline."

3. "Zika Virus: The Next Emerging Threat?" *Science*, accessed September 9, 2016, http://www.sciencemag.org/topic/zika-virus.

4. "WHO Director-General Summarizes the Outcome of the Emergency Committee Regarding Clusters of Microcephaly and Guillain-Barré Syndrome," World Health Organization, February 1, 2016, http://www.who.int/mediacentre/news/statements/2016/emergency-committee-zika-microcephaly/en.

5. Deborah Ancona, Thomas W. Malone, Wanda J. Orlikowski, and Peter M. Senge, "In Praise of the Incomplete Leader," *Harvard Business Review* 85, no. 2 (2007): 92–100; Karl E. Weick, *Sensemaking in Organizations*, Foundations for Organizational Science (Thousand Oaks, CA: Sage Publishing, 1995).

6. "The Last Kodak Moment?" *Economist*, January 14, 2012, http://www.economist.com/node/21542796; Ben Dobbin, "Digital Camera Turns 30—Sort Of," NBC News, September 9, 2005, http://www.nbcnews.com/id/9261340/ns/technology_and_science-tech_and_gadgets/t/digital-camera-turns-sort/#.V83t2j4rJyp.

7. Robert A. Guth, "In Secret Hideaway, Bill Gates Ponders Microsoft's Future," *Wall Street Journal*, March 28, 2005, http://www.wsj.com/articles/SB111196625830690477; W. Joseph Campbell, "'The Internet Tidal Wave,' 20 Years On," *The 1995 Blog*, May 24, 2015, https://1995blog.com/2015/05/24/the-internet-tidal-wave-20-years-on.

8. James Manyika, Michael Chui, Brad Brown, Jacques Bughin, Richard Dobbs, Charles Roxburgh, and Angela Hung Byers, *Big Data: The Next Frontier for Innovation, Competition, and Productivity* (n.p., McKinsey Global Institute, 2011), 41, http://www.mckinsey.com/business-functions/business-technology/our-insights/big-data-the-next-frontier-for-innovation.

9. Viktor Mayer-Schönberger and Kenneth Cukier, *Big Data: A Revolution That Will Transform How We Live, Work, and Think* (Boston: Houghton Mifflin Harcourt, 2013), 59.

10. Jon Gertner, "Behind GE's Vision for the Industrial Internet of Things," *Fast Company*, June 18, 2014, https://www.fastcompany.com/3031272/can-jeff-immelt-really-make-the-world-1-better.

11. David Brin, *The Transparent Society* (Cambridge, MA: Perseus Books, 1998); David Brin, *Earth* (New York: Bantam Spectra, 1990).

12. For an overview of Bayesian networks written for a general audience, see Pedro Domingos, *The Master Algorithm: How the Quest for the Ultimate Learning Machine Will Remake Our World* (New York: Basic Books, 2015), chapter 6.

    Bayesian networks are often difficult to use at large scale, but there are numerous technical approaches to doing so. One that seems particularly promising for applications like those described here is Markov Learning Networks (MLNs) because they allow people to specify many kinds of rules for the likely logical relationships among events without having to estimate detailed conditional probabilities (see Domingos, *The Master Algorithm*, chapter 9).

13. National Commission on Terrorist Attacks upon the United States, *The 9/11 Commission Report* (Washington, DC, July 22, 2004), 344–48, https://www.9-11commission.gov/report/911Report.pdf.

14. Ibid., 272.

15. Ibid., 273–76.

16. In a Bayesian network, the *human estimate* of an event could be linked to the *machine estimate* by conditional probabilities. For instance, the analysts who primed the system might say that if the event is actually going to happen, the humans would correctly predict it 80 percent of the time. This would create a strong linkage between the human and machine estimates, and changes in the human estimates could then have a large effect on many other probabilities in the system. An interesting topic for future research is how to represent the relationship between human and machine estimates when the humans have varying degrees of knowledge about—and confidence in—their estimates.

CHAPTER 15

1. Organization theorists have studied questions about how this process works under the heading of "transactive memory." See, for example, Daniel M. Wegner, "Transactive Memory: A Contemporary Analysis of the Group Mind," in *Theories of Group Behavior*, ed. Brian Mullen and George R. Goethals (New York: Springer Verlag, 1987), 185–208; Kyle Lewis, "Knowledge and Performance in Knowledge-Worker Teams: A Longitudinal Study of Transactive Memory Systems," *Management Science* 50 (2004): 1,519–33, doi:10.1287/mnsc.1040.0257; Kyle Lewis and Benjamin Herndon, "The Relevance of Transactive Memory Systems for Complex, Dynamic Group Tasks," *Organization Science* 22, no. 5 (2011): 1,254–65, doi:10.1287/orsc.1110.0647; Linda Argote and Yuqing Ren, "Transactive Memory Systems: A Microfoundation of Dynamic Capabilities," *Journal of Management Studies* 49, no. 8 (2012): 1,375–82, doi:10.1111/j.1467-6486.2012.01077.x; Andrea B. Hollingshead, "Cognitive Interdependence and Convergent Expectations in Transactive Memory," *Journal of Personality and Social Psychology* 81, no. 6 (2001): 1,080–89, doi:10.1037//0022-3514.81.6.1080.

2. Patrick C. Kyllonen and Raymond E. Christal, "Reasoning Ability Is (Little More Than) Working Memory Capacity?!" *Intelligence* 14 (1990): 389–433, doi:10.1016/S0160-2896(05)80012-1.

3. Megan Molteni, "Want a Diagnosis Tomorrow, Not Next Year? Turn to AI," *Wired*, August 10, 2017, https://www.wired.com/story/ai-that-will-crowdsource-your-next-diagnosis.

4. Dhruv Boddupalli, Shantanu Nundy, and David W. Bates, "Collective Intelligence Outperforms Individual Physicians in Medical Diagnosis," presented at the 39th annual North American Meeting of the Society for Medical Decision Making, Pittsburgh, PA, October 23, 2017, https://smdm.confex.com/smdm/2017/webprogram/Paper11173.html.

5. "International Classification of Diseases," World Health Organization, 1994, http://www.who.int/classifications/icd/en; "Prepare Now for ICD-10-CM and ICD-10-PCS Implementation," American College of Radiology, June 2012, https://www.acr.org/Advocacy/Economics-Health-Policy/Billing-Coding/Prepare-Now-for-ICD10.

6. Scott Wong, Irving Lin, Jayanth Komarneni, and Shantanu Nundy, "Machine Classifier Trained on Low-Volume, Structured Data Predicts Diagnoses Near Physician-Level: Chest Pain Case Study," presented at the 39th annual North American Meeting of the Society for Medical Decision Making, Pittsburgh, PA, October 22, 2017, https://smdm.confex.com/smdm/2017/meetingapp.cgi/Paper/11058.

CHAPTER 16

1. Erik Eckermann, *World History of the Automobile* (Warrendale, PA: SAE Press, 2001), 14; Wikipedia, s.v. "Nicholas-Joseph Cugnot," last modified August 12, 2017, https://en.wikipedia.org/wiki/Nicolas-Joseph_Cugnot; Wikipedia, s.v. "history of the automobile," last modified September 28, 2017, https://en.wikipedia.org/wiki/History_of_the_automobile.

2. Orville C. Cromer and Charles L. Proctor, s.v. "gasoline engine," *Encyclopaedia Britannica*, published March 20, 2013, https://www.britannica.com/technology/gasoline-engine/Fuel#toc47239.

3. Alan K. Binder and John Bell Rae, s.v. "automotive industry," *Encyclopaedia Britannica*, last modified July 18, 2017, https://www.britannica.com/topic/automotive-industry.

4. *Encyclopaedia Britannica*, s.v. "Model T," published June 30, 2017, https://www.britannica.com/technology/Model-T.

5. "Gas Price History Graph (Historic Prices)," http://zfacts.com/gas-price-history-graph; Pew Environment Group, "History of Fuel Economy: One Decade of Innovation, Two Decades of Inaction," April 2011, http://www.pewtrusts.org/~/media/assets/2011/04/history-of-fuel-economy-clean-energy-factsheet.pdf.

6. *Encyclopaedia Britannica*, "Model T."

7. James G. March, "Exploration and Exploitation in Organizational Learning," *Organization Science* 2, no. 1 (1991): 71–87.

8. Hermann Ebbinghaus, *Memory: A Contribution to Experimental Psychology*, Columbia University Teachers College Educational Reprints no. 3 (New York: University Microfilms, 1913); Theodore P. Wright, "Factors Affecting the Cost of Airplanes," *Journal of the Aeronautical Sciences* 3, no. 4 (1936): 122–28; Boston Consulting Group, *Perspectives on Experience* (Boston: Boston Consulting Group, 1972).

9. Abraham Bernstein, "How Can Cooperative Work Tools Support Dynamic Group Process? Bridging the Specificity Frontier," in *Proceedings of the 2000 ACM Conference on Computer Supported Cooperative Work* (New York: Association for Computing Machinery, 2000), 279–88.

10. An early example of the idea of cyber-human learning loops is Doug Engelbart's concept of "bootstrapping" collective intelligence. See Douglas Engelbart and Jeff Rulifson, "Bootstrapping Our Collective Intelligence," *ACM Computing Surveys* 31, issue 4es (December 1999), doi:10.1145/345966.346040.

   Unlike the concept of business process reengineering, which was popular in the 1990s, cyber-human learning loops assume that change is continuous rather than the result of occasional large redesign projects. See Michael Hammer and James Champy, *Reengineering the Corporation* (New York: HarperBusiness, 1993).

In that sense, cyber-human learning loops can be seen as an example of a continuous improvement process. See Wikipedia, s.v. "continual improvement process," accessed October 20, 2017, https://en.wikipedia.org/wiki/Continual_improvement_process.

Image © 2017 Thomas W. Malone, prepared by Get Smarter and Thomas W. Malone.

11. Ricardo Hausmann, "The Problem with Evidence-Based Policies," *Project Syndicate*, February 25, 2016, https://www.project-syndicate.org/commentary/evidence-based-policy-problems-by-ricardo-hausmann-2016-02.

12. Ross D. King, Jem Rowland, Stephen G. Oliver, Meong Young, Wayne Aubrey, Emma Byrne, Maria Liakata, Magdalena Markham, Pinar Pir, Larisa Soldatova, Andrew C. Sparkes, Ken Whelan, and Amanda J. Clare, "The Automation of Science," *Science* 324, no. 5,923 (2009): 85–89, doi:10.1126/science.1165620; Lizzie Buchen, "Robot Makes Scientific Discovery All by Itself," *Wired*, April 2, 2009, https://www.wired.com/2009/04/robotscientist.

13. Kevin Williams, Elizabeth Bilsland, Andrew Sparkes, Wayne Aubrey, Meong Young, Larisa Soldatova, Kurt De Grave, Jan Ramon, Michaela de Clare, Worachart Sirawaraporn, Stephen G. Oliver, and Ross D. King, "Cheaper Faster Drug Development Validated by the Repositioning of Drugs Against Neglected Tropical Diseases," *Journal of the Royal Society Interface* 12, no. 104 (2015), doi:10.1098/rsif.20141289.

CHAPTER 17

1. A. G. Lafley and Roger L. Martin, *Playing to Win: How Strategy Really Works* (Boston, MA: Harvard Business Review Press, 2013); A. G. Lafley, Roger L. Martin, Jan W. Rivkin, and Nicolaj Siggelkow, "Bringing Science to the Art of Strategy," *Harvard Business Review*, September 2012, https://hbr.org/2012/09/bringing-science-to-the-art-of-strategy.

2. Oil of Olay and all other products named here are trademarks of Procter & Gamble.

3. Michael E. Porter, *Competitive Strategy* (New York: Free Press, 1980).

4. Abraham Bernstein, Mark Klein, and Thomas W. Malone, "The Process Recombinator: A Tool for Generating New Business Process Ideas," presented at the International Conference on Information Systems, Charlotte, NC, December 13–15, 1999; Thomas W. Malone, Kevin Crowston, and George A. Herman, eds., *Organizing Business Knowledge: The MIT Process Handbook* (Cambridge, MA: MIT Press, 2003).

5. P&G sold the Pringles business to Kellogg in 2012, so this would no longer be a P&G product. For a description of the invention of the process for printing on Pringles, see Larry Huston and Nabil Sakkab, "Connect and Develop: Inside Procter & Gamble's New Model for Innovation," *Harvard Business Review*, March 2006, reprint no. R0603C, https://hbr.org/2006/03/connect-and-develop-inside-procter-gambles-new-model-for-innovation.

6. Vincent Granville, "21 Data Science Systems Used by Amazon to Operate Its Business," *Data Science Central*, November 19, 2015, http://www.data

sciencecentral.com/profiles/blogs/20-data-science-systems-used-by-amazon
-to-operate-its-business.

7. Martin Reeves and Daichi Ueda use the term *integrated strategy machine* to describe a somewhat similar idea in "Designing the Machines That Will Design Strategy," *Harvard Business Review*, April 18, 2016, https://hbr .org/2016/04/welcoming-the-chief-strategy-robot.

The concept here, however, focuses much more on how large numbers of people throughout the organization and beyond can be involved in the process and the specific roles people and machines will play.

CHAPTER 18

1. Anthony Leiserowitz, director of the Yale Project on Climate Change Communication, summarizes the five key messages about climate change as: "It's real. It's us. It's bad. Scientists agree. There's hope." See, e.g., Kerry Flynn, "Climate Change in the American Mind," Harvard Kennedy School Belfer Center for Science and International Affairs, March 12, 2014, http://www .belfercenter.org/publication/climate-change-american-mind.

2. John Fialka, "China Will Start the World's Largest Carbon Trading Market," *Scientific American*, May 16, 2016, https://www.scientificamerican.com/article/ china-will-start-the-world-s-largest-carbon-trading-market; Lucy Hornby and Shawn Donnan, "China Fights for Market Economy Status," *Financial Times*, May 9, 2016, https://www.ft.com/content/572f435e-0784-11e6-9b51- 0fb5e65703ce?mhq5j=e7.

3. "DearTomorrow, a Promise to the Future About Climate Change" (proposal for the contest "Shifting Behavior for a Changing Climate 2016"), Climate CoLab, http://climatecolab.org/contests/2016/shifting-behavior-for-a -changing-climate/c/proposal/1330118.

4. "Climatecoin 2016" (proposal for the contest "Shifting Behavior for a Changing Climate 2016"), Climate CoLab, https://climatecolab.org/contests/ 2016/shifting-behavior-for-a-changing-climate/c/proposal/1331638; "Sno-Caps: The People's Cap-And-Trade" (proposal for the contest "U.S. Carbon Price 2014"), Climate CoLab, https://climatecolab.org/contests/2014/ us-carbon-price/c/proposal/1305801; "GreenCoin: Start Pricing Carbon Without Governments" (proposal for 2015 Proposal Workspace), Climate CoLab, https://climatecolab.org/contests/2014/2015-proposal-workspace/c/ proposal/1324607.

5. Christian Catalini and Joshua S. Gans, "Some Simple Economics of the Blockchain" (working paper no. 5191-16, MIT Sloan School of Management, Cambridge, MA, November 23, 2016), 9, 24, https://ssrn.com/abstract=2874598.

6. Monica Hesse, "Crisis Mapping Brings Online Tool to Haitian Disaster Relief Effort," *Washington Post*, January 16, 2010, http://www.washingtonpost.com/ wp-dyn/content/article/2010/01/15/AR2010011502650.html.

7. John Schwartz, "Paris Climate Deal Too Weak to Meet Goals, Report Finds" *New York Times*, November 17, 2016, https://www.nytimes.com/2016/11/17/ science/paris-accord-global-warming-iea.html.

CHAPTER 19

1. Richard Conniff, "What the Luddites Really Fought Against," *Smithsonian*, March 2011, http://www.smithsonianmag.com/history/what-the-luddites-really-fought-against-264412/?no-ist.

2. David H. Autor, "Why Are There Still So Many Jobs? The History and Future of Workplace Automation," *Journal of Economic Perspectives* 29, no. 3 (Summer 2015): 3–30.

3. Erik Brynjolfsson and Andrew McAfee, *The Second Machine Age: Work, Progress, and Prosperity in a Time of Brilliant Technologies* (New York: W. W. Norton, 2014).

4. David H. Autor, "Skills, Education, and the Rise of Earnings Inequality Among the 'Other 99 Percent,'" *Science* 344, no. 6,186 (2014): 843–51.

5. For an excellent discussion of the economic reasons for these changes, see Autor, "Why Are There Still So Many Jobs?"

6. James Manyika, Michael Chui, Mehdi Miremadi, Jacques Bughin, Katy George, Paul Willmott, and Martin Dewhurst, *A Future That Works: Automation, Employment, and Productivity* (n.p.: McKinsey Global Institute, 2017), http://www.mckinsey.com/global-themes/digital-disruption/harnessing-automation-for-a-future-that-works.

7. Ibid.

8. Rosalind W. Picard, *Affective Computing* (Cambridge, MA: MIT Press, 1997); Cynthia Breazeal, "Emotion and Sociable Humanoid Robots," *International Journal of Human-Computer Studies* 59, no. 1 (2003): 119–55.

9. James Bessen, "Toil and Technology," *Finance and Development* 52, no. 1 (2015); Autor, "Why Are There Still So Many Jobs?"

10. Paul Osterman, *Who Will Care for Us?* (New York: Russell Sage Foundation, 2017); Eduardo Porter, "Home Health Care: Shouldn't It Be Work Worth Doing?" *New York Times*, August 29, 2017, https://www.nytimes.com/2017/08/29/business/economy/home-health-care-work.html.

11. Autor, "Why Are There Still So Many Jobs?"; James Surowiecki, "The Great Tech Panic: Robots Won't Take All Our Jobs," *Wired*, September 2017, https://www.wired.com/2017/08/robots-will-not-take-your-job/; James Manyika, Susan Lund, Michael Chui, Jacques Bughin, Jonathan Woetzel, Parul Batra, Ryan Ko, Saurabh Sanghvi, *Jobs Lost, Jobs Gained: Workforce Transitions in a Time of Automation* (n.p.: McKinsey Global Institute, 2017), https://www.mckinsey.com/global-themes/future-of-organizations-and-work/what-the-future-of-work-will-mean-for-jobs-skills-and-wages; Kevin Maney, "Need a Job? Why Artificial Intelligence Will Help Human Workers, Not Hurt Them," Newsweek.com, January 18, 2018, http://www.newsweek.com/2018/01/26/artificial-intelligence-create-human-jobs-783730.html; David Autor, "Why Are There Still So Many Jobs?" TEDx Cambridge, November 28, 2016, https://www.youtube.com/watch?v=LCxcnUrokJo&feature=youtu.be.

12. Thomas W. Malone and Robert J. Laubacher, "The Dawn of the E-Lance Economy," *Harvard Business Review* 76, no. 5 (September–October 1998): 144–52.

13. Brynjolfsson and McAfee, *The Second Machine Age*, chapter 11.

14. Danielle Douglas-Gabriel, "Investors Buying Shares in College Students: Is This the Wave of the Future? Purdue University Thinks So," *Washington Post*, November 27, 2015, https://www.washingtonpost.com/news/grade-point/wp/2015/11/27/investors-buying-shares-in-college-students-is-this-the-wave -of-the-future-purdue-university-thinks-so.

15. Thomas W. Malone, *The Future of Work: How the New Order of Business Will Shape Your Organization, Your Management Style, and Your Life* (Boston, MA: Harvard Business School Press, 2004); Robert J. Laubacher and Thomas W. Malone, "Flexible Work Arrangements and 21st Century Worker's Guilds" (working paper no. 004, MIT Initiative on Inventing the Organizations of the 21st Century, MIT Sloan School of Management, Cambridge, MA, October 1997), http://ccs.mit.edu/21C/21CWP004.html.

16. Catherine Rampell, "Support Is Building for a Tax Credit to Help Hiring," *New York Times*, October 6, 2009, http://www.nytimes.com/2009/10/07/business/07tax.html; Jeffrey M. Perloff and Michael L. Wachter, "The New Jobs Tax Credit: An Evaluation of the 1977–78 Wage Subsidy Program," *American Economic Review* 69, no. 2 (May 1979): 173–79, http://www.jstor.org/stable/1801638?seq=1#page_scan_tab_contents.

17. Ira Flatow and Howard Market, "Science Diction: The Origin of the Word 'Robot,'" April 22, 2011, National Public Radio, http://www.npr.org/2011/04/22/135634400/science-diction-the-origin-of-the-word-robot.

18. Future of Life Institute, http://futureoflife.org.

19. Nick Bostrom, *Superintelligence: Paths, Dangers, Strategies* (Oxford, UK: Oxford University Press, 2014); Ray Kurzweil, *The Age of Spiritual Machines: When Computers Exceed Human Intelligence* (New York: Viking, 1999).

20. Peter M. Asaro, "The Liability Problem for Autonomous Artificial Agents," in *Ethical and Moral Considerations in Non-Human Agents: Papers from the 2016 AAAI Spring Symposium* (Palo Alto, CA: AAAI Press, 2016), https://www.aaai.org/ocs/index.php/SSS/SSS16/paper/download/12699/11949.

21. Richard Kelley, Enrique Schaerer, Micaela Gomez, and Monica Nicolescu, "Liability in Robotics: An International Perspective on Robots as Animals," *Advanced Robotics* 24, no. 13 (2010): 1,861–71.

22. "US Drone Strike Killings in Pakistan and Yemen 'Unlawful,'" BBC News, October 23, 2013, http://www.bbc.com/news/world-us-canada-24618701.

CHAPTER 20

1. Robert Van Gulick, "Consciousness," in *Stanford Encyclopedia of Philosophy* (Spring 2014 edition), ed. Edward N. Zalta (Stanford, CA: Stanford University, 2014), http://plato.stanford.edu/archives/spr2014/entries/consciousness; Bernard J. Baars, *A Cognitive Theory of Consciousness* (Cambridge, UK: Cambridge University Press, 1988); Daniel C. Dennett, *Consciousness Explained* (Boston: Little, Brown, 1991); Roger Penrose, *The Emperor's New Mind: Computers, Minds and the Laws of Physics* (Oxford, UK: Oxford University Press, 1989); Roger Penrose, *Shadows of the Mind* (Oxford, UK: Oxford University Press, 1994); David J. Chalmers, "Facing up to the Problem of Consciousness,"

Journal of Consciousness Studies 2, no. 3 (1995): 200–219; David J. Chalmers, *The Conscious Mind* (Oxford, UK: Oxford University Press, 1996); Ned Block, "Consciousness, Accessibility and the Mesh Between Psychology and Neuroscience," *Behavioral and Brain Sciences* 30 (2007): 481–548.

2. The place where the information is integrated is sometimes called a global workspace. See Baars, *A Cognitive Theory of Consciousness*.

3. Thomas Nagel, "What Is It Like to Be a Bat?" *Philosophical Review* 83, no. 4 (1974): 435–56.

4. Chalmers, "Facing up to the Problem of Consciousness."

5. Eric Schwitzgebel, "If Materialism Is True, the United States Is Probably Conscious," *Philosophical Studies* 172, no. 7 (July 2015): 1,697–1,721, https://doi .org/10.1007/s11098-014-0387-8, © 2014, Springer Science + Business Media Dordrecht.

6. Adam Lashinsky, *Inside Apple: How America's Most Admired—and Secretive— Company Really Works* (New York: Business Plus, 2013), 157–59.

7. Jonathan Ive, speaking at the Radical Craft Conference, Art Center College of Design, Pasadena, CA, 2006. Quoted in Lashinsky, *Inside Apple*, 63.

8. Lashinsky, *Inside Apple*, 69.

9. Ibid., 72.

10. Schwitzgebel, "If Materialism Is True."

11. Ibid. Quote reprinted with permission of Springer.

12. Bryce Huebner, *Macrocognition: A Theory of Distributed Minds and Collective Intentionality* (Oxford, UK: Oxford University Press, 2014), 120.

13. Masafumi Oizumi, Larissa Albantakis, and Giulio Tononi, "From the Phenomenology to the Mechanisms of Consciousness: Integrated Information Theory 3.0," *PLOS Computational Biology* 10, no. 5 (2014), doi:10.1371/journal .pcbi.1003588; Giulio Tononi and Christof Koch, "Consciousness: Here, There and Everywhere?" *Philosophical Transactions of the Royal Society B* 370, no. 1,668 (2015), doi:10.1098/rstb.2014.0167; Giulio Tononi, "Integrated Information Theory of Consciousness: An Updated Account," *Archives Italiennes de Biologie* 150, nos. 2–3 (2012); Giulio Tononi and Christof Koch, "The Neural Correlates of Consciousness: An Update," *Annals of the New York Academy of Science* 1124 (2008): 239–61.

14. Virgil Griffith, public letter to Scott Aaronson, June 25, 2014, *Shtetl-Optimized*, http://www.scottaaronson.com/blog/?p=1893, https://www.scottaaronson .com/response-p1.pdf.

15. Oizumi et al., "From the Phenomenology to the Mechanisms of Consciousness," 3.

16. Giulio Tononi and Christof Koch, "Can a Photodiode Be Conscious?" *New York Review of Books*, March 7, 2013, http://www.nybooks.com/articles/archives/ 2013/mar/07/can-photodiode-be-conscious.

17. Marcello Massimini, Fabio Ferrarelli, Reto Huber, Steve K. Esser, Harpreet Singh, and Giulio Tononi, "Breakdown of Cortical Effective Connectivity During Sleep," *Science* 309 (2005): 2,228–32; Adenauer G. Casali, Olivia Gosseries, Mario Rosanova, Mélanie Boly, Simone Sarasso, Karina R. Casali, Silvia Casarotto, Marie-Aurélie Bruno, Steven Laureys, Giulio Tononi, and

Marcello Massimini, "A Theoretically Based Index of Consciousness Independent of Sensory Processing and Behavior," *Science Translational Medicine* 5, no. 198 (2013): 198ra105.

18. David Engel and Thomas W. Malone, "Integrated Information as a Metric for Group Interaction: Analyzing Human and Computer Groups Using a Technique Developed to Measure Consciousness," preprint, submitted February 8, 2017, http://arxiv.org/abs/1702.02462.

19. Philip Tetlow, *The Web's Awake: An Introduction to the Field of Web Science and the Concept of Web Life* (Piscataway, NJ: IEEE Press, 2007).

CHAPTER 21

1. Robert Wright, *Nonzero: The Logic of Human Destiny* (New York: Pantheon, 2000).

2. Jim Powell, "How Dictators Come to Power in a Democracy," *Forbes*, February 5, 2013, http://www.forbes.com/sites/jimpowell/2013/02/05/how-dictators-come-to-power-in-a-democracy/#4a78c04b1082.

3. Wright, *Nonzero*, 3–6.

4. Peter Russell, *The Global Brain: Speculations on the Evolutionary Leap to Planetary Consciousness* (Los Angeles: J. P. Tarcher, 1983); Howard Bloom, *Global Brain: The Evolution of Mass Mind from the Big Bang to the 21st Century* (New York: Wiley, 2000).

5. Pierre Teilhard de Chardin, *The Phenomenon of Man* (New York: Harper, 1959); Jennifer Cobb Kreisberg, "A Globe, Clothing Itself with a Brain," *Wired*, June 1, 1995, https://www.wired.com/1995/06/teilhard.

6. Bloom, *Global Brain*, 15.

7. Jeremy Bentham, *An Introduction to the Principles of Morals and Legislation* (1789; repr., Oxford, UK: Clarendon Press, 1907); Julia Driver, "The History of Utilitarianism," in *Stanford Encyclopedia of Philosophy* (Winter 2014 edition), ed. Edward N. Zalta (Stanford, CA: Stanford University, 2014), https://plato.stanford.edu/archives/win2014/entries/utilitarianism-history; Yuval Noah Harari, *Homo Deus: A Brief History of Tomorrow* (New York: HarperCollins, 2017), chapter 1.

8. Tara John, "The Legal Rights of Nature," *Time*, April 12, 2017, 14; Gwendolyn Gordon, "Environmental Personhood" (working paper, University of Pennsylvania, Wharton School, Legal Studies and Business Ethics Department, March 7, 2017), https://ssrn.com/abstract=2935007.

9. Aldous Huxley, *The Perennial Philosophy* (New York: Harper & Brothers, 1945).

10. Philip Stratton-Lake, "Intuitionism in Ethics," in *Stanford Encyclopedia of Philosophy* (Winter 2016 edition), ed. Edward N. Zalta (Stanford University, 2016), https://plato.stanford.edu/archives/win2016/entries/intuitionism-ethics; John Rawls, *A Theory of Justice* (Oxford, UK: Clarendon Press, 1972).

11. Huxley, *The Perennial Philosophy*.

12. Alan Watts, *The Book: On the Taboo Against Knowing Who You Are* (New York: Random House, 1966), 1.

13. Idries Shah, *The Sufis* (London: Octagon Press, 1964), 311–12.

Index

Index

About the Author

Thomas W. Malone is the Patrick J. McGovern Professor of Management at the MIT Sloan School of Management and the founding director of the MIT Center for Collective Intelligence. At MIT, he is also a professor of information technology and a professor of work and organizational studies. Previously, he was the founder and director of the MIT Center for Coordination Science and one of the two founding codirectors of the MIT initiative on "Inventing the Organizations of the 21st Century." Professor Malone teaches classes on organizational design, information technology, and leadership, and his research focuses on how new organizations can be designed to take advantage of the possibilities provided by information technology.

For example, Professor Malone predicted, in an article published in 1987, many of the major developments in electronic business over the following 25 years, including electronic buying and selling for many kinds of products. Then, in 2004, Professor Malone summarized two decades of his research in his critically acclaimed book *The Future of Work*. He has also published over 100 articles, research papers, and book chapters, he is an inventor with 11 patents, and he is the coeditor of four books.

Malone has been a cofounder of four software companies and has consulted and served as a board member for a number of other organizations. His background includes work as a research scientist at Xerox Palo Alto Research Center (PARC), as well as earning a PhD from Stanford University, an honorary doctorate from the University of Zurich, and degrees in applied mathematics, engineering, and psychology.